ALMOST A FOREIGN COUNTRY

Almost a Foreign Country
A Personal Geography in Columns and Aphorisms

Manfred Wolf

iUniverse, Inc.
New York   Bloomington

Almost a Foreign Country: A Personal Geography in Columns and Aphorisms

Copyright © 2008 by Manfred Wolf

iUniverse books may be ordered through booksellers or by contacting:

iUniverse
1663 Liberty Drive
Bloomington, IN 47403
www.iuniverse.com
1-800-Authors (1-800-288-4677)

Because of the dynamic nature of the Internet, any Web addresses or links contained in this book may have changed since publication and may no longer be valid.

ISBN: 978-0-595-52423-5 (pbk)
ISBN: 978-0-595-62477-5 (ebk)

Printed in the United States of America

iUniverse Rev. Date 11/07/08

For Dana, Michael and Paul

Contents

Acknowledgments

I thank those readers who have responded strongly to some of these pieces, whether with enthusiasm or criticism, principally Marc Chavannes, Nick Despota, Engeline Gregory, Nellie Hill, Marjorie Kewley, Michael Krasny, Tina Martin, Paul Palmbaum, Stan Taubman, Nancy Weber and Paul Wolf. I have often learned from their spirited reactions.

I am also grateful to several friends who have helped me assess the aphorisms and been otherwise helpful with the order and titling of a number of columns, especially Maurice Bassan, William Bonnell, Andrew Chesterman, Jane Cutler, Randy Harrison, Steve Leinbach, Joan Minninger and Dan Wick.

A very special word of thanks must go to three dear friends who looked closely at the final manuscript and made truly helpful suggestions: Elizabeth Davis, Helen Steyer and Marjorie Young. Their encouragement was invaluable.

I am also grateful to my *West Portal Monthly* editor Glenn Gullmes for seeing potential in my column "This Time, This Place" and enabling me to write on so many topics.

Finally, I can't say enough about Stephanie Prescott and Yael Abel, whose editing was only the beginning of their work with me and for me. I can truthfully say that without them this book might not have appeared.

M. W.

Introduction

I started writing columns many years ago, when I first felt the urge to express opinions in print, reveal a train of thought, or present an anecdote I thought was unusual and perhaps even unconventional. Unlike most people, I was in the fortunate position of having people listen to me—mainly my students—but I never wanted to lecture them unnecessarily, or inappropriately. So I occasionally sent Op Ed and general interest pieces to newspapers on such subjects as conversation, the changing things people say, a certain social behavior, or broader social and political trends.

Despite encountering the widespread rejection and indifference which are the prevalent response to most freelance work, I persisted and even managed to get regular slots: for two years, I had a monthly column in *Helsingin Sanomat*, Finland's most prominent newspaper, and for ten years I've had my own column in San Francisco's *West Portal Monthly*, a small but growing neighborhood paper. The latter, especially, provides me with the chance of writing about everything I please, and telling my readers what I think.

And, of course, also how I think. This, it seems to me, is one of many things the column allows and one of its many joys. There are no fixed forms: the piece has to be short, yes, but it can have as many twists and turns as the writer is capable of taking his reader through. Far from the column being only a forum for opinions, it's actually a showcase for a certain presentation of self and outlook. At best, it allows writers to talk uninhibitedly on paper, allowing them to assume a persona, a voice of the author but not necessarily the only one. Thus opinions and attitudes are tested rather than proclaimed, offering the trial balloon of an idea, or the logical consequence of a thought the writer does not wholly endorse.

In this, the column can occasionally slip into the direction of fiction and take on some of the freedoms of that genre. After all, a sketch allows for invention—and not being bound by reportorial obligations, there were times when I happily merged two characters into one, or filled in settings as best I could. My hapless lovers in "Sad, Ludicrous Experiences" practiced their uneasy adultery in two countries as remote from each other as Scotland and Australia , but did not live in either. For the rest, the account of their experience was true to the letter, at least as I heard about it.

That sort of piece is my favorite. I tell a little story, I make some observations, I turn a generalization or two, and that's that. Some columns make a point by telling a story, others tell a story by making a point. Some are more overtly discursive, while the best—in my opinion—blend discourse and personal narrative. Thus, in "Almost a Foreign Country," I attempt to render the feeling of aging and reflect on it: for it has felt to me for years that as we grow older, we become estranged from the familiar country in which we live. Such estrangement, the odd distancing it involves, is a theme in many pieces and indeed a motif in the book as a whole.

As for those commenting on some aspect of the time or some event in the news, e.g. the Littleton school shootings, I am fond of them but aware of how quickly they become dated. True, Littleton will not soon fade from our minds, but it's intrinsically not so different from other school shootings, and while I stand by my remarks about how this dreadful episode relates to our American setting, the event still dims and its singular horror is no longer as emotionally present as it once was.

Nothing fades as fast, it seems to me, as political commentary. At the time this book is published, the Iraq war will still be fresh in our minds, but the reader won't care that in 2003 I wrote that the insurgency was initiated by Sunnis outraged and terrified of having to live in a Shiite-run country. So I have eliminated from this collection many political columns, commentaries on day-to-day public events and even on the figures who dominate them. What's left is what I felt had some abiding significance.

And here we return to the form. The column is best when it comments on central human situations, on the passage of time, on the hundreds of conditions with which human beings have to cope. It is best when the author casts a skeptical eye on the vagaries of his own time, looks at the present as if it were the past (and perhaps looks at history as if it had not passed).

Sometimes it is keenest when it can give the flavor of a situation as well as tell you about it. How best, for instance, to render that strange, relatively new smarminess of our public life? ("Thank you, General, for your long years of service to our country.") How to make readers see that what they accept as normal and ordinary is truly odd? That almost cries out for satire, precisely what I've done in "The Hearing," which, if successful, could stand as a kind of generic account of all congressional confirmation hearings of new CIA or DNI appointments. There the jargon, the opaqueness of the answers, the sense of hyped mystification, and above all the solemn self-importance of the interlocutors is depicted in such a way that my satirical account could serve as a transcript of past and, no doubt, future hearings.

While my readers have not always understood my satirical thrusts—some even expressing sympathy for my imaginary disease CHOIS—this has not been where I've sustained the most criticism. Many have taken me to task for my hostility to "grief counselors," and I was surprised to learn from them that grief counselors and hospice nurses were often one and the same. Well, I am full of admiration for the latter but dislike the former, who seem to be a lugubrious presence in the aftermath of every tragedy and are, I think, especially pernicious in their interaction with children. For me, they symbolize our unfeeling times, which drip with sentimentality but evade sentiment, frequently substituting professional glibness for ordinary emotion, and allowing real facts and true feelings to go unexpressed and unseen. It was out of some such feeling that "West of the Westernmost Point" came, a time in childhood when grief and horror were so raw that they continued to live in me to this day.

Similarly, in "Coming to Terms with the Holocaust," I show that there is no coming to terms with something as unspeakable as the Holocaust. My own childhood experiences of that time and place make me suspicious of those unbrushed by it who seek now to draw lessons from what they do not know. The idea that the Holocaust can be integrated or somehow accommodated strikes me as naïve and rather callow—either an unthinking reflex or a well-intentioned desire to give it meaning, to find transcendence in enormous suffering. Not that I think one can do nothing with its legacy. On the contrary, we are all enjoined to do what we can, however little, to mitigate suffering, to relieve wherever we are able the pains of those who are victims here and surround us now. My view of this in no way encourages quietism. Those real acts, not unlike the acts of heroism that took place during the Holocaust, both relieve suffering and constitute the real antidote to the facile and formulaic distortions to which our time is prone.

In like vein, the genuine heroes of 9/11 cannot be recognized as long as we impute heroism to the victims of 9/11 in its aftermath. This seems a reckless disregard of what they were and a sentimentalizing urge to turn their victimhood and the sheer pity of their deaths into something manageable, and perhaps politically useful. In the process, their reality—and the reality of their situation—is violated.

Such critiques of time and place have a context, of course. In "Places on the Map and in the Mind," I try to sketch my own relationship to the America I came to at age sixteen and portray what I have seen in other places, such as Holland and Finland. I also present the views of others about us and about people in distant places. America makes me infinitely comfortable and yet also makes me gnash my teeth. The Holland of my childhood is a source of abiding curiosity and fondness, but it is no longer mine. Finland I was privileged to get to know somewhat but could never give myself to wholly. All are here in some form.

But finally, I take most pride in rendering my sense of the varieties of human behavior and the ambivalences we're all prone to. Many columns and almost all my aphorisms have that as their subject. The aphorism seems to me the most introspective of forms. And while I see an aphorism as a column in miniature, and a column as an expanded aphorism, I am conscious of how quaint the shorter form looks. Odd that in a time of one-liners we do not seem to value aphorisms. I have sprinkled them throughout, but could just as well have located them all in one place. After all, an aphorism that requires a context is not an aphorism.

Most of these pieces have, in slightly different form, appeared in print before. Some were given as radio talks to BRT 3, the Belgian Broadcasting Service. Where necessary I have received permission to reprint. My thanks to the *Los Angeles Times*, the *San Francisco Chronicle*, the *San Francisco Examiner*, the *East Bay Express*, *The Sacramento Bee*, *The Daily Californian*, the *San Jose Mercury News*, *Helsingin Sanomat*, *Hufvudstadsbladet*, *Tikkun.org*, *The American Scholar*, *Kruispunt*, and, of course, the *West Portal Monthly*.

Prologue: Almost a Foreign Country

"Do you want a shtraw?" asks the young man in the coffee shop.

When did "straw" become "shtraw"? I wonder sourly for a long minute.

Relax, I tell myself. Language changes, and pronunciation changes too. What does it matter?

But I stay annoyed. He should say "straw," I think, and nobody should say "inshtrument," "shtrategy" and "shtreet."

A few minutes later I overhear two young women talking. They speak with that odd kind of croak, the sounds seeming to emanate from deep, deep in the throat. A friend of mine reports that linguists call it "throating," as if that explains anything. "Yeah," rasps one to the other in a way I can hardly mimic, "she ought to . . . like . . . give it up."

I take my examples from language and speech, because these illustrate small changes that in no way affect me and should therefore be of no consequence. They're irrelevant to my well-being.

Which is why I try to account for their effect on me. Is it that they are mindless imitations? One person does it, and another follows? Sure, but we all learned language that way. Probably my irritation derives from nothing more than difference—just not what I'm used to.

Language is the pool in which I swim. Now the water is chillier, less inviting. I miss my comforts; my world has become defamiliarized.

But why should more important social changes bother me less, changes that could have an impact on me?

Maybe because I can take a stand for or against them. I can formulate and express an opinion on them, judge them, or grapple with them.

Manfred Wolf

I recognize that in part I can say this because some of those social changes have pleased me. I'm content with many alterations in manners and morals. Our more realistic family values I approve of, though they clearly drive some to distraction. Our present-day views of sex I find altogether more sensible than our views, say, fifty years ago.

On the other hand, the ubiquitous noise of our jingle-jangle ADD society—cell phones ringing, people talking too loudly, too fast, and saying little—upsets me. And the slogan culture, the platitude culture, the piety culture—these I detest.

Still, it's the little changes of language and fashion that bother me most.

The older years are made difficult by changes. We live in the same country but it looks strange; it's almost a foreign country. That combination of familiarity and unfamiliarity is stressful.

It's like living in the same house but your bedroom is now oddly, disorientingly located. In the kitchen, the dishwasher is gone and so are some small utensils. Sure, other things take their place, but you never quite know what they're for or how to use them, so you don't. Some young person explains them to you, but he talks quickly and carelessly, and you can't quite hear what he is saying, and he has an unpleasant manner, and you want him to go away.

Unaccountably, the house has stairs now, which weren't there before, and they're steep and a little hard to climb. It might as well be a different house—in a different country.

2005

Lost and Happily Found: On the Borders of Sadness and Hope

LOST AND HAPPILY FOUND

I was on my way to the swimming pool of the Pinnacle Sports Club at the Jewish Community Center, something I do two or three times a week. Before my swim, I often sit in the Royal Ground coffee shop on Sacramento Street and read the newspaper or a book. Sometimes I scribble down notes for an article, and once or twice, I have even written a column there.

On this particular morning I was eager to read an article in a Dutch paper on the Surinamese author Astrid Roemer. I had tucked the paper into my jacket pocket before leaving the house and was looking forward to reading it while drinking my decaf and eating a small oatcake, which is also part of my ritual.

When I got to the café, I patted my jacket pocket. No paper. How is that possible?

I now walked back to the car, thinking that the paper had fallen from my pocket when I got out of the car. I checked next to the car, under the car, in the car. Nothing. No paper.

Well, what could I do? I decided to skip the café and have my swim.

Gradually, I was getting used to the loss. It wasn't a great loss and I started thinking of other things. Still, I could feel, in an almost tactile way, the article I wanted to read and could see before me the picture of the author who was its subject. I felt a slight, continuing regret for not being able to do so.

After swimming, I decided to go to the café, but changed my mind at the last moment when I remembered I had lost the paper and so had nothing to read.

I got back to the car and suddenly saw next to it, on the sidewalk, the familiar small print and narrow format of my Dutch newspaper. It was just lying there, and though people had stepped on it, the paper was clearly intact.

My mood soared. I felt a surge of energy. Since I now had the paper I might as well go back to the Royal Ground for coffee and a snack. I returned to the café, ordered, sat down and realized that a page was missing, the one with the article on the author from Surinam.

My spirits fell somewhat, but not badly, because I still had the paper, though not the part I really wanted.

For a moment I thought self-pityingly, 'Of all pages, just that one had to be lost.' But then I thought I would go and have yet another look around the car.

So I looked next to the car, under it, scanned the whole sidewalk. Nothing. No page with funny Dutch print. I checked in the car again. No.

Well, time to give up. I got into the car and saw wrapped around the tire of the car in front of mine a page of funny Dutch print! I quickly got out and unpeeled the page from the tire. It was indeed the missing article. What luck that the car had not moved for a whole hour!

My spirits now were very high, and two feelings, two thoughts, came to me:

1) A small, fortunate event can turn the day around. We seem to need this bit of luck, a little break, the perfect cup of coffee, that incredibly convenient parking place. Well, maybe we don't need it, but we certainly want it.

2) I couldn't help but experience this episode symbolically. Something was restored to me, some loss made up. I had been careless or unlucky, and the world did not punish me but set things right.

Just that realization made me almost jubilant, just the sense that something could actually be given back. If what I have lost can be recovered, then what I have handled badly can be undone, set right.

And, oh yes: the article, how was it? Just so-so, not all that interesting. Not worth all the effort I took to retrieve it. But somehow that did not matter.

1998

LUDICROUS, SAD STORIES

When I was a boy reading Dutch books, I always liked stories in a certain very popular Dutch genre, which consisted of ludicrous, sad tales.

This category of stories had a name in the Netherlands, which I can't recall, but I do know that it is the sort of genre that couldn't possibly thrive in America, where, after all, every cloud has a silver lining and every tragedy occasions the thought that "the healing has already begun."

But because I have been weaned on this genre, or because I have a certain unhappy quirk in my temperament, I tend to see it everywhere. If you look at things a certain way, you will see these stories played out all around you.

Here's one:

A friend of mine, a middle–aged Scot, has been conducting an affair for many years with a married woman who lives in Australia. I can speak freely here because this book has limited distribution in Edinburgh and maybe none at all in Sydney.

Vincent and Maggie met while he was on sabbatical in Australia and she was a university librarian. Since that blissful time, now nine years ago, they have been corresponding, then faxing, and now e-mailing. Occasionally they speak on the phone. E-mailing is especially satisfying, because they can write every day and occasionally almost feel as if they are having a conversation.

But of course it's not like being together. Much of their correspondence consisted of how wonderful it would be to be together again and lie once more in each other's arms.

Academics are happily mobile, and my friend arranged to give several lectures in Australia, one of them in Sydney ("The effect of indoor-plumbing on Victorian fiction"). He would have two and a half days in Sydney, and asked Maggie to do everything possible so that they could spend much of those days with each other.

She got very excited, told her husband she had to go to a librarians' conference during that time, made hotel reservations in a charming beach town up the coast, etc.

I make it sound easy, but anyone who has ever been unfaithful knows that timing and logistics are demanding, and a thousand and one arrangements necessary. This sort of trysting has to be carried out with military precision.

In one of his e-mails, Vincent also asked her to obtain an overhead projector for his lecture. This was foolish of him. Such an arrangement should have been made with his academic hosts, but I think it betrays the folly of the lover whose vanity makes him think that everything about him is of consummate interest to the beloved.

She e-mailed back that she would see to it, but in her excitement, and her need to organize things, and in her tension about possible discovery—was the charming beach town far enough away, might she bump into a friend of the family there?—forgot all about the overhead projector.

Vincent arrived, was met by his girlfriend, whisked off to the lecture—but there was no overhead projector and the lecture was a fiasco.

Several of the finer points he wanted to illustrate about flushing and emotional release got lost.

They spent the next day and a half quarreling with each other about *her* failure to remember, *his* lack of understanding for her situation, and everything else that this sort of relationship can cast up. The last day was better but still raw.

Occasionally it almost felt like old times, but they were both imbued with the melancholy of their impending separation and the realization of having wasted precious time in a nasty fight.

When she drove him to the airport for his flight to Melbourne, neither Vincent nor Maggie had any sense of when they would see each other again.

1999

Gone Fishing: A Sad, Ludicrous Adventure

Readers of my column know that I am very fond of the sad, ludicrous story, a genre that (along with "small humiliations of daily life") has flourished in the Netherlands but would have scant chance of success in this country. Such stories are both funny and disheartening, a combination, I think, Americans frown on.

This time the story is from my own life.

When my children were young, I had a persistent feeling of guilt about never having taken them fishing. I knew that taking them fishing was a good thing to do, but I did not know how to fish, and I was not much interested in learning.

On my youngest boy's twelfth birthday, I was beginning to have that sense of Now or Never. I told him about my guilt, and after a few weeks he mentioned that it was not too late and that his eleven-year-old friend Chuck across the street had a fishing rod and knew how to fish. (His father had taught him.)

First he and then we asked Chuck if we could take him and if he would instruct us in the art of fishing.

He was very eager, and my son Paul, always good-natured, was happy with the whole arrangement.

Shortly thereafter, we set off for Lake Merced. The eleven-year-old said he had fished in Lake Merced many times and "knew the best places where to go." In the car, Chuck held on proudly to a shiny new fishing rod. I asked him about bait, but he said it wasn't necessary. His dad did not use any.

Lake Merced was as usual enveloped in a dense fog, but never mind: the object here was to learn to catch a few big ones, not to get a suntan. Both Paul and I followed Chuck as he resolutely walked over to the edge of the lake and somewhat slowly unreeled a line. It did not look right to me, but who was I to argue with Chuck and his father, as outdoorsy a fellow as I was indoorsy?

Chuck stood there for a long time. At last Paul called, "Are they biting?" I added, "Chuck, are you sure that's all there is to it?"

Chuck did not answer, and we all stood around for a while.

I looked at the brand new fishing rod. "How often have you gone fishing, Chuck?" I asked blandly. Paul was starting to grin.

Chuck looked at us and then at his rod and said, "Well, we haven't gone yet. My dad has been too busy." When he saw us both smiling, Chuck started to smile too.

Paul, who at this moment could have been very disappointed, once again showed his good nature and laughed hard. Chuck joined in, and so did I.

As we were heading back for the car, Paul said, "Let's go to Safeway and buy a fish."

"Good idea," I answered. "This lake doesn't seem to have any fish, but we can still have fish for dinner."

At this point, the story stops being part of the sad, ludicrous Dutch genre, which is supposed to leave the reader feeling bleak. Now it is becoming an American story, with hope and optimism at the end, a *Reader's Digest* story or a TV human-interest segment. The always obligatory healing can now begin.

Why? Because Chuck remained pleased with himself and Paul always laughs when he tells the story, and I do too. We think of it as a funny story rather than a fiasco.

I may feel guilty about many things having to do with parenting, but I don't feel guilty about not having taken my kids fishing. And in good American fashion, I can even say I learned from this episode:

Above all else, kids love to laugh—and have an adult laugh with them.

1999

Another Sad, Ludicrous Adventure

As I get older, I feel more and more that certain experiences will never recur. It's a sad feeling: the thought that you may never again expect your whole world to change, that you'll never be inflamed enough to think that finally, what you have always wanted has arrived.

And yet, I am also often surprised by a kind of perpetual recurrence of certain feelings and even episodes.

The other day, my friend H. asked me to go to a Great Gatsby dance with her. I really did not want to go: I do not do the Charleston, and my Foxtrot leaves something to be desired. Besides, I have sore feet.

But I said yes to please her and not appear the constant naysayer.

As soon as I had said that I would go, my mind started racing: was there time for me to take some lessons—secretly, surreptitiously—so that I could surprise her when the twenties event arrived?

My mind traveled back two decades. My then-girlfriend M. and I had taken a class in Greek dancing. We had been to Greece the summer before and wanted to stay in cultural touch with that time and place.

Every Tuesday night, M. and I went to a church in Noe Valley and met up with about ten other couples. Soon the teacher put on a record and the whole line of us would move to the "Kritiki Syrto" or to any number of dances whose names I have now forgotten.

The teacher was a small, bald, rather old man, who was an excellent dancer. Unfortunately, he was an impatient teacher. Every time we mastered a dance, he instantly went on to the next. He never gave us time to enjoy what we had mastered with such pain. We never really got to dance.

9

(He clearly wanted to teach "graduate school" dance. Imagine you're teaching at a junior college when your whole being cries out for a position at Harvard!)

When I say "we" mastered a dance, I mean M. and perhaps some of the others. It is debatable whether I ever really did. But as I said, we did not get a chance to enjoy what we did learn, because our teacher was already explaining and demonstrating the intricacies of the next dance.

Because of this frustration, we quit—I happily, M. somewhat reluctantly.

But the dream died hard. I wanted to master Greek dancing and, above all, surprise and impress M..

So I decided to take lessons on my own.

Somewhere in the Avenues, a rather bewildered young man was teaching me, his only student, the intricacies of Greek line dancing.

I lasted in the lessons for three months and did some practicing on my own. And then I forgot the whole thing. And, of course, M. never brought up the subject of Greek dancing again.

But about two years later, M. and I were at a wedding in San Diego. Suddenly out of nowhere came loud Greek music. M. looked at me expectantly, hopefully. She was in full Greek dancing mode. Several other people were already in line. It was the moment to shine.

But the two years had done their awful work. I remembered no steps, neither from the original teacher nor from the private lessons. Nothing. Too much time had passed (for me, not M.). I hopped along like a fool, hoping nobody would notice my total lack of Greek finesse.

The only thing I ever got out of this career in dance was the story—the wry kind of sad, ludicrous story so beloved by Dutch writers, so uncommon in America.

2000

Two Celebrities in One Place:
Mulisch and Milosz

Almost twenty years ago, the famous Dutch novelist Harry Mulisch spent a few months at Berkeley as a Regents professor at the university. In the course of his stay, the head of Berkeley's Dutch Studies program, my friend Johan Snapper, organized an elegant dinner for about forty guests—prominent members of the Bay Area Dutch community, academics from various universities, and other notables. Among the guests was the Polish poet and Nobel Laureate Czeslaw Milosz, a professor at Berkeley.

Seated at six or seven round tables, we were each introduced by our host, who made a brief mention of our accomplishments. Professor Snapper has a very un-Dutch fulsomeness, as much due to a slight tendency to flattery as to an innate generosity of spirit.

Perhaps the only ones whose accomplishments did not have to be inflated were Mulisch and Milosz.

The two celebrities sat far apart from each other, and at each table there was a mix of Dutch and non-Dutch, and the former were not necessarily familiar with the books of either giant. When Johan Snapper mentioned Milosz's essays on totalitarianism, *The Captive Mind*, I heard a very Dutch voice exclaim,

"God . . . did Mulisch write that?"

To which someone else replied, "I thought he wrote novels."

It dawned on me that Milosz sounded to several people like Mulisch. True, in Polish, he's "Mi-wosh," but English—or Dutch—speakers don't say it that way.

As the evening wore on and the wine flowed, it became ever clearer that some people were confused about there being two Mulisches, or thought there was one with any number of diverse talents, or that there was one who was both Dutch and Polish, poet and novelist—and that at a certain point they had stopped caring whether there were one or two.

The university people who were present, mainly American, did not share this confusion but, not knowing Dutch, were unaware of it. Anyway, they spent much time beaming and nodding, which is what Americans often do at such occasions.

Milosz, who sat at my table, suddenly announced to his tablemates, "Under the communists . . . they do this when you speak up," and he rapidly slid the side of his hand over his throat. Shortly thereafter he fell fast asleep at the table.

Mulisch, on the other hand, was being the hardworking guest, utterly charming, talking to four or five people at his table, no doubt strategically placed there by our host.

The evening ended happily, with the relatively short good-byes that distinguish American from European dinner events. On the way out the door, I heard a pleasant Dutch businessman from San Francisco say, "There, there he is," pointing at the dapper, stocky figure of Czeslaw Milosz disappearing into the night.

The whole experience made me acutely conscious of how vaguely we are perceived, how indistinctly—and it made me wonder too . . . if achievements and events become so blurred in the present, how will they be perceived in the future?

When both of these formidable authors are gone, their lives will be owned by those who have only the feeblest grasp of what they achieved. Even so, they are among the lucky ones. After all, they've left something real and tangible, and, though not fully known, they at least remain behind in some fashion, however muffled and distorted, while the rest of us disappear without a trace into the forgetful night.

2006

Epiphany in Finland

It was my first trip to Finland. Like other tourists, I visited Helsinki's majestic cathedral, stood in the famous market at the harbor, and marveled at the "white nights" of summer. I drove to the resort of Hanko and visited the old city of Porvo. Soon, I was taken by my hosts to their *stuga*, their summer home. I had heard about the Finnish obsession with summer homes, the cottages on lakes or the little houses near the sea, sometimes on islands. Theirs was actually a large farmhouse, which had been until the fifties a working farm, magnificently situated on an inland sea near Salo, some sixty miles west of the capital.

My Finnish friend's mother was as warm as the day was chilly. A dignified woman, gray-haired and straight in bearing, she had an easy, humorous way about her. It was clear that she loved this house where she had settled after a life of rootlessness and wandering as the wife of a Finnish ambassador. Now widowed, she had come to rest in this setting. She gave me a tour of the lovely red house with its large kitchen and cheerful windows. An indoor veranda looked out on the rolling land between house and sea. A low red barn stood to one side of the house. She pointed to it and smiled. "We have no facilities here. But there is the outhouse."

No facilities? I wondered. We had just turned on the electric light in the handsome, large kitchen. A telephone was visible in the little sitting room facing a lush garden with a cheerful pavilion. The mail had arrived, and a number of letters lay on top of the latest edition of the *New York Review of Books*.

As a still somewhat jet-lagged tourist, I pondered the question doggedly, then had an urge to wash up from the train trip. There was no bathroom, but here in the kitchen, beneath the gleaming copper pots and pans, was a small sink. No faucet though.

In the next hour or two I kept trying to turn on nonexistent taps. In the outhouse there was a bowl, water in a bucket, soap, a towel, everything to get clean, but still it all felt awkward. Why were there no "facilities"?

The last time I had been in an outhouse I was five years old, in Holland. World War II had not yet begun, and my parents had taken my brother and me to a farm on a lake, and to this very day I remember gleefully swinging a cat by the tail there and my father standing stiffly on a sailboat in a suit and raincoat.

But now my thoughts were almost crassly American. Why have electricity, a phone, the latest magazines, and not running water? And when my friend showed me the sauna and said that ever since she was a child she had felt that you couldn't get as clean anywhere as when you washed in a sauna, I took it for a bit of harmless Finnish kitsch.

That night I told her my puzzlement. And she answered, "Not having all these conveniences brings you closer to the past, and to the way people lived then." She is a writer whose books often dwell on the importance of the past, on memory, on the settings of our lives.

It is now a year later. I am in the same place. Finland is having a rare, prolonged heat wave. Off the black rocks at the bay's edge is a view of almost biblical purity. Reeds grow in profusion along the shore, and a lovely wooden pier divides these rushes and leads into the glistening water. Only two other people are in sight: a small boy and girl, the neighbor children, idle quietly in an old row boat.

Again we sit around the big, square kitchen table and talk. A warm glow pervades me after the long swim. The conversation turns to some Americans who had visited earlier in the summer and had been made uncomfortable by the absence of their creature comforts. I think of my own doubts.

"Why, actually, don't you have running water?" I ask my friend's mother.

"I like getting it from my own well and checking it periodically," she replies. "I like to think about the water level. It gives me a feeling of control. Also, I like to think about which tree I'm going to chop down. And when I bring in my own wood for the woodstoves or to heat the sauna, I feel I'm working on my own sustenance. It's not exercise but work. I am part of a process, of a natural rhythm. Unlike tennis—where first you play, then you rest—this exercise is part of what maintains me."

I understand that. After all, back in California I teach my students Wordsworth and the English Romantic poets. Didn't these sages preach that when we are part of the natural process, we are most whole? And doesn't this ease with our natural setting quiet an ever-aching human aloneness?

Probably, in this glorious summer, many Finns are explaining, each in their own way, some such thing to their foreign guests.

Suddenly my friend's mother adds: "You know, when I'm in the kitchen, drawing the water, I'm aware of doing the same thing, making the same gestures, that my mother did."

I walk out into the garden and collect some water from the well to add to the kitchen supply, and inexplicably remember a bucket of water held up by my parents for me, and my small hands gingerly but happily scooping out water to splash over my face outside of that distant farmstead, under a lowering Dutch sky.

Late, after the long meal, some semblance of dusk seems finally to be falling. Outside of the windows the Finnish forest beckons, and my friend and I go for a walk.

Around a sudden bend in the clearing of the forest we see great umbrella-headed mushrooms, and I crouch down to look at them and think again of the time when my parents had taken my brother and me to that farm near the Dutch lake. But now I remember too that we had gone mushrooming in the woods, on that warm afternoon half a century ago, when my parents were still young. My father was bending down to press the underside of each mushroom and he told me, then five years old, to see if they were turning blue. I can still feel the excitement and warmth of that childhood day, in that happy and eager-for-the-future time before the war.

Now, in this Finnish wood, on this warm evening, looking at a huge gaudy mushroom, picturing my father bending over the mushrooms excitedly, agility and youth in his gestures and pleasure in his eyes, I realize that I never saw him so excited again about anything so ordinary, so common, in all the war-wrecked years since. He and my mother had saved us from the Nazis by fleeing Holland in 1942 and wandering with us through Belgium, France, Spain, Portugal, to Dutch Guyana and Curaçao. But he had lost his parents and all his brothers except one. Long after we had reached safe haven, he was distraught by what was taken from him. For me, as a growing boy, that was frequently difficult: other children had fathers who could get excited by football games or nature walks, but mine seemed always to stand to one side with distant and haunted eyes, seeing nothing before him and everything that was not. In all the years of loss and pain and exile since that time, he could never absorb himself in an everyday event again. I cherish the image of when that was not yet so.

Now that I no longer live in Holland but in California—that paradise of refugees where everyone's past is elusive—I feel a sudden sense of luck to recover a bit of my own history. The poets I teach my students speak not only of the wholeness of life but of the necessity of the memory. It seems essential that the past not disappear altogether. Perhaps the long summers in the country do something like that for Finnish people—remind them a little of how their parents and grandparents lived, and even how they themselves once lived. My own brief summer days in the *stuga* were no doubt very different from those of most Finns, but they helped me to recover some distant memories. How far I had to travel to find a small part of myself that lay buried in the past.

1990

ABOUT WRITING A MEMOIR

For several years now, I have been working on a memoir of my childhood and adolescence in the forties in Curaçao, a Caribbean island in the West Indies.

Several sections have been published in a variety of literary magazines, and the generally warm response I have had has encouraged me to keep writing.

But I often ponder this strange activity. Why am I really doing this? In the great glut of memoirs, is one more really necessary? What will mine accomplish?

Well, aside from the satisfactions of ego, I think something is gained by rescuing this odd slice of life from oblivion.

The late forties, as lived by Dutch-speaking refugees in an exotic outpost of the Kingdom of the Netherlands, under the long shadow of the war—isn't this worth reviving?

Who would know anything about it after the handful of people who lived through that experience are dead?

So my aim is to show something about that time and place, to tell something about my family, and finally to reveal a bit of myself—and to depict how all of it was affected by the European catastrophe that changed all the principal characters forever.

And the place makes it a story of three cultures.

Here you have the local Curaçaoans, resilient descendants of slaves; the Dutch, colonial functionaries, well-intentioned but myopic; and the Jewish refugees, relieved to have escaped, but bewildered and upset. Even in this latter category, to which our family belonged, there were serious divisions. The recent refugees from Europe were Dutch, while earlier Jewish settlers on the island came from Eastern Europe.

Most important to me is to tell the story and show how we all collided, lived together, got along, and to do so, I tell certain incidents that should bring it all to life.

Whether these concern my grandfather entertaining an American gangster who pretended to be an orthodox Jew, or the time one of my teachers tried to capture a small wild donkey and put the animal in the back seat of his car, from which it promptly escaped, or a hapless, furtive, deranged man in our Surinamese detention center who had to leave his family behind in wartime Europe, my aim is to have them be real and thereby show the pathos, the humor, and the oddness of that time.

And that's of course where the problems of turning memory into writing begin.

For instance, my father comes across in a much livelier way than my mother, because my father had certain peculiarities: he was self-absorbed and unseeing, but eager to dispense a kind of Jewish folk wisdom; he was often unintentionally funny.

My mother, on the other hand, whom I felt closest to, was a peace-maker, a diplomat, a woman with strong opinions but mild, soothing manners. She tends, at this stage of composition, to be a paler character in the book.

Some of this is not only due to problems of literary form but deficiencies of the writer. I may not be able to handle subtly difficult characters, just as I'm not very good with descriptions.

I have the most difficult time bringing out the sound, smells, sights of the island. I am not as observant of landscape and setting as I am of people, their moods, the way they think, their turns of phrase. And I appear to be most retentive about what they said and how they spoke all those years ago. So I find it easy to render dialogue, much of which I remember, some of which I reconstruct.

Which leads, of course, to one of the dirty secrets of memoirists.

Do they, we, remember or invent? For myself I say that I remember a good deal, but, oh, how I wish I had kept a diary or a journal! Nothing will bring back all the detail of that period the way a journal would.

Still, even without a diary, I remember with the utmost clarity when my fifth-grade teacher lit a whole series of cigarette lighters and asked the kids which one gave the brightest light, or the day our biology teacher was told, in that curious, chanting way the Curaçaoan kids had, that the "missing link" was actually a fellow pupil in class.

While some memories are astonishingly clear, I do stylize and retouch, and I do occasionally streamline two characters into one. To that extent, this memoir, like others, is a kind of fiction. And a similar artistry is at work in the structure of the book.

Each chapter is a kind of short story, polished, finished, able to stand on its own—which makes me worry that a publisher will say, "Don't give me a book of interconnected stories; give me a memoir that is sequential and reads like a memoir."

But as I write it, that is still not my biggest worry.

My biggest worry is that the sort of kid I was is just not exciting enough for a book: I was observant, old for my years, cautious, judgmental, level-headed, well-read.

I had my hopes and dreams and conflicts, and I tried to escape pain by dreaming of the future, but is it enough? Would anyone really want to read about it?

1999

Related Aphorisms

Those who set preconditions for happiness will not achieve it.

After we die, we belong wholly to the distortions of the living.

People want God to answer their prayers in part because they want to be noticed.

Character and Perception: To See Ourselves as Others See Us

To See Ourselves as Others See Us

All my life I have regarded myself as a bit of a diplomat. It was always easy for me to see both sides of a dispute and, given the occasional chance, my own mild manner allowed me to succeed in bringing the contenders closer together.

Sometimes the two sides did not know I was involved. This was part of the pleasure for me: I enjoyed working behind the scenes.

It's one of my frustrations that my working life afforded me little opportunity to exercise these nascent diplomatic skills. Though a lifetime of university teaching and writing added up to a good career, I could have done some part-time administration or served on boards of organizations, as I do now. But I was always so focused on doing my immediate job—teaching—that I did not pursue this other inclination, except on a personal scale.

All this by way of introducing another subject.

A few years ago, I arranged a lecture for a retired colleague. A dynamic but difficult man, he had published an interesting World War II memoir. He seemed to feel that he never got his due at retirement, and equally, the powers-that-be thought that he was voracious in his need for recognition and praise.

Both sides were probably right.

I introduced the idea of his lecture on campus to my former department chair, a generous, reasonable man, who was not enthusiastic but certainly helpful. I then persuaded the retiree, who was willing but still nursing his grievances. I made several calls to both sides. It was not diplomacy on the grand scale, but it required effort and tact.

Other people got involved and promoted the talk. When the time came, the speaker performed well. The audience was gracious, attendance excellent. The event was a success.

Afterwards, I thought no more about it, having then turned my sights on larger game. After all, the Israeli-Palestinian quarrel still needed to be resolved.

But a few weeks later, a remark was reported back to me, made by a colleague who had promoted the lecture. "Oh," she was quoted as saying, "Manfred is a fixer."

A fixer? Isn't a fixer a somewhat shady person who arranges shady deals?

Suddenly I caught a glimpse of myself as seen through another's eyes. To her, I was not a tireless, well-meaning diplomat but a manipulator with an unpleasant agenda.

And of course, manipulation is part of the diplomacy game. Didn't Henry Kissinger, when he arranged the Golan Heights Accord (which has now held for several decades), tell both sides how much they were admired by the other? Lies and tricks, no doubt, but I'm glad he used them.

And I have to confess that small manipulations and indirections are part of my character. I hate telling people the unpleasant truth.

So this woman saw something in me that was there. That she highlighted it and, at that moment, probably saw no other part of me is unfortunate and regrettable—but not incomprehensible.

If we knew, really knew, how our friends talk about us, would we still like them?

There are several ways to look at this. One, the other person sees a side of us we don't. Two, the other person twists and distorts some part of us. Three, and worse still, we're seen quickly, one-dimensionally, superficially.

That's probably how we are viewed after death, if remembered at all—quickly, one-dimensionally, and casually appropriated in some fashion by the survivors for their own psychological comfort.

But while we're still alive, there may be a gain in seeing ourselves as others see us. We get a new view of ourselves and, for a moment, may actually overcome a certain perpetual self-delusion.

Worth it?

2005

Mind Over Mattress

My friend H. thinks I need a new mattress. "How old is it anyway?"

"Oh, about 20 years," I say, shading the truth somewhat. I actually think it's closer to 30.

"If you got yourself a new mattress, your sleep would improve," she added. "Your insomnia would get much better."

She thinks I won't do what she so sensibly recommends because I'm set in my ways, used to all my old things, hate change, etc. She is right about that.

I think she recommends this because she has a tendency to think in categorical, quantitative terms. If you're depressed, you'll get help from anti-depressants. If you can't sleep, get a new mattress.

This advice comes from that certain way of thinking. I am right about that.

So we're both right about each other, and yet there is more to it: I know that I have had many good, restful nights on this mattress, and that other things —mainly my mental state of the day—are responsible for my occasional, severe insomnia. I feel that she does not see the whole picture and that a mattress is a tiny and insignificant part of my sleeping problem.

I can see myself from the inside, while another person gets an image of me, quickly settles into that image, and then sees me accordingly.

It is what we all do with each other—she with me, and I with her. You could say we see each other ideologically. We have a certain view of each other to uphold.

Again, neither of us is wrong. These images we have of other people are remarkably accurate. But they are not complete. And people do not necessarily conform to their image all the time. No one is always in character.

"To myself I am subject; to everyone else object," goes the aphorism—but there is a sigh in that pronouncement, a wish that it were otherwise. We dream of being fully seen, wholly understood.

Some people, of course, do not want to be fully seen, because they fear they're not worthy enough, not lovable, but most people hope that if they are truly, really seen for what they are, they will be loved.

That is the great urge, and yet what arrogance resides in that wish! Why should we be fully known, what right to it do we have? Do we deserve such a painstaking love?

It reminds me of the corresponding urge many people have, to be loved unconditionally. Why should they be? Fortunately, most love is conditional.

And maybe fortunately too, some people can love and be loved while still feeling they are not fully understood.

1997

HER YELLOW HAIR

It was one of those startling comments you rarely hear in conversations, which for the most part tend to be tame and conventional. The striking, fiftyish woman said, "I'd love my husband less if he had less money." I think I would have found this comment horrifying twenty years ago, maybe even fifteen years ago. I would have thought that it wasn't much of a love that could be affected by something as crass as the amount of money he had.

But I now see this attitude as wise. It is one of the few things about which I've drastically changed my mind as I've grown older. I don't believe that people should love each other only for their money, but I now recognize that a person's money is part of who he is—an attribute he has acquired, a goal he has accomplished. This woman's husband, for example, certainly had more to do with gaining his wealth than he did with his fine features, with which God or Nature supplied him.

Why do we feel we can love people for a pretty smile or a handsome face when they themselves have had nothing to do with creating these? Even intelligence is probably something we are born with. And yet it is acceptable to love someone for her fine mind or attractive shape but not for her wealth or fame.

And even aside from the matter of separating what a person created from what she or he was simply blessed with, there is the matter of what can only be called "context." Every person has a context, and I have lately begun to appreciate that we are both ourselves and our context, and that the two are almost one.

A person's money is part of his context, his setting, his milieu; it goes with him. He is not only the person with nice manners and a warm smile but the one who can call for the best theater tickets or keep horses or drive an expensive car without thinking twice about it.

I believe that when we are young we are likely to think of ourselves as discrete entities; yes, we know we come from somewhere, we have a background, but so what? We are what we are. Now I realize that there's so much more to each of us—a setting, an atmosphere, our talents, our accomplishments, our friends. They are all a part of us, indivisible from the *gestalt* we are. A beautiful face may be less important than a warm heart, but without it, its owner would be a different person.

The great Irish poet William Butler Yeats wrote about this subject in his poem "For Anne Gregory," addressed to the daughter of a friend. The girl in the poem wants to be loved for herself and not her appearance—not for her "yellow hair." She remonstrates with the older man that she can always dye her hair and force the young men smitten with her to love her for herself alone and not her yellow hair. To which Yeats replies in the last stanza:

> I heard an old religious man
> But yesternight declare
> That he had found a text to prove
> That only God, my dear,
> Could love you for yourself alone
> And not your yellow hair.

In other, plainer, words: though God can draw the distinction between what we are and how we appear, human beings cannot.
2000

Self-Criticism vs. Habitual
Self-Disparagement

We all know people who habitually disparage themselves. Comments like, "I'm really not smart," or "I haven't got much to offer," litter their speech. It sounds like self-criticism but really isn't.

When you criticize yourself, you acknowledge flaws, you see faults, you reveal weaknesses—all laudable, in that, presumably, your self-scrutiny will lead to some correction, some self-improvement. It's constructive to look at yourself occasionally and wonder where you go wrong or what you've done in the past that could have led to present difficulties or pain. Just understanding helps—and if remediation ensues, all the better.

But when you habitually dismiss yourself, you're not engaged in anything constructive. Such utterances are mere psychological tics, which might even be the opposite of honest self-criticism. They do not induce introspection but create brooding, depression, or anxiety. While they inevitably stem from deep impulses, their impact on you, though negative, is superficial. You are not grappling with a problem but wallowing in a murky self-image.

And when you verbally express this self-disparagement, the effect on the conversation is generally not wholesome. The person you're speaking to has two possible reactions: (1) "Well, I wonder if there isn't something to that self-assessment; maybe he's not a worthwhile person at all, or else he wouldn't be saying that," or (2) "Oh, please, you're not at all what you say; you're really quite wonderful."

Some would argue that it's really the second response the speaker has solicited by criticizing himself—that he says he's awful because he wants to hear he's great—but in fact I doubt it. Usually the self-disparager is unhappy, and usually the positive rejoinder won't persuade him or even make him feel better. So I doubt that a compliment is desired.

But if it is, that compliment isn't worth much. After all, the compliment is meant to make the self-disparager feel better, and that sort of verbal rush-job has no substance or meaning, and he ends up knowing that in his bones.

My readers might argue that it's all well and good to point this out but that it won't keep a person with genuine low self-regard from saying self-dismissive things. Perhaps. But couldn't something be gained, at the very least, as a matter of etiquette almost, by not expressing these things, or trying to curb yourself from saying them? After all, you might actually think a bit better of yourself by not repeatedly asserting your worthlessness.

This verbal tic has always been with us and has drawn much sardonic commentary over the ages. "All censure of oneself," wrote the great Samuel Johnson, "is oblique praise," while another aphorist, the equally great La Rochefoucauld, said that "to refuse praise reveals a wish to be praised twice over."

But aphorists are notoriously unkind. Surely our psychologically attuned age can see a more heartbreaking weakness revealed here, requiring compassion. And yet the cure is, as it always was, "Please look. Try not to do this. It doesn't do you or anyone else any good."

Perhaps we are all ultimately reduced to such homely remedies.
2006

CHARACTER IS ALMOST EVERYTHING

The longer I'm around, the more I resist the easy explanation. Both in my day-to-day life and in my teaching, I am dismissive of the cliché, the pat response, the slogan-like solution to questions and problems.

It's not as if nothing is simple—it's just that most things are not. My students know that my attitude is connected to my definition of an intellectual as someone who thinks for himself, without being swayed by all the facile explanations that are always around, someone who looks at as many aspects of things as possible and says, "Yes AND no" or even, "On the other hand" frequently.

But though so many things are so complicated, some can be seen, and certainly responded to, as simple and good. Growing older, I find myself moved by quiet, inspiring stories, the sort of thing the *Reader's Digest* often features or *20/20* does on TV around Christmas. I give myself wholeheartedly to the stirring account of the young Irishman who lost his legs, became an athlete, achieved a medical degree—and turned into one of the now-famous Three Irish Tenors. Similarly, I am moved by the story of the door-to-door salesman in Portland whose cerebral palsy did not stop him from walking up- and downhill seven miles a day to sell household articles to often hostile, but frequently sympathetic, city dwellers.

The man—a Forrest Gump–like soul if there ever was one—never lost his sweet buoyancy, except when his ever-loving, beautiful mother developed Alzheimer's disease. The thought of her not wanting him to leave the house still brings him to tears. But even without her, his sole companion, he carries on. And not only has he borne his suffering with such sweetness, he also seems to bring it out in others.

I am becoming ever more convinced that the ancient Romans were right to insist that "character is destiny." This man had everything against him, and yet he met his lot with such radiance that his life became a success. And he worked at his good fortune too, never asking others do for him what he could do for himself.

Correspondingly, I have less patience than I used to with failure. It seems to me I know many people—myself included—who are too bowed down by troubles, by inabilities, by regrets. They have let too many things stop them. At one time, I may have thought failure interesting; now I see it as boring. I even see it as a lack of character. Why not work harder, try harder, do things differently? Why bemoan that you made a mistake in 1991, or that you did not have time to write that novel, or that they overworked you on the job, or that your kids did not turn out the way you hoped? Why not do what you can? For yourself—and for others?

These inspiring stories show how little difference there is between doing for yourself and for others. In each case, there is an absence of self-absorption, of self-involvement. You work, you try, you do something for someone—it hardly matters for whom. Both you and others will be better off for your having done so.

2000

Everything Is Mixed, Alas

She is more likely to do what Mother Teresa did than anyone I know. If she sees someone suffering, she will immediately give help. I have seen her overflow with kindness and concern. Especially the young and helpless bring out a rush of warmth in her. Children, dogs, cats—she will not turn away from them if they need her help.

This kindness is unaffected and has no sense of show about it. Where there is pain, she will do her utmost to relieve it without regard to how others view her. Nor does she pause to wonder why other people aren't helping. She is too busy giving help, too immersed in doing what she does, to give that unconcern any thought.

A saintly nature, you will say. Well, yes—but the odd thing is that she is more likely to impute narrow, selfish motives to other people than anybody I know. If a friend who is single does a favor for a man, then that must mean "she is interested" in him. If a reporter writes a certain story she doesn't like, then she supposes he must have been "bought off." She has a way of seeing people act entirely out of self-interest, though she herself is the living disproof of that.

Does she exempt herself from the mechanism she sees at work everywhere? Evidently, but she probably does not give that inconsistency much thought. Is her imputation of nastiness a result of a certain disappointment that others aren't more like her? Maybe. Could she be making up for an innate selfishness in herself by being so kind? Possibly, but I really don't think so. It's more as if the two sides of her nature live in separate realms.

I can't reconcile these two sides, and I won't try. What strikes me, though, is that they coexist and that one of them is beautiful and the other really unpleasant. And such two-sidedness marks my experience of most of my friends. Some are perceptive and then, suddenly, presented

33

with a different aspect of things, utterly unseeing. One is warm and humorous—and yet crass and callous. Another is intuitive and quick, while at the same time abysmally foolish. Yet another is interesting and generous, but ultimately narcissistic. Everyone is mixed.

I don't doubt that that is how I strike them also. Inevitably, sometimes they are pleased with me, sometimes truly disappointed.

And that is certainly what we must accept as we grow older: that everyone, everything, is mixed, that all experiences are flawed, that almost nothing is whole and pure. Something in us, maybe the child or adolescent, still hungers for the ecstatic wholeness of things, but our better self, our wiser self, knows that we must accept imperfection and love what can be loved. Even life, it turns out, is the art of the possible.

One reason human beings are ever eager to be infatuated is that in such passion they can feel, for once, wholly without ambivalence. Such fierceness of feeling is single and clear; such wholeheartedness is precious. But though we yearn for the uncontaminated experience, and may even find it, we will never keep it. Some contamination is always present; some radical imperfection is forever palpable. The only sane way to live is to accept what is less than whole and to embrace our ambivalence.

2001

APPEARANCES AND REALITIES

When I recently sat in my favorite West Portal café, a woman at the table next to me said, "You should smile more often."

It was a little hard to smile after that. I had heard this many times before, and it's advice I try to keep in mind but seldom put into practice. When I'm not smiling, which is most of the time, the two vertical creases running down from the corners of my mouth give my face a severe, disapproving look. If a plastic surgeon could guarantee success, I'd consider cosmetic surgery to have them removed.

Much as I dislike those ugly creases, I have to admit to a certain justice in them. "At fifty," said George Orwell, "we all have the face we deserve." Even truer at sixty. These lines speak a truth about me; I do disapprove.

I disapprove of a whole lot of things, many of them petty and insignificant: men who wear their caps backward; the frequent use of *like* in conversation; the thoughtlessness with which people indict others and excuse themselves; the common practice, especially among the young, of body piercing... Need I go on?

But this sort of disapproval is unattractive. I would prefer to hide it. And, to take a somewhat wider view of the whole matter: to what extent do any of these appearances really point to a reality? I may disapprove of a lot of things, but I also approve of a lot of things, so how do those vertical lines really express me?

I have no qualms about plastic surgery. People who oppose it have a way of saying that those who undergo it disguise their age, refuse to be themselves, and vainly try to improve on what nature has given them.

Well, are we not all doing that much of the time anyway?

Nature is what human beings try to suppress when it suits them, which is most of the time. That perfectly shampooed, coiffed head over there: is that natural? What about the woman at the far end of the room, with her silky legs and her expensive party dress? Or the man with his Armani jacket coming out of Schwab on our suddenly upscale avenue?

We can no longer say what is truly us because we have done such a fine job of hiding us.

Once in a while, to be sure, we let nature peep out, but only when we're in the mood. The rest of the time we are civilization's creatures.

And in fact we begin to identify with the artifice we create. To quote George Orwell again, "The face grows to fit the mask."

Just so: play a role long enough, you become that role.

But what about those people who say they're tired of playing roles?

It seems to me that most of them are no more natural when they let go of their inhibitions than when they restrain them.

They have merely taken on another style, assumed another way, embraced another set of mannerisms, which they convince themselves are truly genuine.

Usually it is a clamorous, insistent, unpleasant style, and so persuades them that it is less artificial.

Actually, it is another guise, and no more real than the rest of their guises, just as the post-cosmetic surgery me (hopefully with those frowning, disapproving vertical lines finally removed) would not be less me—or more me—than the one I am now: that severe-looking man you see at the next table.

1997

Related Aphorisms

Everyone is a mixture of low and high self-esteem. Both are usually unwarranted.

Beware of those who have never caught a glimpse of their own masks and disguises.

Admitting a vice doesn't turn it into a virtue.

Innocence always fails to recognize ambivalence.

We forgive people anything if they have genuine charm, but we condemn even the finest qualities of those without it.

Some people so crave admiration that they bask in the admiration of those they dislike.

Another's dislike for you could be the path to self-knowledge but seldom is.

Character is the degree to which we fight our nature.

However guardedly you criticize someone, you will not acquire a reputation for judiciousness. Only praise achieves that.

Some people embrace asceticism with an eagerness resembling sensuality.

We are often more proud of our faults than of our strengths.

We are less knowable than predictable.

We love to categorize others as much as we hate being categorized.

If you praise yourself, no one else will.

Patience, a solid and rare virtue, is frequently indistinguishable from sloth.

Some of our most reasonable judgments are formed less by reason than by taste.

Men and Women: The Way We Love Now

ALL KINDS OF LOVE

As I get older, I become ever more convinced that in the same way we now accept all kinds of living arrangements between romantically involved men and women— from marriage, to living together, to romantically linked but not living together—we should accept that there are all kinds of relationships between men and women, from conventionally romantic relationships, to romantically involved but not committed, to romantic friendships to simple friendship.

Something like this turned up in David Lodge's novel *Therapy*, in which a married man is once a week seeing a woman with whom he has a clandestine relationship.

It is clandestine because the relationship is erotic and illicit, yet the two do not sleep together. As I recall, Lodge compares it to what the French call an "amitié amoureuse," a loving friendship.

A different kind of relationship shows up again in Lodge's later novel, *Thinks*. Here we have the main character and a woman who is not his wife going in for some regular "snogging" in furtive moments, especially at academic dinner parties.

Why are we so intent on pinning down love relationships? Why is it all so either/or? Are they a couple, we ask, yes or no? Is it sexual or isn't it? And the minute things are so defined, so circumscribed, then certain roles and rules are assigned to the pair.

I don't doubt that what I'm describing is being practiced by some truly hip people.

Surely somewhere there must be couples who make out like in high school but don't see each other otherwise? And maybe right now there is a couple, right here in the neighborhood, who get together because *her* husband doesn't ever want her to dress in a certain way and he wears a certain outfit which *his* wife would find ridiculous? And they may or may not have sex.

All these in-between relationships should be called love relationships. To the people involved, they are probably as important as their other, more conventional relationships.

Aging does not seem to lessen their importance, as it does not in what is more conventionally called love.

Here is how the poet and playwright Tina Martin expresses that thought in her poem *What to Do with Love.*

> The heart, unlike hair,
> doesn't have to turn grayish
> Or stop turning
> Edna St. Vincent Millayish.
> Love's for all time
> And with infinite merit.
> It would take higher math or
> Elizabeth Barrett
> To count all the ways
> Love counts in our days.
> There's no need to weigh love,
> To count, or conceal it.
> Just know it and show it and
> What?—Oh, yeah. Feel it.

2001

Six (Not Wholly Related) Thoughts about Love and Romance

The other day, someone asked what, as an older man, I now thought of love and romance. It was an interesting question, all the more so because he vaguely recalled my having written a column about many kinds of love, in which I argued that there was a whole range of romantic feelings between friendship on one end and consummated passion on the other.

So what else do I think? Some of these thoughts are embarrassingly obvious, others hopefully not: I apologize for the inevitable generalizations, and I confine myself to the relations between men and women.

1) The desires, needs, wishes and hopes of men and women are often somewhat incompatible. The old cliché that men express affection in order to have sex, and women engage in sex in order to get affection, is probably true. I pass over this quickly—it has been said many times before.

2) Although there is that difference between men and women, I also believe that men and women have this in common: they can love several people, passionately, at the same time. A man can love several women, and a woman can certainly love several men at the same time. Although it is understandable when the victim of infidelity, male or female, rages, "OK, then. Choose one of us," this ultimatum does an injustice to the situation. He doesn't want to choose. He loves his wife *and* his girlfriend.

3) Whether simultaneous or serial, every relationship, however good, is limited, partial, not wholly fulfilling. With Roger she had wonderful sex, but he was selfish to the core. Now, years later, she

sometimes thinks of Roger with longing, especially since deep in her heart, she doesn't feel all that sexy with the man she is with now. Henry is much more thoughtful, he listens, he talks, he is considerate—and yet.... If you have had a number of relationships, some will have been better than others, but most, maybe all, are wanting in some crucial way.

4) Perhaps for this reason, people are so in pursuit of that drug called infatuation. When you're in that heightened state, nothing feels limited or partial. Your feelings are whole and boundless. You have no ambivalence. Human beings will do almost anything to shake their habitual ambivalence.

5) But, alas, infatuation makes way for what Freud dryly called the reality principle. You adjust to the world that is. Certainly that is the somewhat less-than-shining path to good health. Yet good health, however arrived at, whatever its compromises, is enjoyable. Unless you're a complete malcontent, you will learn to live with restrictions, and you will learn that happiness—or at least contentment—comes from not dwelling on what the relationship doesn't give. You may even learn to like the politics of the relationship, for, to paraphrase Phyllis Rose in her book *Parallel Lives*, our relationships are the greatest experience with politics we will ever have.

6) Which leads to my last proposition. Paradoxically, learning to love what you get in a relationship is a good way to learn to do without almost anything. To accept limitation is to learn to do without. My point is one that young people cannot possibly know: you do not need a relationship to be content—you do not need love in order to be happy. Nor would you really want young people to know that rather unromantic truth.

2006

Men and Women, Continued

Whatever the changes in the relations between men and women—after the sexual revolution, the feminist revolution, the whatever revolution—some gestures in the courtship between the sexes seem constant. I remember them from my first dating days in the fifties.

Here's one. You embrace the woman; she lets herself be embraced, and then gives you a few rapid pats on your back.

It means, "Don't come any closer. Have no expectations. I am not attracted to you."

Or it means, "I might be attracted to you, but don't get closer. Not until you say a few magic words, or you make a commitment of sorts."

You might well ask what a commitment means when you're in your sixties, but that's another story.

Here's another of those classic, immemorial gestures: you have had a good time together, you have talked and laughed, and now you bend toward her, desiring a kiss on the lips. At the very last possible second, she turns her face and offers you her cheek.

It means roughly what the rapid pats on the back mean: "I'm not interested, or I'm not interested unless you make a declaration, some kind of statement."

Or, "I'm not so attracted to you that I'd risk showing you more of me."

Of course, I write all this from the male point of view, being male. And I realize that you would have to be a John Updike to describe it all gracefully and in much more detail.

There are two explanations, as I see it, for the persistence of these two gestures.

One is that the women I write about are roughly of the same generation as the ones I knew in college in the fifties, and they adhere to the same codes. The second is that something less time-bound, perhaps even less culture-specific, is at work here—some deep-seated, ancient gestures in the rituals between women and men.

I hold with the second, but before I return to that thought, let me just add that such behavior becomes more common with age. It is unfortunate but true that the older years yield up more rather than less of their share of rejection.

Why? It seems unavoidable—for one thing—that each side has more to fear. She is ever more afraid of displaying her body, thinking ever more of her own imperfections, while he, though he presses on, has his matching anxieties: anxieties about the incapacities of the older years, and all that they entail.

I view all this with a mixture of irritation and wonder, even awe: despite the slogans, the exhortations, the pervasive encouragement from the helping, healing, and geriatric professions, the ancient, beautiful dance of avoidance and invitation, of rejection and communion, between men and women throbs on, in the same way, then, now, forever.

2004

John and Clara: A Valentine's Day Story

He was thirty-five, she twenty-nine. John and Clara had been dating for a while, which meant that they had seen a movie together, had dinner twice, and once went for a long hike at Point Reyes.

It was almost old-fashioned the way it all took place; he even once picked her up at her house and afterwards dropped her off—without going in.

So since they kept seeing each other, it was inevitable that the matter of making love would come up, and one evening, after another pleasant date, Clara took the initiative by asking John to come up. Her roommate, as John knew, was away for the weekend.

Clara served a drink, put on some music, and soon enough nature took its course. John was ardent, Clara passionate, and after a few hours in her pleasant, large bed, they decided that next time he would spend the night.

As he got up to get dressed, John felt distinctly infatuated. The lovemaking had been good, and Clara, in the light of a lone, dim lamp, looked fetching in her half nakedness.

She, also in the afterglow of this experience, looked up at him and smiled. "So," she asked, "What Does This Mean?"

His mood instantly turned. He looked at her first quizzically, then, as he began to grasp the question, coolly. How could she ask this? What was it supposed to Mean?

She saw the change in him and sensed a certain chill. Did he not think enough of what they had done together to see a meaning in it? Did it mean so little to him?

His mood was spoiled; so was hers. She was clearly leading him somewhere else, away from this exciting experience, into another place where rules would be made, parents met, arrangements discussed. She

49

wanted them to board the train heading for Commitment. "Like all women," he thought acidly.

Seeing his hesitation and disapproval, she thought that he just wanted to have his way with her; he wasn't interested in anything more than that. "Like all men," she thought bitterly.

While still in bed with her, John had fantasized about returning weekly, twice weekly, as often as he could. Beyond that he didn't think.

And Clara wanted that, wanted him to come back weekly, twice weekly, whatever; but it just couldn't stop with that. They had to go somewhere.

John and Clara did not see each other again. The conclusion each drew about the other was too devastating.

And, oddly, that conclusion, and maybe the generalization that went with it, was correct. Most men fear—and have experience to base it on—that women will have sex in order to maneuver them to a place men do not want to go. Once she maneuvers him there, he thinks, she may no longer be interested in sex.

Most women fear—on the basis of substantial experience—that men are interested in sex, but not in the larger things that make up a relationship, i.e., companionship, homemaking, parenting.

Could there have been ways to overcome this gap between John and Clara? Of course. Each could have disguised his or her own disappointment, could have made an adjustment to the other's wishes. Clara was unusually quick to show her hand, and John was unusually impatient to run as he did.

You could accuse either one of being ungenerous, immature, impulsive, or naïve—or, for that matter, uncompromisingly honest.

1999

AN INCONVENIENT INFATUATION

When I lived in Helsinki from 1989 to 1991, sometime toward the end of my first year, I met a soft-spoken American woman, fine-looking, tall, with just a hint of gray in her beautiful brown eyes. More than her appearance, I liked the way she spoke—quietly, warmly, directly. We met at a large university gathering to which she had been invited as a prominent member of the foreign community. As I recall, she was an executive of a Finnish corporation. She lived in Helsinki, while her husband, a Finn, lived in the United States.

The Finnish woman with whom I then lived was on one of her many out-of-town speaking engagements, and I lingered at this gathering not only because I enjoyed my new friend Eva's company but because I didn't relish the thought of returning to an empty apartment in a foreign city. Eva had just returned from a visit home and was funny and bright about her experiences.

We soon agreed that, living in Helsinki, we both longed for an occasional American voice, and we decided to meet again, at her house. This time we were joined by an American friend of hers, and while I did not like the friend, it was still a pleasant evening, the three of us talking animatedly about Finland—Finnish ways, customs, habits, some of them charming, some annoying.

I invited both to be my guests the following week at a Chinese restaurant and also invited my Finnish lady friend, but she had yet another lecture engagement in Stockholm. So the three of us—Eva, her friend Joanna, and myself—met.

While Joanna nattered on about meeting a Frenchman named Jean-Claude "who really knew a lot about wines," I looked at Eva and suddenly knew the meaning of someone "taking your breath away." For the occasion Eva wore a black-bordered white dress, which was both beautiful and wrong for her because it made her look plump. The attempt to dress up—for what? for whom? . . . for me?—and the elegance of the dress together with its heartbreaking imperfection, the white material too taut against her brownish skin, stunned me, got into my heart, and did not leave it for a while. The evening was memorable, not for anything that was said or done, but only because I was now utterly infatuated.

How inconvenient, how ill-timed, how absurd! I was devoted to the woman I lived with, and certainly not inclined to start a love affair with a second woman in Finland. Nor, if truth be told, did it seem that Eva felt anything much about me. She clearly did not.

I taught my classes, got on well at home, but had no friend to confide in. I tried and, to an extent, succeeded in talking myself out of my inappropriate infatuation. This attempt consisted in part of listing all Eva's faults, which included the choice of her friend Joanna.

For our next meeting, the two of us took a walk in a summery Nabokovian park, the northern trees I couldn't name interspersed with wonderful, slender birches. Eva was upset, because her husband had delayed his vacation home, and her teenage son was making teenage trouble. As if to punctuate my disappointment, a cold rain squall suddenly swept in from the Baltic, making our lunchtime walk even shorter.

Our next and last meeting was to be again with Joanna. We met at Stockmann, Helsinki's largest department store, whose lunchroom was a favorite of loud, rich Russian tourists and old Finnish ladies wearing stovepipe hats.

My efforts to talk myself out of love had been relatively successful, and anyway I was soon to return home for three months. We talked about our reading, and Eva told about a new book, a California self-help book, which proposed that we all make our choices and therefore "have to take responsibility" for our moods. If we are unhappy, it's because we not only choose to but want to be unhappy.

She went on, in the manner of someone who was not used to talking about ideas, and as her tedious summary lengthened, the last of my infatuation drained away. My spirits soared. I was going to buy flowers for my intelligent, attractive housemate, who would never have swallowed these trite and tawdry ideas and passed them on as wisdom.

Lunch over, I lightly kissed Joanna and Eva goodbye, happily relieved of my burdensome feelings. But then Eva said, "Manfred, one other book I've been reading . . . . Brian Boyd's new biography of

Nabokov. So much better than Andrew Field or Alfred Appel's work on him. I love Nabokov."

Nabokov? Eva loved Nabokov? My heart did not skip a beat: it simply paused. My favorite author? How could the woman who had just expounded on Choosing What We Are, how could she love Nabokov, the subtlest of sorcerers? Of course Brian Boyd had written the best book on him—I hadn't read it yet, but the reviews had already convinced me. And Eva, this gorgeous, heart-stopping woman, knew the book.

Many years later, long after I returned to the United States, I met Brian Boyd, a charming New Zealander, at a conference. We talked for five seconds. I wanted to tell him the story, so Nabokovian in its absurd intensity, but he was surrounded by admirers and well-wishers, and I could not and did not tell him.

2004

An Older Man's Perspective on Older Women and Romance

I am blessed with a great many women friends. Not only do I find them more interesting than men, but they also give me a glimpse into the world of women—their lives, their ways of thinking, their worries and complaints.

If they are single, which many of them are, and if they are older, which most of them are, then one thing weighing on them is loneliness. They all would like to meet a man who would become more than a friend; they would like some sort of romantic involvement.

But we all know the dreary statistics. Over a certain age, available women hugely outnumber available men. Longevity is only one factor; another is simply that more older men than women are married.

So these women make do. They go to the movies with a girlfriend or occasionally with an unattached male friend. They travel with women friends, and some even do things alone (though almost never do they eat in restaurants alone). A few of my friends say they would "like to have a man to go to the theater with once a week," a kind of steady escort. But in fact—dare I say it?—their psychology does not really allow for that. They want more.

If they meet a likely, perhaps responsive man, something happens. Whatever the age of the women, if they feel attracted to the man, and if he responds and they start seeing each other romantically, then a kind of female hormone kicks in. What happens most often is that these women long to enlarge and intensify the fledgling relationship. However busy they are, they start feeling they should spend more time together, move in, set up housekeeping, buy a house—create some kind of family unit.

These are all arrangements that the (few single) men of my acquaintance never initiate when they get involved, and I don't think it's an exaggeration to say that they tend to resist such exhortations.

Seeing this male reaction, my female friends do the mature thing and resist pressing the point. They moderate their demands. Now they just want a "commitment."

Actually, this too is a counterproductive move on their part, because the men are often all too happy to commit themselves; they just don't want to say so. And since commitment grows organically, like trust, how exactly can it be negotiated?

My observation is that some men run and are then pronounced hopeless, others give in grudgingly, still others "commit" themselves without quite knowing what they're committing themselves to.

So, I think in most cases, it would make a lot more sense for that dread word not to be uttered. "I love you" sounds fine—but "commitment" has the inevitable feel of standing in long lines at Home Depot with household articles in hand.

My column ends here, but I have an irrepressible afterthought, a kind of modest proposal. If the world and love were run along rational lines—try to imagine that absurdity for a moment—wouldn't it then be logical for every single, older, still amorous male to have two or three lovers? Yes, of course, many men may also lack the desire or the emotional energy for more than one lover. But, look, certain sacrifices are in order: if women can learn to put up with sharing their men, certainly men could learn to spread themselves a bit thin.

2000

The Mysterious Case of the Available Man

I have a friend in Amsterdam who is now closing in on sixty. He was married at one time to an architect, but she got tired of what she called his "underachieving." In twenty years he has not remarried, but he has been in any number of "serially monogamous" relationships.

In one respect he differs from the many other divorced, single men I know. Jan really doesn't like to work. Though not Jewish, he wryly quotes a Yiddish proverb to explain himself, "A job is all right, but it interferes with your work."

But that proverb implies that some larger, more important work is to be done—study, wisdom, the art of living—and that's not exactly the case here. He is not a big reader, not exactly a Student of Life. He plays the piano and once a week gets together with friends to play— but he is not passionately devoted to music. He sees films, but not more than anyone who might have a job. He volunteers once a month at a soup kitchen in Amsterdam's center, but he is no Mother Teresa. So what does he do?

And, an American might ask, how does he support himself?

Well, that's a little easier in Europe than it is here. He draws some money from the state, and his health care is free. Occasionally he works in a restaurant, and his earnings can be legally added to his monthly check from the state. He is surprisingly good at doing taxes, and during tax time he helps people with their paperwork. Once in a while, he does house cleaning, but he refuses as many of those jobs as he accepts. He lives frugally but not well.

A mutual friend called him a hippie, but that doesn't completely fit. He is neat and tidy and would prefer to live in an orderly household with a woman—he would do a fair amount of housekeeping.

He had one relationship with a woman who took him to Greece one summer, and to this day she talks about what a fine time they had.

The trouble was that they had to come back home. She was a schoolteacher, and after two months in sun-baked Greece she missed the Dutch rain, her pupils, and even the colleagues she often complained about. He could have stayed forever—he had made friends with the people living on the beach, the older crowd who ate in the tavernas every night, the tourists who came there for the day. Like many Dutch people he speaks several languages fluently, but his greater gift was being able to talk to all sorts of people. He also picked up Greek dancing. Marie was just a little more subdued about cavorting in line, but still, Jan proved to be an ideal travel companion.

Why am I telling you all this?

Because I'm thinking of all my female friends—in both America and Holland—who are always complaining about being unable to find a decent, available man.

Here he is, unmarried, fun, more than willing to be faithful. Why is he not snapped up by any number of fifty-plus women I know? He could give companionship, sex, fun, maybe even love.

I know four or five comfortably-off Dutch women who long for male companionship and could easily spare an extra thousand euros monthly for his support. But if Jan placed an ad, an honest one, no self-respecting woman would answer.

How to explain all this? The psychologist Yolanda van Ecke says, "A man may advertise for what he wants, and a woman for what she can give."

That's a bit crisp for my taste. Lots of women advertise for what they want. The crux of this problem seems to me to be that a woman can't be seen as supporting a partner, while a man can.

Or is there more to it?

2001

WHY LYING ABOUT SEX CAN BE A GOOD THING

Everyone lies about sex, we've had much occasion to hear during the Clinton years. It's always said as if it were true but also regrettable.

We shouldn't lie, but, yes, we do lie about sex. It's a pity we do, but understandable, too.

I don't think it's regrettable at all. Lying about sex can be a good thing.

Certainly when it comes to sexual indiscretions, it's better to lie than to tell the truth.

The idea that lying is always wrong is baseless. We lie quite often, and for good reason. We lie to save the feelings of others.

We conceal in order not to hurt.

Lying about a sexual indiscretion strikes me as almost mandatory. Why?

1) Can anything really be gained from telling, i.e., hurting, those who will feel enraged by our actions, hurt, betrayed, etc.? Who has ever benefited from disclosing all to a distraught spouse?

2) Lying about sex protects one's partner in crime. She (he) has a right to privacy, which your disclosure would violate. If the other party wants to confess, that should be their choice, though in doing so, she (he) will violate yours.

3) We should all have the right, where no crime is committed, to our privacy. Secrecy is the only thing that will ensure it. And that privacy is not only a gain to you but to the rest of society. Why is privacy so earnestly advocated and so commonly violated?

4) Confession is supposed to counteract hypocrisy, but actually it will only lead to further hypocrisy and concealment.

Suppose you tell your spouse about your affair—are you also going to tell her about all the feelings that led up to the affair? About your

58

sense of her shortcomings, or even your own inadequacies? The whole truth can never come out. It's an illusion to think it will.

5) Confession leads to hysteria and badgering others to confess. In that sense, confession is bad for the soul. It leads to pride and exhibitionism and the forced involvement of others not inclined to confess. It leads to the Jerry Springerization of life.

Sometimes it even seems a substitute for the activity that is confessed, since the drama of confession is frequently a lurid replay of the act and an adjunct to it. It prolongs the tumult of the original trespass. Here is your chance to revive those sensations once more. If for some reason you can no longer do it, then you can at least talk about it.

Confession in sexual matters is a kind of pornography.

All in all, wouldn't we be better served in these matters by judicious concealment of our faults and sensitive concern for the feelings of others?

2000

Simple Truths and Complex Lies

Lately, a number of studies have suggested that most people give themselves away when they lie. Their facial expressions can be decoded by a skilled investigator.

This is good news for law enforcement, but it seems to me that only the most simple, uncomplicated, straightforward lies could possibly be identified that way.

A question such as, "Were you at the scene of the crime last night?" requires a fairly simple Yes or No. The emotion registered on the face may well reveal the respondent's truthfulness or lack of it.

But most lies are necessarily more complicated, neither fully lie nor fully truth.

Take the answer to the classic question, "Does this dress make me look fat?"

Even aside from the important fact that one person's concept of fatness differs from another's, something indeterminate in the question brings out a variety of possible responses.

And aside, too, from tact and diplomacy, there are so many reasons to answer No, even if the answer might more narrowly, more honestly, be Yes.

Here are some possible reasons, as they could play through the other person's mind. How would you gauge their truthfulness? Could they even be labeled true or false?

1) This one makes you look no fatter than any other combination, so the answer is Yes. It's not the dress that makes you look fat—that has nothing to do with it. It's your general appearance. Therefore the answer is also No.

2) Most of the time you don't look fat at all. This outfit makes you look a little fat, but if I say that, you're going to keep thinking of

yourself as a fat person, which would be downright false. So all in all No is more accurate than Yes.

3) You look so much thinner than you did a few years ago. While these clothes might be a bit unflattering, it's just not worth mentioning, in view of your greater overall thinness.

4) This is really an attractive outfit, even if it makes you look a bit heavy.

5) You are fretting too much about this. Though you're a bit fat, and the dress accentuates that, there's nothing wrong with the way you look. The answer is No because it accurately reflects the general state of your appearance.

6) I'm so glad you're not wearing your white slacks. Those make you look heavy—this dress much less so. Here the answer is what, exactly? Yes or No?

Ad infinitum.

They may all be lies, in some abstract sense, but I contend that none of them constitutes lying.

Lying is simple only as a violation of a factual statement. There are lies which we can't really call lies: ambivalences, exaggerations, shortcuts, etc. If someone asks me whether I've read a certain book and I haven't, am I lying when I say Yes? Technically I am—but suppose I've read excerpts from it, reviews of it, and heard the author speak about it . . . have I not 'almost' read it?

Would a simple No be more truthful than a complex Yes? Would the expression on my face lead an observer to know I'm shading the truth?

Doubtful.

2008

We want to be loved for what we are—despite what we are.

Most couples have only one argument, endlessly repeated.

People love being in love, which affords them a refuge from ambivalence, however transitory.

We are considered less interesting when we marry than when we divorce.

Sentiment and Sentimentality: The Way We Feel Now

West of the Westernmost Point

When I was twelve and living on the Caribbean island of Curaçao, one of my classmates drowned. He and his family had gone swimming in Westpunt Bay, and Lauie Tramberg (I remember his first and last name) had swum too far out and was seized by a current, which took him out to sea, west of this most western point on the island.

Fifty-five years later, I still remember hearing the news at school and being sent reeling by it: I saw Lauie, small, helpless, his white body ever heavier in that black-blue sea, west of the island's westernmost point. I thought of it for days, weeks, and always it stunned me.

Of course, after a while, time brought some relief, and this melancholy picture visited me less often. But it has never entirely left me.

On the day it happened our teachers did not discuss this news with us, nor did we expect them to. I mentioned it to my older brother that afternoon, and to my parents that evening. My brother was grave, and said little, and my parents were sympathetic and quiet.

I do not remember feeling the need to talk to anyone about it. Talking could not change the utter finality, the dread weight, of the event. That is what I thought of—the heavy immutability of it, poor Lauie struggling against the darkening sea and heavy sky. Only its not having happened could console me; nothing else could give much comfort.

It's not that I believe talking never helps. We know the relief that comes to anyone from airing a grief, or bringing up a problem. It's just that some things are too deep for speech and too irrevocable for mediation.

It is for that reason I feel skeptical of our present habit of dispatching "grief counselors" to the scene of any tragedy. Would I have felt better if I had talked to a grief counselor on the day of Lauie's drowning?

I doubt it. How could anyone have made me feel better? Who could make the death of a young person light? Who could even make it lighter?

What is the point of sending a perfect stranger, however sympathetic, however well-trained—two big howevers—to comfort children after a tragedy? Is their sorrow not precisely the appropriate emotion? Why should we desire its instant conversion to something easier?

I think it is our sentimentality, our desire to make it all feel better, that guides us in this impatient hope of transmuting grief and pain to wholesome "healing."

And isn't there something odious about that tribe of grief counselors, feeding on death and tragedy? I'm sure that they are well-intentioned. But I'm equally sure that most of them cannot do more than mouth a few well-worn platitudes. And some, no doubt, would be all too eager to have their charges start bucking up before their mourning had even begun. And not one, not one of them, could possibly undo the awful knowing that a friend was floating west into an unfathomable sea.

2003

American Psychological Catchphrases

For decades now, America has been subject to a stream of psychological catchphrases, as if the whole country were a patient eagerly awaiting the latest self-help book. As a society, we are much better at creating catchy new phrases than at remedying the conditions they describe.

A recent American psychological catchphrase is "emotional literacy." Suddenly one hears that many Americans, especially children, are lacking in the ability to handle their emotions or manage their relationships with others. There is even a call for teaching "emotional literacy" in the schools—to be added to more common fare, like science and mathematics and English and history and geography.

Whatever the outcome of this particular plan, it is the latest in a whole series. Not so long ago, we heard a good deal about "low self-esteem." Self-esteem was somehow going to be taught in school. And not only in school: years ago, a member of the California State Legislature, John Vasconcellos, created a task force of citizens and experts to promote self-esteem and personal and social responsibility.

To no one's surprise, this task force found that low self-esteem was a crucial weakness in many lives and that American society would be healthier if somehow this lack could be overcome. Many of the ills of society, from substance abuse to random violence, would be remedied or at least improved if people's self-esteem could be raised. Vasconcellos's report was sometimes respectfully received, sometimes ridiculed—but its implementation has, of course, been difficult.

It is not that such studies are unsound or even that they ignore the conditions that create the problems they label. It is widely understood, for instance, that a greater sense of community and family cohesiveness would lead to more self-esteem. But in practice, these popular phrases appear to announce a mechanical solution for a larger societal problem: they lead people falsely into thinking that the remedy is at hand.

We are told we're an "addictive" society, that some of us are "co-dependents," supporting and furthering others' addictions; that some of us have "toxic parents" and come from "dysfunctional families." Many of us need to heed the "inner child" or the "wounded child" before we can undergo the "healing" process. Our divorces cause "separation traumas," a kind of death requiring us to go through the long phases of "mourning" or "grieving." And those of us living in violent cities are often said to suffer, like Vietnam veterans, from "post-traumatic stress syndrome."

Something is positive about all this, some attempt to deal with human problems, some humane impulse to remedy human suffering. And it is liberating for sufferers to discover that there is a name for their condition.

But there is also something false here. Even aside from the fact that the underlying conditions are not subject to a quick remedy, the terms become imprecise and fuzzy very quickly. Is it "emotional child abuse" for a parent to yell at a child? Well, yes and no: depends on how it's done, how often, and for what reasons. But the phrase requires a yes *or* no answer and does not allow for subtleties and fine distinctions.

This vagueness means that all too often these psychological terms become mere slogans. They seem to explain but do not. They have the atmosphere of a diagnosis without diagnosing anything. In the end, they accomplish very little, and like political slogans, they merely narrow our thinking—and lessen the chances of bettering human difficulties. They do the opposite of what education is supposed to do.

1991

Sentiment, Sentimentality, Mawkishness

I am, by all accounts, rather unexpressive. Many think of me as unemotional. I don't go in for the usual displays of feeling, and I have never been fond of the give-me-a-hug style that so many people still favor.

My conviction, or my inclination, or my practice, tells me that if I listen to you, consider what you're thinking and feeling, then I am responding to you, and potentially doing so with feeling. Attention is my way of displaying interest, fondness, emotion. Should such attention develop on both sides, then the intimacy of friendship can result.

This is widely misunderstood. I am regarded as "cold" because I'm not being emotive and don't say "I love you" to people I don't love.

Someone who tells me how much he cares for me but has forgotten what I told him yesterday does not win my affection or persuade me that he cares. Someone who asks me a question but doesn't really hear my answer is not someone I'll ever care for.

My response to such people will be correct but by their lights "cold," no matter how often they declare their affection, esteem, or even love.

In fact when they do, I hold it against them. Such people allege what they demonstrably don't feel. It's easier to say "I love you" than to love. It's even easier to say "I like you" than to really like someone.

I'm thinking of one man in particular, who frequently tells me I'm "a great man." I cringe when he does—he has known me for over ten years but doesn't know me, he hasn't taken the time to find out what I think or feel, and it's inappropriate and intrusive for him to say what he does. When he asks for my view on something, he is too impatient to hear my answer and starts talking before I'm through.

His statement isn't even about me—it's about his need to be loved. He wants me to say in return that I think he is pretty great himself, which of course I do not, being "cold."

Evidently his form of admiring or loving is not based on any knowledge of the person he allegedly admires. It's based on his need or his wish—it has nothing to do with me. It is a form of rampaging sentimentality, an indiscriminate yearning to express emotion and to quickly, quickly, quickly gain a return of feeling. He wants his emotional high, but it's the unearned emotion of the drunk.

"Unearned" is the key. Genuine like or love has to be earned, to be won; it cannot be solicited, or seized. His expressions of "feeling" are ways of leaping over the usual ways of earning love or esteem. Like the person who praises himself because others won't, he seeks to gain an instant assent from you—he'll con you into stating your admiration by first flattering you to the point where some similar response seems called for.

None of this would be particularly significant if we didn't see this pattern at work as a style in the culture at large, which is nothing if not mawkish, which always avoids the hard job of gaining trust in favor of exhorting you to trust, which holds candlelight vigils for victims it refuses to truly mourn, which favors sloganeering sentiment and gushy words over thoughtfulness, attention and care.

It's so much easier to say indignantly, "What about the children?" than to show (or make) one less violent movie or video game. So much easier to say "I love you" to a friend than put yourself out for that same friend. So much easier to settle for the sentimental tear than the actual experience of sorrow. So much easier to talk than to listen.

2007

CANTING

I've often thought we should revive the word "cant." What is our present day equivalent?

Here's what the word used to mean and still should.

To say you believe something without actually believing it is not exactly canting. There is a difference between mere insincerity and cant. When you're canting, you have half persuaded yourself that you believe what you're saying or even thinking. Some of it may be pretense, but much of it is real enough.

Canting satisfies the need for having fashionable, approved-of opinions. You cant about things you feel are good—it shows your earnest concern, your attention to the world's welfare. Canting has always been common, and though this particular word has fallen into disuse, the activity isn't any less popular than it used to be. There are still many widely sanctioned virtues we profess, and it remains important for us to believe that we believe certain things.

Unfashionable opinions are tolerated but regarded as perverse or charmingly whimsical. How far would you really get in polite company if you expressed the belief that children are better off not going to school, or that the English language is in fine shape, or that some cultures are better than others, or that animals should have the same rights as people? Although I much prefer the permissiveness of American society to the orthodoxy of many others, it is a mistake to think that widely divergent views are widely considered here. And most people, even fine, thoughtful people, will not brave disfavor; they will want to be with the majority, or at least the trend-setting minority.

Each social group seems to have opinions it insists on and its members take for granted as self-evident and good. Such beliefs create a bond between the members of the group. An academic will signal and underscore his membership in one of the two subgroups of American academia by saying, "Naturally it's the scientists who get all the research money." The comment places him squarely in the humanities and cements his connection to other humanists. Students will adopt such views from their professors and may even use them to gain entry into the group.

Sometimes it is not the implicit pressures or attractions of a given group but our self-image that requires certain opinions. Approved-of notions help us to deny our faults, both publicly and privately, by sketching a picture of a somewhat idealized self. But since this idealized self seems genuine to us (most people who recognize their faults see them as charming weaknesses), we easily pay lip service to what we are unwilling to see or unable to question. And such lip service involves pretending to feelings that are not felt.

Is it merely a harmless way of speaking for someone to say that he is "terribly concerned about world hunger"? Perhaps. Certainly it is appropriate occasionally to say things out of politeness, and no one should be held responsible for every word they say. But when you start thinking a canting way, when you believe in the genuineness of what you are ever-so-politely uttering, when you have convinced yourself that you are deeply concerned about world hunger and yet have not given a shred of evidence of being so, then true canting begins—with your conviction of sincerity.

Canting occurs in the most unexpected places. In his book *Crazy Talk, Stupid Talk*, Neil Postman lists among the books he has learned much from Karl Popper's *The Open Society and Its Enemies*, declaring it "the most brilliant discussion of the roots of fanaticism I know of. When I have depressing days, weighted down by excessive exposure to crazy talk, it helps me to get through if I remind myself that Karl Popper is alive and *thinking* in England."

Well, Karl Popper is dead now, and so is Postman, but no depression that is a depression worthy of its name is going to be lifted in the slightest by that thought, no mood is going to be changed by a book. I don't doubt that Postman liked Popper's work and I don't doubt that good books are a genuine pleasure; but I *do* doubt that (1) he has ever been depressed by crazy talk—annoyed yes; amused, yes; angered, yes—and that (2) his spirits can be lifted by the thought of a brilliant man being alive.

There is a lovely passage in Boswell's *The Life of Dr. Johnson*:

JOHNSON. "My dear friend, clear your *mind* of cant. You may *talk* as other people do; you may say to a man, 'Sir, I am your most humble servant.' You are *not* his most humble servant. You may say, 'These are bad times; it is a melancholy thing to be reserved to such times.' You don't mind the times. You tell a man, 'I am sorry you had such bad weather the last day of your journey, and were so much wet.' You don't care six-pence whether he is wet or dry. You may *talk* in this manner; it is a mode of talking in Society: but don't *think* foolishly."

(May 2, 1783)

As usual, Dr. Johnson has it right. If we start to believe what we say, then delusion and self-delusion have triumphed. Our platitudes leave the realm of etiquette and enter our psyches, and we end up saying and believing things like, "Life in the city is too hectic. I'm moving to the country," or "The pace of life is faster than ever."

Such clichés either put us in the company we admire or affirm us as the kind of people we want to seem, the kind of people who not only have the right opinions but even the right feelings. But we probably persuade others less than we persuade ourselves.

1985

The Tao of Irritation

As we get older, we have more irritations, and one reason why we do is the fact that we have more to be irritated about. I have written before of that sense of dislocation many older people experience, the familiar slowly being replaced by the unfamiliar, the human landscape ever so slightly but ever more bewilderingly looking out of focus.

And yet I am ready to admit that some of these irritations are irrational. There is no good reason why caps worn backward should annoy me as much as they do. Relax, Manfred, it's just a style. Styles always change. Maybe in another ten years people will wear caps on their feet. So what? Why get irritated?

But I do: the sight of anyone over fifteen wearing the bill backwards makes me want to retch. I need to see a therapist about that.

And the sound of anyone saying, "I was so, like, insulted, I felt, like, so harassed. You know what I'm saying?" annoys me too. And again, I shouldn't be annoyed; it doesn't matter. I'm being unreasonable.

The other night I watched a concert on TV, and there were the musicians gyrating away. Didn't bother me at all. I rather liked the music and found their body language entirely appropriate. They were putting out maximum effort and producing a fine show. But then the cameras panned to the audience: hundreds, thousands of arms in the air, clapping, waving, swaying, all of them in unison, "grooving" together.

Why did that seem so silly? Another irrational dislike? All they were doing was "getting into" the music, having a good time, abandoning themselves to the rhythms and sounds. How could I possibly object?

Well, I'm not sure that they were abandoning themselves to the music. I think they *thought* they were, felt themselves overcome; but I doubt that any such emotion was really involved. They were merely behaving the way they thought they should, in that conventionally stylized form that has now been the fashion at concerts for the last thirty years. It's like applauding when a speaker has given a speech—you just do it. You do it because everyone else does. It's the appropriate behavior under the circumstances.

What I dislike is the pose of naturalness when people are being most unnatural. I see my annoyance about this as being less irrational than many of my other dislikes. The unwitting pose has become such a hallmark of our time: we spout clichés with tears in our eyes ("I just want to give back to the community"), we utter pieties while "visibly moved" ("I need to spend more time with my family"), we make sentimental references at a moment's notice ("We must do this for our children's sake"). It's everywhere in the culture; the media, of course, play a huge role in this kind of talk.

And maybe the worst of it is that we have snowed ourselves into believing we are sincere. We don't quite know it's something we have heard other people say; we don't recognize we're just imitating someone else's display.

Just like those kids swaying so demonstratively to their music. It may feel like feeling—but I don't think it is.

2001

American Sentimentality in Action

Just a few weeks ago, the longtime director of the CIA, George Tenet, quit. It was his good fortune that former President Reagan died immediately afterwards, or Tenet's resignation might have been subjected to a lot more scrutiny than it got. Or maybe not. Hard to say these days.

I would hereby like to reopen the matter. It doesn't interest me whether Tenet jumped or was pushed—I am much more concerned with some of the details in and around his resignation and what they say about us and our time.

He said he was eager to spend "more time with my family." This is one of those ridiculous things people say with a straight face and everybody accepts—I myself am waiting for the day when someone announces his entry into politics by stating that he would like to spend less time with his family.

In the process of saying this, the man became quite teary-eyed. It turned out he has a son, a senior in high school, and Tenet wants to help this son prepare for college admission. Or some such thing.

Surely no one else has ever had a full-time job and seen a son off to college at the same time!

It is entirely typical of our time and place that Tenet would become tearful about his son's going to college but not about all the men and women—to date—his lies or miscalculations or simply dumb errors helped send to their deaths in Iraq. Whether he mistakenly deduced that Iraq had weapons of mass destruction or concluded that it did not—but did not want give the "bad" news to his president—either way, he let down his country and is indirectly responsible for the deaths of many of our young men and women.

But no, that wasn't worth any emotion—or any explanation, or any accounting. Nor did the press ask him. Maybe they would have if Reagan hadn't just died, but I doubt it. The press is not noted for its attention span. It too, I'm afraid, has a lot to answer for.

So what have we got here? A man who blubbers about his son going to college, but evidently doesn't see, or doesn't want to see, or can't see, or can't be made to see, that he has responsibilities infinitely greater than his family. What information did he give the president— and why? What was the threat Saddam posed to our country? Why was Tenet sitting behind Colin Powell when the latter gave his now infamous speech to the United Nations?

And yet I'll bet he thinks of himself as a truly thoughtful and richly patriotic man, who has served his country well.

I've said it before: sentimentality always stands in the way of sentiment. If you can say something smarmy about family, then you don't have to feel very much else, then you can feel yourself to be a feeling person but you sure as hell don't have to feel.

Unfortunately, it's all around us. Tenet is a perfect example of what happens every day and why Americans, despite their friendliness, and unmistakable generosity, are widely detested overseas. That smarminess, that easy attention to something gushy, that innocent lack of attention to what really counts, that inability to see the obvious and unwillingness to hear what is shouted at them . . . unfortunately, that's our culture, that's us.

This column was written in 2004 when George Tenet left the CIA. His new book, *At the Center of the Storm: My Years at the CIA*, published in 2007, confirms that he is not only sentimental but also self-serving, self justifying, and terminally self-deluded.

Related Aphorisms

Human beings always have the courage of their conventions.

The rapture that is not ours is embarrassing.

Changing Times, Changing Styles: The Way We Think Now

Changing Thoughts in Changing Times

When I first started teaching at San Francisco State University in the fifties, we had a strict No Smoking policy in our classrooms. The message was clear, and I don't believe anyone ever violated it. If you were a student, you did what you were told, and the faculty enforced the rules that came from on high. The classroom might be relaxed, but faculty and administration acted *in loco parentis*, in the place of parents, and few questioned that arrangement.

The sixties changed all that. The No Smoking signs were still up, but I remember many classrooms where students and teachers were puffing away. We were all adults; students called us by our first names—why treat them like children? It would have seemed quaint and anachronistic to ask students not to smoke—after all, they were free to do what they wanted. And those who did not want to smoke, well, fine, they didn't have to. This perspective probably lasted well into the seventies.

We now come to the eighties and later. Anyone smoking in a classroom would be stopped, by faculty and other students alike. How dare smokers impose smoke on their classmates? Freedom was expressed not in smoking but in being able to tell someone to stop polluting the clean air we all had a right to breathe. If a professor did not enforce this position, these same protesting students might well cause quite a bit of trouble for smokers and teacher alike.

What is my point? Why am I rehearsing these small historical examples?

I have gone over them because they show how our thinking changes over time. What we approve and disapprove of is extremely malleable. Prominent opinions in one time are not necessarily prominent or even respectable in another.

And perhaps more important is that they also show that the reasons for our approval or disapproval change, and do so rather quickly. In each instance, a different set of arguments and a whole new cluster of values are in place.

After all, in the fifties, it was a matter of civility, of respecting one's elders, of adhering to some simple do's and don'ts that counted. In the sixties, it was a matter of individual freedom, of having the right to do as one liked, of being treated as an adult, of demonstrating the equality of student and teacher. The underlying value was a new, expanded view of freedom: light up, and do so wherever you happen to be.

Since the eighties, extending into the present day, the value of independence bolstered by good health is the main concern. My freedom lies in not being subjected to your unhealthy habits. Your freedom to smoke deprives me of my freedom not to be smoked at.

The reader might say, well, yes, but didn't this change come about because nowadays we know so much more about smoking, including the damage of secondhand smoke? To be sure—but it's the uses to which we put that knowledge, and the way we express it, that makes of this series of events a kind of study of the changes in our thinking wrought by time.

Not that anyone sees those changes in the moment itself. At each point, our views seem natural and obvious, and anyone who questions them a bit strange.

2003

Are We Still Doing Self-Help?

The other day I thought of all the "self-help" things I had done in my life and wondered why I wasn't doing any of them now. Did I grow up—or grow old?

In the seventies I did a lot of faddish things. Maybe I just didn't want to be left out, like a friend who some years ago lamented that he had "slept through the sexual revolution."

My very first venture was a class in self-hypnosis. I had hoped that it would give me greater control over my moods, perhaps make me more tranquil. On the first night of class, the instructor—a rather grim-looking man in his forties—burned himself with a cigarette to show how successfully he could put himself under.

To further demonstrate that everything was possible, he recited Kipling's poem "If," that great Edwardian exhortation to self-reliance and manly courage, oddly out of place among the rosy faces and miniskirts. After his first instructions, almost everyone was in a deep trance—except me. I wasn't fighting it; I wanted it to work. I wanted to lose my skepticism, but I didn't.

Self-hypnosis having failed me, I turned to the management of alpha waves. In a grungy basement sat twenty of us, attached with electrodes to a box that registered our brain waves. Alpha waves are associated with peacefulness. The theory is—or was—that if you can see them, then you can produce them almost at will and become peaceful. I was skeptical, but since this is the principle of biofeedback, which has medical respectability, I had to try it. To my distress, I seemed to have few alpha waves. And I certainly couldn't make any. Around me my classmates were oohing and aahing about their production of these magical lines on the registers of their boxes, and I felt more than an occasional twinge of envy.

One time, when I found myself thinking about an article I was writing, I registered more alpha waves than before. "Fine," said the instructor, seemingly the obligatory instructor response in these classes to whatever you experienced.

Some years later, after many people had already done so, I tried transcendental meditation. I will never forget the eagerness of forty or so people at the initial session. The speaker promised us well-being, happiness, and health. I would have settled for two. Touchingly, one young woman asked, "Will TM improve my social life?"

"Of course it will," answered the instructor.

On the last day of my initiation I was to bring flowers and a neatly pressed white handkerchief and receive my mantra. The instructor and I mounted four flights of stairs to the sacred initiating room. He was a young man, but at the third flight of stairs he started huffing and puffing. "These stairs always get me," he said, slapping his chest.

What about the calm strength that daily practice of TM was supposed to bring? What about life-affirming energy coursing through the veins?

It was another unwelcome triumph for my skepticism.

And since the seventies and eighties? Did I give up? I think so. Or maybe I'm going back to the fifties, when the Existentialists preached embracing a cause, committing yourself to something outside of yourself.

Oddly, that way of living, while not exactly in the self-help mode, offers a fair amount of it. Lessening the attention you give yourself may be the biggest help you can give yourself.

1985

Remembering the Men's Movement

It used to be said about the town of Berkeley that the people there supported themselves by giving therapy to one another. So it was not surprising that my first encounter with the new men's group should take place in Berkeley, perhaps twenty years ago. In the cafeteria of a small high school, a slight, excitable man was talking about the need for men to be *more* than sensitive and tender—qualities which were too reactive, too much in response to what women wanted of men. The question was, he said solemnly, without any sense of irony, what do men want?

I don't recall if there was an answer from him or from the several dozen men—and a fair number of women too—that evening. I do recall that there were bongo drums and that someone read poems by Robert Bly, a well-known poet and translator, and that I thought at the time we might be in for a new wave of poetry and therapy.

What has happened in the intervening years is far more than I expected. Robert Bly became for a while the guru of the Men's Movement. He preached the gospel of the Real Man, the Wild Man, who has come to terms with his own masculinity. This new man must heal himself of the grief left by absent or over-demanding fathers and must learn to be at ease with his own strength as well as his own feelings.

On college campuses, in large auditoriums, on weekend retreats in the woods, Bly had himself become a father figure to thousands of men who not only listened to his sermons but also beat on drums and sweated in ceremonial sweat lodges. In between, they embraced, they cried, and they told their stories of confusion and pain.

Men, it turns out, want to be with other men. They have a need for "bonding." Their self-definition must not depend on modern society's plans for them or on the needs of women. Their maleness must be allowed expression, whether through a sudden uninhibited yell in the forest or through closeness with older men or tutelage of younger men. To befriend this Wild Man in oneself is to finally make peace with one's father, and oneself.

The men who went on these all-male weekends raved about their newly acquired independence and assertiveness. I asked one if you could really get a new identity in a weekend. His answer: "It's not new. I realized before that there was something like it deep inside me."

Fair enough. This is often the way new converts feel. And there have certainly been enough of these groups in the American landscape to make one feel that this too shall pass. But actually, the phenomenon is more than that of yet another therapeutic support group: this one sprang up in reaction to the women's groups of the sixties and seventies. It's not exactly that men were frightened by feminism and needed a counterweight. No, they envied women their new togetherness, their sense of purpose, their newfound ideology, their friendships, their discussion groups. Men needed their own thing now.

And where women had the ideology of men's oppression, men had a vacuum. Not at all calculatingly, but in all earnestness, Robert Bly filled that vacuum. And once he provided the ideology of men needing to make peace with their fathers, he started casting around for other traditions: the sweat lodge in which Indian adolescents were at one time purified into manhood, the drums, the dancing around campfires, the chanting.

The participants in these events did not necessarily swallow the ideology but enjoyed the group experience, the flirtation with communalism, before they went back to their isolating jobs or nuclear families. And even if this experience is nothing more than what the writer Tom Wolfe once cynically called "Let's Talk About Me," it may still be better than silence, aloneness, or alienation.

So what has happened since those days? Is there still a Men's Movement? Or has it vanished without a trace?

Perhaps it survives in an attenuated form—in certain gay identity groups, or even in Christian organizations, like the Promise Keepers— but it seems largely gone from our ever-changing social scene.

2000

Ever Hear of 'Scarification'?

Once again I'm in my observation post, my café, my clean, well-lighted place—as life-enhancing a spot as that of the marvelous Hemingway story in which I first came across the concept. Reading, writing, musing, I watch the world go by.

In walk three young people in their twenties. Two of them are pierced.

I give a little involuntary shudder. The ear clips are one thing, the nose ring another—but why, oh why, that dreadful thing through both eyebrows?

In the sixties, I had no problem with long manes. In the seventies, I did not find pink or orange hair abhorrent.

But in the eighties and nineties, I have loathed piercings. Is it my problem?

Of course, it's an irrational prejudice. Why should I care? I know it's not The End of Civilization As We Know It, because that has already taken place. So what is going on?

Well, I tell myself, if I knew why people did this to themselves, then I would mind less. And yet when I come up with reasons, they do not seem to lessen my annoyance.

OK, what are the reasons? I read a book about "scarification," but still did not get any kind of meaningful explanation about why people did these ghastly things to themselves. Recently I asked a friend's son why he did it (asked in a smiling, friendly way).

His reply: "Yeah, I thought it would be…like…cool, man."

That didn't help much either.

So it's up to me to come up with reasons. I can think of several:

1) It's a fad. If one person does it, another will want to. If several do it, it becomes almost irresistible.

2) It's a way of rebelling against established ways of dressing, self-presentation, being. This is enough to make most parents shudder, so why not do it? And even if the perpetrators of this self-mutilation are in their twenties and thirties, there are still parents or parent-figures or society or something—though God knows society isn't going to mind one bit, and soon enough you'll see models with nose rings or athletes with pierced tongues or politicians with a few "tasteful" piercings.

3) Being pierced, you can signal to other pierced creatures that you are one of them, with them, cool, stylish, new. Not that different, I suppose, from two guys in suits and striped ties recognizing their joint membership in a certain kind of club.

4) When you are properly marked—and this goes for tattoos as well, and of course pierced people are often tattooed people—there must be some pride in having endured pain. It's a kind of self-imposed hazing that allows you to walk with an added spring in your step; you are not faint of heart, you are, well, like, brave.

5) You have taken adornment many steps further. People wear decorative watches, bracelets, earrings—the piercer has merely taken this to its limits, "pushed the envelope," as the inane phrase goes, taken adornment to new heights. You are a happy extremist, and if you experiment with all this, maybe add a few more nose rings, then you may even have created a new identity for yourself—you have reinvented yourself.

6) Identity is important. Altering it, finding it, creating it. When you pierce, you change what is given.

Maybe humanity has always chafed at all the things that were merely given us, that seemed immutable.

Maybe we started wearing clothes to make an impression, to be different, even to ourselves; maybe we just couldn't accept what we were handed down from on high. Maybe our efforts have always been to make us less "natural."

Maybe "scarification" is an attempt to change what is so recalcitrant in life, so resistant to our will. Maybe it symbolizes our desire to change what we cannot change. Only this last reason makes me feel a little kinder.

But I'm not at all sure I've got any of this right. Can my readers come up with more reasons?

1998

GENERATION GAP IN THE SUNSET

It was an uncommonly warm early spring day. From West Portal Avenue, I made my way to Taraval Street and walked right into the sunset, which looked beautiful over the pastel and white houses of the Avenues. I had errands to do but enough leisure to enjoy this spectacular setting. More people than usual were out, and for a while the Sunset District looked like a slow-paced resort.

In front of Walgreens stood a boy of about fifteen. He wore a heavy black winter jacket, a kind of ski cap and woolen gloves. One of his pant legs was rolled up in a way I had noticed in other kids as well.

Dropping the paper wrapping on the sidewalk, he greedily ate a hamburger and, somewhat incongruously, drank a Diet Coke. Although he was eating, his eyes were half-closed, looking contemptuously at the peaceful scene around him.

His boom box blasted angry rap, and occasionally he nodded at the lyrics, evidently in full agreement with what was asserted about what should be done to whom. I could just make out a strident rap voice asking, "You know what I'm sayin'?"

Two streetcars went by, and he let them pass. He was clearly waiting for something or someone. I now came a little closer, dangerously loitering to get a better view.

I was grateful for my drab clothes, since I did not want to give offense by wearing the wrong colors. I have a mail-order blue suit that might just provoke a member of, say, an orange-wearing gang to violence. On the other hand, my aging eyes could not make out any signal colors on him.

Soon I saw who he was waiting for.

A little clump of kids ambled down the street, two boys of about fourteen wearing those droopy full-diaper pants, three girls in T-shirts and jeans. It's almost as if the boys and girls lived in different climatic zones; boys ready for the Arctic, girls on a tropical beach.

Though impeccably multi-cultural, they were segregated by gender. The boys were silent, the girls mugging and talking and saying "like" all the time. Even the most innocuous comment was met by shrieking; things such as, "Oh, yeah, like, look Joseph, you're out on the shtreet." Kids nowadays say "shtreet" and "conshtruction" and "grosh-eries"— assuming they use those big words at all.

Were they a new species? Bred on television, pizza and rock videos, these boys and girls had already witnessed 100,000 murders on TV. They could not possibly have anything in common with the bookish, eager-for-good-grades kids I grew up with.

Now I walked behind them, riveted by the exotic sight they afforded as they gamboled along, interrupted only by high-fives, shouts, high-pitched interjected phrases. Language had become subservient to gesture, and the boys had virtually given up words altogether. Because of the frequent stops and starts I was able to keep up with them and also hear them quite clearly.

But imagine my surprise when after a few blocks of going in one direction they turned back and slowly climbed up the steps of the Parkside branch of the Public Library.

Only then did I notice that three of them were carrying books.
1997

"So Many Bleating Sheep—So Little Wool": Schooldays in a Faraway Land

Every few years, we hear alarming reports about our schools—falling test scores, or violence, or drug use, or the schools' overall poor performance.

Maybe we should get used to the idea that what goes on in school differs from what we want, and that our plans for the children somehow clash with the interests and even passions of those children.

Are there in fact two cultures, the school and the adult culture, which are almost always and inevitably in a state of collision?

Teachers brought up on books and TV are now dealing with students raised on computers, video games, and a host of strange gadgets. Students are "texting" each other, where another generation passed notes. One generation doesn't even speak the language of the other—sometimes literally so—and cultural collisions would seem to be inescapable.

I think back with some amusement to my own school days, and an even greater culture clash, immediately after World War Two on the then-Dutch colony of Curaçao in the southern Caribbean. The language of instruction was Dutch, but the Curaçaoan children spoke Papiamento, a Creole mix of Spanish and Portuguese, its grammar partly derived from West African languages.

I distinctly recall the following exchange between teacher and students:

"Hipólito, when did the Romans come to our country?"

"The Romans came to our country in 50 AD, sir."

"Where in our country did they have a large settlement, Benjamin?"

Never mind that "our country" in the textbooks was five thousand miles away. The pupils knew what was expected of them and how they were supposed to answer.

At the same time, though, a curious underground life went on in class, a kind of counterpoint to the formality and rigidity of the instruction.

For instance, one day in sixth grade our teacher asked about his lost pointer. He had pinned up some fine Dutch sayings and proverbs, which were supposed to impart order on disorderly native ways. And he also needed his pointer for the coming lesson in geography on the Dutch East Indies, later Indonesia, half a world away.

"Sir," called out Wilmoo, a tall, light-skinned lad in a pale-blue sport shirt. "I saw the pointer yesterday."

"Yesterday, Wilmoo, you saw the pointer yesterday?"

"Yes, sir, I saw it on a car."

"And so did I," interjected Benjamin, a small, very lithe boy, with an elegant head and fine, noble features. "I saw it on a car too, tied with twigs to the front bumper."

Now a chorus of voices. "Yes, I saw it also; no, no sir, I was the one who saw it. How can you say you saw it, when I was the one who saw it? It was speeding by without a car. It flashed by my house like magic."

Wilmoo stood up. "I saw it pass my house in the middle of the night. It was beautiful and shiny. I had never seen anything so fast; it whipped by me."

Several boys were standing up now, turned to each other, grinning, gesticulating, all of them clamoring and chorusing.

"And I heard it singing; I heard that," chanted Ricardo, and he started swaying in his seat, singing, his body throbbing and shaking.

"Well, boys," said the puzzled teacher, "these tall tales aren't getting us anywhere. The good old Dutch saying applies here, 'So many bleating sheep—so little wool.'"

What the boys were doing, half jokingly, good-naturedly, but also hypnotically, they would do again and again. Whether as a pun on somebody's name or a ritualistic repetition, the buzz started spontaneously, both when the kids were happy and when they were bored. As a consequence, there was often a hum in the classroom, a subterranean sound, a distant rumbling, a languid undulation, which was bewildering to the teachers from the Netherlands, who had signed up for a stint in the Caribbean colonies because they needed a job and wanted to get away from the bleakness of postwar Europe.

I realize this is an exotic example of a school culture clash, from a faraway colony in the last days of colonialism; but is it really so different from what goes on in most classrooms everywhere? Isn't there always a conflict of interest, or at least a clash of preoccupations between them and us—between what we want them to learn and what their heads are full of?

2007

Let's Go Metric

Recently, I saw on TV the sort of thing that I'll never get used to in America, a program on how we're doing with the conversion to metrics in the schools. There were long earnest conversations with two teachers, one of them stressing the traumatic effects of "metricization," the other looking somewhat more brightly at the long-range, positive gains to be derived from such a transition, whatever its difficulties for the "youngsters" (only educators use this word in place of "children").

This same television program also featured a little cartoon concocted for the young, with the usual jibber-jabbery creature, saying things like "Let's all go metric." This nerve-wracking animal was supposed to be reassuring, no doubt, but it introduced a clamor and an over-animation into the whole scene that tends to give me a headache and probably gave the "youngsters" a good case of hyperactivity.

I couldn't help but remember my own experience, as a child, with similar changes and conversions. I was ten or eleven years old, in the classroom of our dusty old school building on the island of Curaçao. The Caribbean heat was, as usual, stupefying. Suddenly, a stir. The "Inspector of Education," an old, white man with a round, bald head and a long beard, was at the door. He was the only person for whom we had to stand up.

He walked slowly, clumsily, to the teacher's desk, and whispered something at him. The teacher, also standing, looked startled, reverential, then whispered back. The next moment, the old man was gone.

We all sat down. The teacher looked solemn. But the build-up of tension clearly required that he be less formal than the occasion might warrant. "As you know," he said, "the Inspector of Education represents the Queen here on this soil.

"At least, of course, in matters of Education does he represent the Queen, especially by way of the Minister of Education, whom he directly represents.

"You might say he represents the Crown. At any rate, he has come by to inform me personally—as well as the other teachers—that The Hague has ordered that henceforth in the Secondary Schools of the Kingdom, Spanish shall be on the same level with German as the fourth language, that is to say, after Dutch, English and French. From now on, you may choose one of these two, and your choice will fulfill the fourth language requirement."

There were no questions, because there couldn't be. If it had been so decreed in the nation's capital, in The Hague, then there could be no further discussion. The whole problem was now solved. Gone was the puzzle: German in such disrepute during the War, Spanish considered somewhat lowly by the Dutch authorities... Both were restored, though not yet to the level of languages that really mattered; after all, those were mandatory, no choices there!

If we had had to go to yards and inches, pounds and ounces—off the metric system—the Inspector would have just walked in one fine day and said so, and the announcement, formal or informal, would have had to take care of the pains of "transition" and the trauma of "conversion." No federal funds needed. No discussion of wider implications. No jibber-jabbering cartoons. Just an old man with a long beard.

1974

Nostalgia for Lost Community and a Movie

I have often thought about the American loss of community and sense of family and about the hunger to replace it with something else. In the mass society, with lives lived anonymously, it is often celebrities who become family figures and mass entertainments that replace familial occasions. For better or for worse, this sort of thing now binds us in community.

Something like a movie can have everyone talking and can even stir passions. One such movie was Kevin Costner's *Dances with Wolves*. Some have dismissed it as a revisionist Western; others praised it as the beginning of a certain mental and psychological redress for the American Indians. Some argued that Hollywood had once again fooled us into accepting a glossy action-packed adventure as truth, while others pointed out that to hear the Sioux language spoken seriously and thoughtfully was itself a major departure from the Hollywood tradition.

Whatever its merits, this film about a Civil War soldier who slowly becomes converted to the Sioux Indians has stirred something deep in us—in the American psyche. We have felt guilty about Indians ever since their defeat, and the movie is a collective exercise in wish fulfillment: if only it had never happened; if only whites and Indians could have lived together harmoniously. This dream of reconciliation is by no means ignoble, but it is predicated on a mental recasting of some of the realities of the past.

For the culture clash of White and Indian was extreme. The two ways of life could not exist side by side. Largely nomadic tribes with a reverence for the spiritual sanctity of the land were utterly alien to property-loving, thing-obsessed Westerners. A victorious culture in an exercise of nostalgia can now afford to dream of living harmoniously with its antagonist.

In fact, that dream existed before a final victory. It was the dream of the Noble Savage, the primitive who had not succumbed to the blandishments of civilization. But while the dream never really died, it did not do very well in close proximity to the Indian, for it was a private, urban dream, dreamt by idealists, and it could not withstand the alienness of a totally different civilization.

Since that early time in American history, the Indian has had a rich existence in the imagination of whites. To this day, we speak of the Wild Indian, the creature free from the restraints we all feel. The incredibly popular children's books by the German Karl May encapsulated that image for Europeans as well: Indians were free, they had the freedom of the forest, they did not feel the constraints of Western society.

In our time, the image has changed again. Indians are now seen as the original ecologists, the ones who did not waste and despoil the land but lived in utter harmony with it. It is part of a larger wave. We in America perceive the Indians as exemplifying all we have not done, all we have lost, all we have forgotten. Indians are now venerated for their spiritual connection to the world that we *wasichus*—the Sioux word for whites—must learn to emulate. The various sixties movements, the Make Love not War ethos, the political idealism, are now to be found in a reverence for the earth as former hippies join yuppies in sweat lodges, where they celebrate the ritual of purification.

The actual knowledge about American Indians is still not great. A process of some sentimentalization is at work: never mind that most of the Indian tribes were warlike and fought each other fiercely—at least they revered the environment. They had what we so desperately lack, a sense of the land and a sense of community.

The film *Dances with Wolves* very clearly reflects this present-day image. The community to which the soldier escapes is an ecological utopia, a perfect antidote to the world we in the West have created. But ultimately it tells us less about the Sioux Indians than about our own dissatisfaction with our own world.

For what the movie also brings out is that no two cultures could have been more different. If that was so then, it remains so now, with the Indian in total defeat. Our longing to somehow integrate the two is understandable, but finally it is nothing more than an exercise in nostalgia. And yet our collective longing also binds us together; we may not have the actual Indian community to merge into, as did Kevin Costner's Civil War soldier, but we have at least the movie to create for us the shared sentiment of community.

1991

What Technology Can't Do for Us

A friend from the East Coast faxed me a humorous piece about toilets. She evidently thought I would find it hilarious. I worked my way through it, but just barely. Funny it wasn't; strained would be a better word.

In my e-mail I receive four or five "witty" stories a week. The last one was about Adam and Eve and was as unfunny as most of them: something about a rib. Why am I getting these?

Here's why: because they're easy to send. The technology is there. Someone sees something funny or has a funny idea, sends it off to a bunch of friends, and they pass it on. It beats writing a letter.

Very little is gained from all this lightning-speed sending of material. Certainly it would be folly to regard it as having anything to do with dissemination of knowledge. Most of the stuff we read is not even information; it's just stuff. So many messages, so little content. So much material, so little knowledge. So much information, so little wisdom. Knowledge is hard to acquire; you don't get it from quickly scanning your monitor. And wisdom is even harder.

This point has been made before, but it seems to require constant reiteration. To a lot of people, wiring up a class of kids to the Internet spells knowledge. The children will learn from looking things up.

Not really. It's a little like having an encyclopedia in the house. Did that ever guarantee that Johnny learned something? No, all it guaranteed was that he could look something up—and then if he thought about it, studied, reflected on it, he might learn something.

We had plenty of information, plenty of stored data, long before the Internet. A good school library thirty years ago contained infinitely more than most kids will assimilate in their entire school career. What we do not have enough of is studying, learning, thinking. Mindless copying of data does not promote any of these.

Is that possibly why the United States, with its great wealth, does not turn out students who perform well on the international tests we've heard so much about recently? We have all the materials at our command and spend vast sums of money on schools, but these do not seem to produce the bright, intelligent kids we yearn for. Do we need any further proof that technology by itself does not breed either intelligence or understanding?

Not that any of this clutter is intrinsically harmful. The only harmful thing in it is the idea that it has anything much to offer us.

1997

Abstract Meditation on Conspiracy Theories

To force an arbitrary, invented order on events so as to make them bearable is a revising of reality, a reshaping, a remaking that is oddly akin to certain other mental processes. Surely wishful thinking, daydreaming, and occasionally dreaming itself are ways of making happen internally what failed to happen externally. These activities can be useful and even creative, as we all know; but when the mind does not recognize, and will not acknowledge, a fairly plausible version of events, and willfully substitutes *its* constructs and insists *they* are real, then a certain conspiratorial madness has taken over.

In finding someone to blame, we are creating order. In outlining a conspiracy, we are making meaning. And while the initial impulse may be a petulant lashing out at what angers us, the subsequent process is understandable and even admirable. For to find order and meaning is an act of analysis. To discover explanations, determine responsibilities, reveal underlying structures, is hard intellectual work. Even in cases of real paranoia, the mad constructs, weird though they may be, are ways of accounting for a problem, desperate attempts to forge understanding.

Not only does conspiratorial thinking allow the creation of a certain meaning, it also gives one the chance of exercising control. To organize information is to leave little to chance. The power of the imponderable and unpredictable and unforeseeable is denied. Because events are now perceived as occurring in a carefully orchestrated fashion and then acted on accordingly, the illusion of power over them is possible. Totalitarian societies are often notoriously "paranoid." Such societies use explanations to help them achieve control over their

100

problems and enemies by seeming to make them part of a plausible, orderly pattern.

Conspiracy theories have always been with us. For over a century, *The Protocols of the Elders of Zion* has convinced some people that a handful of Jews was about to take over the world.

But what I personally find more disturbing than the insanities of a few is the presence of such thinking in the minds of so many otherwise sane, pleasant people. I am not arguing, of course, that conspiracies do not ever exist. I am saying that conspiratorial thinking is all too common.

Complicating the matter is that healthy problem-solving and weird conspiracy-mongering are related activities. Part of intellectual activity is to find underlying schemas and connections. Freud said that philosophic systems resemble paranoid constructs. And if structuralists like Claude Levi-Strauss are right, then human beings are indeed pattern-making, structure-finding creatures.

"For some," said the novelist Norman Mailer, "it is unendurable to live without a hypothesis." I suppose it is when the hypothesis becomes extreme or cut off from reality that paranoid thinking thrives.

And a further complication is that the same way the "party-line" in an ideologically based totalitarian state rules the truth, so the self-image of a person can rule his psyche. That is to say, it operates in a "totalitarian" fashion by controlling the flow of perceptions and by eliminating unacceptable versions of what happens.

Internal conspiracy theories fester when explanations have to be invented and blame formulated to explain away failures, weaknesses, unpopularities, and so forth, without the person blaming himself. The totalitarian part of the psyche requires a system that allows for control over unpleasant realities. At its most extreme, self-image does to personality what ideology does to the state. Politics and psychology frequently run on parallel tracks, and governments and people often behave in similar ways, with a curious mixture of pride, self-interest, and self-justification dominating their sometimes self-serving, sometimes self-destructive behavior.

It is in the ideology of personality that conspiratorial thinking may well have its beginning.

2005

ENVIRONMENTALISTS WHO OVERLOOK
THE ENVIRONMENT

When I was in Amsterdam last spring, the story went around that an American couple from California walked into the famous Dutch poet Remco Campert's favorite bar, which he had patronized for more than thirty years to drink, smoke and discuss poetry. The couple looked around, overwhelmed by the noisy, smoky crowd, strode up to the bartender and almost in unison asked, "Could you please tell those people not to smoke?"

A few days after I heard this story, I was at a large dinner party in Amsterdam's elegant canal district. Before dinner, drink in hand, most guests were chatting and smoking. Once food was served, cigarettes were put away. But as the wine flowed and the conversation grew more animated, it seemed to become permissible to smoke between courses. Toward dessert, people were eating and smoking at the same time.

Not too long thereafter I accompanied a Dutch novelist to a protest meeting in the little town of Ruigoord, slated for destruction as part of an expansion of Amsterdam harbor. The event took place on a sunny afternoon in a church. Some important figures in the Dutch environmental movement were present, as was a whole slew of poets and writers. The readings were long, but the speeches short and to the point: the pretty little town had to be saved, the developers had no reason to touch it, the government should step in to scrap all these plans.

With the applause for every talk, the dogs that had been brought in by their owners barked. People smiled good-naturedly. This could have been a meeting in California in the early seventies, or for that matter now. Except for one thing:

Many in the audience were smoking.

I do not for a moment question the sincerity of the environmentalists who spoke up at the meeting to save the town.

It's not hypocrisy we're dealing with here, but blindness. Somehow smoking seemed to have no connection to the environment; in their minds, it was a different matter—if they thought about it at all. But I don't think they thought about it.

No need to go to Holland to observe this sort of blindness. How many environmental rallies in beautiful parks end up with litter all over the grass?

And how many people protective of the environment would be willing to forego the modern conveniences we are all addicted to—water-wasting flush toilets, emission-spewing automobiles, convenient but indestructible plastics? Maybe only the likes of Gary Snyder and Jerry Brown—and we suspect them of being austere people with a love of austerity for its own sake.

Somehow we human beings define what we need and then protect those things from attack, insulate them even from our own convictions.

We exempt what is convenient to exempt. And we do so unconsciously, which adds a layer of self-delusion to the whole process. So ingrained is our habit of making exceptions for ourselves, so innocent are we of what we do, that most of us do not even see a conflict.

Ask the people in that pretty Dutch town to do away with their cigarettes and they would think you were making a highly irrelevant point—or at the very least must be a strange, intrusive Californian with rather absurd ideas.

1999

The Plague Years

Not very long ago, the best friend of my youngest son died. He had been a hemophiliac, and sometime in the early eighties, long before blood supplies were screened, one of the many transfusions he constantly needed was infected. A few years later, he was found to be HIV-positive, and about two years ago he was diagnosed as having AIDS. Erik was a brilliant graduate of Yale University, a harpsichordist of some renown, an artist of immeasurable promise.

A former student of mine, now in his late thirties, is HIV-positive. Unlike Erik, he is gay. *When* his condition will turn into AIDS, he doesn't know. Right now he feels fine. Some years ago, Robert was beginning to make a name for himself in London as a playwright. A young, attractive, gifted man, the world was his oyster. Now it's an inky squid, a sinister, ever-threatening danger.

In a friend's apartment house, three of the six flats are inhabited by men with AIDS. My friend, the oldest person in the house, used to call downstairs when the boys were making too much noise at their wild Saturday night parties. They affectionately called her the "housemother." Now she occasionally shops for them when they are too weak to do so themselves, a mother to her sick children, except that these won't get better.

"I have seen the best minds of my generation destroyed," wrote the poet Allen Ginsberg in the late fifties, when there was little reason for him to say so. He was in a hyperbolic and metaphoric mood, assailing the conformity of American culture. But now he could have said it with more justice, and it would have been literally, factually correct.

The artistic community has been devastated. Many well-known painters, musicians, dancers, have lost their lives. But it is not the loss to art that one mourns the most. I have heard people ask about the

Holocaust, "How many Freuds and Einsteins perished there?" I submit that the world can more easily do without another Freud or another Einstein than a mother can do without her child. It is the human cost that is so appalling.

What is the effect on a city like San Francisco, where almost ten thousand people have died of AIDS?

The tragedy has touched many personally, but even those who have been free from a personal encounter must confront its horrors. The young are understandably afraid. The linking of sex and death threatens to undo all the hard-won ease about sex of the last twenty-five years. Whatever the deeper metaphysical links between sex and death, so favorite a theme in literature, young people cannot possibly experience sex this way. For them, it has always symbolized the pleasure of the future, the hope of the adult life.

That hope is now checked. And in fact, the greatest casualty of this epidemic for the society as a whole, for the old as well as the young, is the decline of optimism. Maybe every generation, even in America, has that optimism knocked out of it: young men going off to war in the forties, the threat of the atom bomb in the fifties, the curse of Vietnam in the sixties.

But America has a harder time with that pessimism than other cultures. We don't like limitations, and we don't like things we can't fix. The various radical AIDS groups do not only agitate for more government research but also play out a psychodrama of denial: if you shout enough, you lose yourself in the shouting, the anger, and then you have for a moment defeated doom. The American attitude continues to be that every problem has a solution: sooner or later someone will come by to fix what ails you.

And, of course, sooner or later someone will. But till then, this optimistic society cannot face the fact that so far no one has come by to cure what ails it.

1990

The Death of Common Sense

"All they need," said the waitress, "is a bit of common sense... common sense is dead in this country."

We had been talking about the way people sue each other at the slightest provocation, the craze of litigation sweeping the country.

I couldn't agree with her more. When you look around you, you certainly see how much common sense seems to be missing. And yet, I think, are we completely sure what common sense really is? Isn't common sense sometimes counterintuitive?

Who would have thought in, say, 1965, that those fast adding machines, computers, would be of any interest to more than a few specialists? The common-sensical thing to think at that time was that it was a passing fad.

Who would have thought that rock 'n roll would stay around as long as it did?

Common sense does not allow us to see any number of things— and yet sometimes it does. I go back to what the waitress said, that we need more of it. Here are some of the things I think of as just plain common sense:

TV Violence:

It is absolutely obvious to me that the more violence children see on TV— people shooting each other routinely, bludgeoning each other when the need arises—the more these children will perceive that behavior as, somehow, normal.

It does not mean that after seeing the mayhem a child will necessarily go out and shoot someone, but that there will be just a bit less surprise than there should be when someone actually does get shot.

The argument that kids know that what they see on TV is not real is partly true, partly false. They know it is not real, but it becomes part of their world anyway, a bit less unthinkable than it would have been without so many hours of TV violence.

Pornography:
While I think graphic violence is far worse than graphic sex, I strongly feel that the depiction of sexual violence toward women will inevitably affect the climate of violence, which will inevitably breed more sex crimes against women.

Violent pornography doesn't create violence, but it makes it just a little more acceptable.

Guns:
The easy availability of guns, their sheer spread throughout the country, helps account for our ghastly murder rate.

Of course people kill people, not guns on their own, but people will use what is near at hand. And of course if there were fewer guns, criminals would still have them, but the man subject to a sudden impulse would not—and this is not even to speak of the accidental discharge of the parents' gun found by playing children. An old Dutch proverb, "Opportunity creates the thief," states the matter well.

Let's lessen the opportunity.

Why are common-sensical things rejected? Sometimes, I admit, because they're wrong. More often, I think, because they are at odds with people's desires: for violent movies, for pornography, for guns. Emotion tends to beat out common sense.

The denial of sense afflicts all sides of the political spectrum.

The Right wants guns without restriction. The Left wants no tampering with pornography. In each case, good reasons are brought forward, but in each case, the emotional claim is far greater than the claim of sense.

Having said this, though, it sounds as if I'm urging us to *do* things. I myself would love to see more gun control, and I would have no qualm about limiting violence on TV, but my point here is not to urge action. My point is to say, This is what I think is *true*. If it is, let's admit it.

Once we do, we can decide what, if anything, to do about it.

That would be the common-sensical thing to do.
1997

Another Time, Another Way of Doing Things

During the Arab oil embargo of 1973, when all over the country long lines of cars waited at gas stations, I was visiting my Aunt Anna in White Plains, New York. My mother's sister was then a young-looking sixty, energetic and enterprising. As I recall, she, my brother, and I went to visit her mother, my grandmother, in a retirement home in New Jersey.

But first we had to get gas.

Anna drove to a gas station, but rather than joining the mile-long line of waiting cars crawling toward the two pumps that were being used, went right to a third pump, next to which a car was parked.

An attendant came over immediately, and I thought he would point us to the end of the line.

Not at all.

He smiled warmly ("Hello, Mrs. Fay"), opened the hood, made a show of looking in, and called another attendant, who then placed himself in a way that concealed a hose and nozzle being inserted into the gas tank.

The operation concluded, no money was handed over, and we swiftly drove off. To this day, it isn't clear to me whether any of the other motorists had seen us, and if they had, why there wasn't a riot.

I was embarrassed, appalled even, but very curious. "How did you do that?" I asked.

"Well," said my aunt expansively, "I've been over-tipping him for the last ten years, giving him gifts for his wife, you know, just being friendly."

"How could you know that some day you'd need him?" I said, one step ahead of her explanation.

"I didn't. . . I do it with everyone—my dry cleaner, the 'Super' in my building, my dentist's nurse. I learned that in Europe."

I knew it was a European style, though not favored by the parents of my Dutch friends when I was growing up in Holland or in the Dutch colony Curaçao. I remember disapproving of it when I was a child. My mother had a Russian friend who lavished gifts on her hairdresser, not just at Christmas. Why would she do that, I wondered?

These were Central European or Eastern European habits, I thought severely, always a rather judgmental child. (My aunt had grown up in Germany, not Holland.)

As an adult, I saw another aspect. People like my aunt considered such people "The Help," and gave them rewards the way nowadays we tip in a restaurant, or give something to a delivery person, or remember the "paper boy" at Christmas. It was merely an extension of how most people in our own time and place define "The Help."

But I continue to feel troubled by this habit, because somehow related was the attempt—which I also remember disliking as a child—to create an intimacy with people who were not intimates: you tell your maid about your troubles, or confide in her that you're having marital problems.

Those people worked for you, were subordinate to you—how could they really be your friends?

It used to be that the farther west you went in Europe, the less of this you saw. Western Europeans thought of themselves as able to respect certain boundaries, while Eastern Europeans felt the West was cold and impersonal. Both were right.

Is there a reason for such differences in cultural style?

Now, looking back after all these years, I see yet another side to it all. The urge to be on good terms, to buy, woo, or finagle someone's goodwill, may well have its origin in fear. If you feared that at any time Cossacks might set your house on fire, wouldn't it be a good idea to have some advance information, or some trusted local who would give you shelter?

And is it at all possible that this habit of my aunt I so disapproved of had saved her life when in 1942, she—as we were—was fleeing Europe during the Nazi occupation?

2007

Related Aphorisms

Yes, those who forget the past are condemned to repeat it, but so are those who remember the past.

Ecology, like Freudianism, made us realize that nothing can be discarded. Garbage exists after it's thrown out, and the unconscious clings to debris which a higher self has cast off.

We stylize our past, mythicize it, and, advertently or inadvertently, rewrite our history. We are all revisionists, and memory is nothing if not ideological.

The paradox of ideas is that they affect us emotionally.

Nothing is so serious that it can't be trivialized.

The most rigorous censorship is exacted by unvoiced assumptions.

The invention of God may well be the ultimate conspiracy theory.

We are not "condemned to be free." We are condemned to be free to indulge the illusion of freedom.

A Conversation Gone Awry: The Way We Speak Now

We Have, Like, Body Language

Have you noticed? The word "like," which was used often in the sixties to add an irrelevant pause in the middle of even the shortest sentence (as in, "He was, like, upset," or, "We had, like, snow,") has become part of some larger conversational drama.

The speaker may say, "She goes, 'You can't do that here,' and I'm like [long, significant pause] I can't believe this is happening."

Here "like" signals high emotion, in this case astonishment, anger or outrage. The speaker is saying, "I was shocked, I was in a total state," and the listener is supposed to gasp.

However, the speaker isn't really saying it but *acting it out.*

Often, this kind of dramatic utterance is part of some larger story, in which an important dialogue is reproduced. We have all heard it:

"So she goes, 'You're back in town' and I go, 'Yeah I think so,' and she goes, 'Why didn't you call Jack?' and I'm like (long pause, mock astonishment, mouth open, eyes wide in disbelief)."

We get the direct quote rather than the indirect comment on it. Dialogue is replayed rather than summarized. The story is not reported so much as it is rendered. Even speechlessness is mimed.

This kind of talk attempts to show rather than tell. Especially among young people, speech is turning toward performance. We're asked to hear, to experience, the speaker's astonishment. And if other people's reactions are quoted, then we hear what they said and how they said it, in their own tone of voice.

In fact, the use of "go" instead of "say" is also evidence of speech turning into drama. "Going" suggests activity, acting, both in the sense of doing something and of performing.

One theory I have about the origin of this sort of talk is that it started with a generation brought up on cartoons, where everything was always spoken with great emphasis, and any conversation had to be acted out. The kids liked the energy, picked it up, copied it—and a new style was born.

Cartoon talk needs the inflections, the gestures, the mugging, the clowning, to accompany it. You say, "You know, I mean, wow, I'm like…" You can only give those words meaning by creating a highly charged context. Eyes grow wide, mouths fall open, tongues hang out.

In such exchanges, body language replaces oral language. This is the great American perkiness, the over-animation that never fails to impress (or distress) foreigners. Our smiles and chirps are legendary.

American movies and cartoons may spread this new way of speaking all over the world, especially among the young. What's lost is a certain precision of language, a suppleness of vocabulary that comments on the action. What's gained is that emotion gets into the conversation as part of a performance.

1997

Standard English?

Like many older singles, I spend a certain amount of time in coffee shops. Mostly I'm surrounded by older people who, like me, are reading or writing or musing. Sometimes, though, young people come in, usually in groups of three or four.

Overhearing them has given me a whole new view of the Ebonics debate. We now know that whatever else the Oakland School Board had in mind, their ultimate goal was that African American kids should be proficient in Standard English.

No one can disagree with that goal. But where *is* Standard English these days?

The kids I'm listening to now, in my favorite West Portal café, are not speaking Ebonics; they are non-minority—white, privileged, boisterous. Are they speaking Standard English?

"I treat you good— you treat me good. Know what I mean?"

It's a kind of stripped-down English, almost a pidgin.

Other times, it's a language that seems to have done away with words and substituted looks, gazes, postures. Body language has taken over from verbal language.

"I was like—"

[long, astonished pause]

"And my mom went, 'What?'"

"And I'm like, 'Whoa.'"

"And my mom's like—"

[open-mouthed bewilderment]

"Like I talked to my cousin? And she like couldn't believe it? And I like yelled???"

It isn't Standard English—maybe a sort of Standard Body English.

Older people have always objected to the slang of the young, but has there ever been a time when so much talk relied on non-words, pauses, eye-rolling, looks of disdain or horror?

Linguists always tell us that language forever changes and with it the Standard language, but I can't help wondering what it's going to take to get these kids to that Standard language, however modified it may be at the time.

Perhaps all school boards, not just Oakland, ought to try and reiterate that important but evidently so distant goal of Standard English.

1998

CHOOSING YOUR OWN VOICE

Students of history know that in other times people thought differently, felt differently, behaved differently. We are, as they say, creatures of our time. If the prevailing ethos is that you're a victim, then chances are you'll feel victimized; if the times dictate that you have nothing to complain about, then the likelihood is, all other things being equal, you'll think so too.

We feel what we're allowed to feel, and we experience what we're sanctioned to experience. Only the rarest human beings rebel genuinely against the prevailing modes and feelings of their time.

In smaller ways, we copy the styles of others. Role models, whether on TV or not, are particularly influential in pressing their style on ours. Anyone who has watched a lot of TV can see the effect on the surroundings—people will, unwittingly, imitate the people they admire on the screen. And not only the ones they admire, but everyone who happens to be on the screen.

Little mannerisms, body language, even the way the language is spoken, are quickly imitated. Kids copy gestures they see in the cartoons they watch. TV is as much a part of their environment as other people are.

This we know; it is so obvious it hardly needs stating. But what is less obvious is that even our voices—so peculiarly our own, so tied to our personality, even our biology—are also often copied from popular styles around us. I notice it more in girls, but I don't doubt a similar phenomenon exists in boys as well.

I remember when girls' voices were much huskier than they are now because any number of movie stars had—or affected—husky voices. Nowadays it strikes me that young girls frequently have three types of voices:

1) The little girl voice. Probably modeled on TV cartoons, this is so common that nobody looks surprised when a full-grown woman speaks in a voice much more suited to an itsy-bitsy thing.

2) The scratchy, slightly croaking voice, sounding as if it were coming from deep, deep in the throat. There is supposed to be an ironical effect here; probably it started with a scornful, quizzical manner rapidly imitated by thousands. This voice seems always to be marveling at the folly of other people, mainly other girls.

3) The metallic voice, penetrating and twangy. I theorize that this one originated in loud, busy households, because there's a piercing, unavoidable quality to the voice. The speaker does not have to raise her voice to be heard; the metal bites through all other things. For some reason, this voice is in vogue.

Inevitably there are other voices, some beautiful, some mellifluous, and I'm a grouchy bear for not devoting a column to those. And, of course, some voices sound as they always have. But these three types seem very real to me. And every time I hear them I marvel at our human malleability.

1998

A New View of Bilingual
Education in California

The eternal fuss over bilingual education and ballots in California may not have been scrutinized from enough points of view. I got a fresh one the other day when my friends Carol and Paul came up to San Francisco from Los Angeles.

Right after breakfast at the St. Francis Hotel, we all went up to their room. They wanted to call Michael, their four-year old, who had stayed home. Father talked first:

"Hi, Michael, how are you?"

"_____"

"*Buenos dias, a tí también,*" said Paul.

"_____"

"*Si, tengo un regalo para tí.*"

"_____"

And so it went. Michael speaks Spanish better than English, and prefers it anyway because that's what he speaks with Margarita, my friends' live-in maid from Nicaragua.

Paul and Carol both work all day—he's a successful stockbroker, she a buyer for a well-known Beverly Hills shop—and Margarita is at home with the kid.

"The other day," said Carol, "I asked him if he had seen my watch, and he didn't understand, so I said, '*Dónde está mi reloj?*' and he answered, '*Mamá, allá, en el cuarto de baño.*' Smart as a whip."

Paul and Carol tell the story wryly but don't seem to find it noteworthy that they too are becoming bilingual. After all, they need to communicate with their son as well as their maid.

For that matter, I wonder if language learning hasn't progressed farther in the fancy suburbs of LA than we know, and if it doesn't involve the affluent Anglo classes more than the Latinos, who are always thought to be the ones chiefly affected by the problem.

Language acquisition, as the language theorists tell us, thrives when there is a genuine need for the second language.

This was brought home to me again when I stayed with Carol and Paul in their beautiful house in Brentwood.

At a certain point, their large German shepherd, mistakenly thinking that we were ready to go out for a walk, pressed rambunctiously against little Michael.

"*Bleib*," yelled Carol. The dog stayed. And then, when we all did go for our walk, she commanded, "*Bei fuss*." The dog heeled beautifully.

After an uneventful stroll (Michael happily chirping, "*Mira, mira*," from his stroller), it was "*Sitz*," and the creature sat.

Some time in the evening when I was mulling all this over, I heard "*Platz*," and there was a loud plop as the eighty-five pound animal crashed to the floor, frozen in place.

I got quite used to speaking German to the dog, warning him to "*Pass auf*" (Watch—a good, all-purpose order) and itching for the chance to bark "*Fass*" (Seize) at him, so he could chew any would-be burglar about to intrude on this happy household to pieces, and thereby fulfill his sacred mission of *beschützen*, protecting.

The dog, I found out on this anthropologically significant weekend in Los Angeles, had been trained by Klaus, a fashionable dog-trainer in Santa Monica. Klaus' background and methods are staunchly Teutonic.

Once, to train a neurotic old dog to stop being upset at loud noises, he shot off a gun every time the dog bent over his dinner. That way, the animal would associate noise with pleasure, see?

So whatever you may think of teaching Hispanic kids arithmetic in Spanish, or of having a section of the ballot written in Chinese, some form of "bilingualization" is already going on. And as usual, the rich are way ahead of the rest of us: they're working on being trilingual.

1980

The Language, Again

I have said it; you have probably said it. Many people have said it. "The language is growing coarser."

That means a whole lot of different things. Sometimes it means that more swear words are being used in polite company; sometimes it means that these days English speakers appear to have a narrower, more stripped-down vocabulary.

And it means yet other things.

But when it means seeing certain words as inferior to other words, watch out. It seems almost impossible to assess the worth of individual words.

People always say certain words are pretty or ugly, but does that mean anything? Are they intrinsically one thing or the other?

The same words can be viewed as beautiful or ugly. Compare these two passages, written eighty five years apart:

"Has anyone reflected what a touch of grossness in our race, what an original shortcoming in the more delicate perceptions, is shown by the natural growth amongst us of the hideous names–Higginbottom, Stiggins, Bugg!" (*Matthew Arnold, "The Function of Criticism at Present Time," 1865*).

"There's a kind of peacefulness even in the names of English coarse fish. Roach, rudd, dace, bleak, barbell, gudgeon, pike chub, carp, tench…The people who made them up hadn't heard of machine-guns." (George Orwell, *Coming up for Air*, 1950)

If you look at the two passages, you realize that they have in mind two similar kinds of words. Though the former is a set of proper names and the latter is a set of common names, they are both Anglo-Saxon in origin, or at least not Latinate. And yet one author denigrates them, the other celebrates them.

Why? What's the difference? The difference lies in the point of view of the observer.

Matthew Arnold laments the lack of aesthetic good taste in the England of Victorian times and celebrates the classical elegance, the love of beauty and ideas he finds in France and the ancient world. In view of that attitude, the words he cites merely represent the crassness he abhors.

George Orwell, on the other hand, worries about the totalitarian drift of the future, and in post-World War Two days sees in the old English words a wholesomeness, a resistance to the evil of the approaching times, an English antidote to chaos.

It is this difference in point of view, in overall purpose, in context, that creates such a different evaluation of each word. Arnold stresses that side of the word that is displeasing and ugly because of his overall concern for beauty, while Orwell finds in its very crassness a comfort and a reassurance.

It is like two points of view, two attitudes, towards one person's behavior.

Two people can regard the same comment as either blunt and tactless or charmingly direct. It all depends on what else interests them, both in that person and in themselves.

And this, it seems to me, makes it almost impossible to evaluate any word for beauty or ugliness. Just about every word is both and a lot more.

Individual words are not easily typed as pretty or ugly, beautiful or vulgar; their context and the general orientation of their speakers make them one or the other or something else.

This ambiguity in each word makes of language a kind of poetry and of speech a kind of magic. And, it can be added, of the analysis of speech a kind of philosophy.

In light of that, who can be sure that words we find so ugly nowadays – symptoms of the decay of language—*docudrama, infomercial,* jargon words from TV, or super-crass expressions like, "This movie *sucks,*"— won't some day be considered beautiful, the former a sign of lush creativity and the latter an example of naïve immediacy?

It will all depend on the total point of view brought to them at that time.

1999

Related Aphorisms

Even lowly professions breed their own special pompousness.

A Conversation About Conversation

Do's and Don'ts of Conversation

Now that the holidays are upon us, we will all be thrust into the obligatory dinner parties, family get-togethers, and convivial meetings, and we will be amused or bored, depending largely on the conversational styles of those around us. I'm offering the following suggestions in the hope that you at least will not contribute to someone's tedium and may even brighten a fellow creature's day.

Aside from the usual advice always given—listen more, don't flip the conversation back to yourself, smile—I recommend the following:

1) Talk, yes, but don't narrate. Most people are not good storytellers and, more important, most stories are not very good. They go on too long, don't come to the point, and, if they're meant to be funny, often miss their mark. What happened to you at the Frankfurt airport may have struck you as funny at the time, but it's boring and pointless to most of your audience. However polite they are, they'll feel trapped in your monologue quickly. Also, you're taking up more time than you deserve.

2) Be sure that you're not talking longer than the other person. It may be your turn to speak, but don't hog the floor. As soon as there is a discrepancy in talking time between the two of you, there is a big conversational problem. It should be as close to fifty-fifty as possible.

3) Do give an opinion, do state a feeling, but try to do it lightly and with a certain originality. It's not as if every opinion has to be fresh—or even can be—but it's best if it's not recycled from the morning's newspaper. Your conversation partner has also read the morning newspaper. And try to avoid crass, sweeping statements like, "The candidate with the most money always wins." You may think this is heavy thinking on your part, but someone else just sees a sledgehammer mind.

4) Be personal, but not too personal. You can say what you like, why you like it, how it strikes you, but I think the particulars of your therapy or the seriously flawed character of your ex-spouse should be out of bounds. Details of trouble at work, the annoying habits of coworkers—shoptalk of any kind—is deadly. On the other hand, if you're a cancer researcher talking briefly about the nature of your work, or a lawyer giving a few hints about your latest interesting case, that's just fine.

5) If you're there with a partner, please do not indulge in either hostile sniping ("Harry never remembers the kids' birthdays") or cute marital byplay, however fond you feel ("Carla, you were always the first to find a pastry shop." "No, John, it was you: remember that time in Siena . . .") And above all, just because you have a partner at the table, don't feel that he or she has to verify every statement you make: "And that guy, his name was Bregonzi, do I have that right . . .?" Since nobody at the table gives a rat's behind what his name was, why bother with verifying that factlet? A simple and irritating variant on this is the familiar, "And so we left Tuesday. Was it Tuesday or Wednesday we left, honey?" "No honey, I think it was Wednesday; remember you had gone to the office first . . ."

6) Avoid canting, gushing, overpoliteness. Of course you want to compliment the host and hostess on a fine dinner, and certainly you want to politely acknowledge the trouble they've taken with the meal. But it is not the BEST dinner you ever had, nor is it the most WONderful evening of your life. I realize this is American party talk, the social code especially prominent in my own older generation, but it is obnoxious and not worth the paper it isn't written on.

Now that the milk of my human kindness is really flowing, I must stop. Happy Holidays!

1999

PLEASE DON'T SMILE WHEN YOU DON'T LISTEN

My favorite *New Yorker* cartoon appeared during the aftermath of the Vietnam War, when each day seemed to bring more sad news of Vietnamese refugees being intercepted and sometimes rescued in boats on the South China Sea.

The cartoon showed a man and a woman at an elegant cocktail party. Both of them looked bright and perky, and when he said, "Isn't that terrible about those Boat People?" she replied: "Oh, yes . . . do you *sail?*"

There is a certain style of non-listening going around that I'm well acquainted with these days. Here's my story:

I'm editing an anthology for The Traveler's Literary Companion series published by Whereabouts Press. My volume, *Amsterdam*, will bring together, in English translation, stories and fragments from longer works by Dutch authors that will give the traveler to Amsterdam a certain amount of cultural background to that city.

My friends know that I've been working on this project for at least a year. My labors have included selecting the Dutch stories, overseeing their translation, and dealing with various editing problems as they have come up, such as reconciling the translators' wishes with those of the copy editor employed by my publisher.

I have been so busy with this project that inevitably my friends have heard a good deal about it.

But that doesn't keep them from occasionally asking, "Say, Manfred, will these be all your own pieces in the book?"

No, of course not. I don't write about Amsterdam, and, what's more, how could my writing introduce the sort of cultural background only a diversity of writers could give?

When I explain this, some of them persist and say things like, "Why not show off some of your own work?"

These friends are, on the whole, literary people and very bright, and they know better. They just haven't been paying attention. When they finally understand that my writing will not appear in the book, they sometimes question why I'm not translating everything. "Why translators?" one of them asked. "Haven't you translated all the pieces yourself?"

Well, no. Why should I? With many excellent translators from Dutch, why should any one person translate eighteen different stories?

This is still forgivable, but the other day I heard a new one from someone who was ostensibly interested in my project: "Is the book in Dutch or in English?"

Why would a book introducing a foreign visitor to Holland be in Dutch? And why would I have been dealing with translators if the book was to come out in Dutch?

I explain again what this anthology is all about, and my friend nods. "But your publisher is in Holland, isn't he?" Is anybody listening? Does anybody care? Are we all so flooded with messages that we can't take them in? Or is it genuine indifference and total self-absorption I'm seeing?

But this is churlish of me. Here I'm turning against my own friends. Surely I myself am often not listening, and people have to repeat to me again and again which date they leave for Paris or when Aunt Millie is flying in.

Fair enough. But what I think I don't do is *pretend* to be interested. The prevailing style in these parts (California? The United States?) is to feign a great deal of interest, to affect much enthusiasm, to smile, to chuckle, to be perky—while all the time not listening. For some people, the smile and the furrowed brow are almost substitutes for listening.

They seem to feel it's worse to show no animation than not to listen. For me, it's the other way around.

2000

A CONVERSATION GONE AWRY

As usual, we meet in our pleasant West Portal café, and I look forward enormously to our talk. I like Joseph; he is warm, thoughtful, knowledgeable. Proud of being an independent scholar, unconnected to any university, he has published many scholarly articles.

Occasionally, he cannot help tweaking me a little about my having been a lifelong academic, and he refers once in a while to my sheltered life.

The topics of his articles range from foster care to drug addiction among suburban middle class youth. They are well regarded, both by members of the academic community and the general public.

I have heard him talk about these subjects with knowledge, compassion and understanding, with a real awareness of the complexity of the subject. He avoids the clichés of outsiders and stresses the complicated motives of people who are foster parents, or the intricate realities social workers have to confront when they, let us say, place a child in foster care or steer one into adoption.

It is this quality of mind I admire. It is this quality of mind I myself try to show, especially in my classes, where I frequently tell students that the best answer is "Yes and no" or, "On the one hand...on the other," preferably with a long explanation attached to it.

I truly believe that almost everything we really look at is complicated and that people act out of a mixture of motives—which still doesn't mean that there is no right and wrong.

So when my friend arrived and had taken off his sopping raincoat and his wide-brimmed hat, I was happily awaiting our usual good conversation. We talk about any and all things and rarely irritate each other, though on occasion I am annoyed by his lunging in the direction of gross over-simplification, as when he says that Republicans win more elections than Democrats because "they have more money."

When I bristle at that, he compounds the annoyance by saying that I'm "sheltered, naïve."

I counter that this is simplistic. Isn't there a mixture of reasons why the Republicans swept Congress in '94 and were less successful thereafter? What about Democrat Clinton? Did he win because he had more money than Republican Dole?

He intimates that in the academy, we live in such a cozy hothouse world with our like-minded colleagues, and our classes where we rule the roost, that we couldn't possibly know the real world.

But this sort of irritation is rare. Today we start talking agreeably enough about movies, and I ask him if he has seen such and such a film. He says he hasn't and adds that Siskel and Ebert reviewed it favorably, but that their reviews lately have been so uniformly favorable as to be unreliable.

"Yes," I agree. "They just like too many movies. It's hard to trust their judgment."

"Definitely," he replies, now puffing at his pipe. "I wonder how much they're getting to be so positive."

Now I'm really annoyed: "You know, you have too good a mind to say something like this. You coarsen your opinions by saying that."

He answers angrily: "That's a terrible way to put it. Don't talk down to me."

I reply testily, "Do you really think someone pays Siskel and Ebert big bucks to voice positive opinions? Do you think they're bribed?"

"Manfred, you tend to be really gullible. I'm more of a realist than you are. As an academic, you have no idea of the corruption that obtains in the real world."

At this point I have a choice. I can prolong this argument or end it. I choose the latter, but my mind is racing.

How could he believe that Ebert and Siskel are for sale? And how would he account for their occasionally negative reviews? Not enough money?

And how would he feel if someone said crassly about his specialty, drug addiction: "You know, I think the only reason we have drug addicts in this country is because of poverty." Wouldn't he instantly counter that the truth is more complex, that his own research has shown lots of rich middle class kids to be on drugs, and that while poverty might be a factor in someone else's addiction, it isn't with middle class suburban kids?

Why acknowledge complexity only in the situations he knows? Why ignore complexity in everything else?

He thinks I'm naïve and living in an ivory tower, not familiar enough with the real world to know how it works.

I think he is simplistic and coarsely ideological and allows his emotional beliefs to guide his thought. Each of us thinks the other has a fatal flaw in his thinking.

1998

MRS. BLOWFIELD: SCENE FROM A MARRIAGE

This happened in Sacramento, but it could have happened anywhere.

They came into the restaurant, a handsome middle-aged couple, obviously married, since they had what the late Mary McCarthy once called, "that linked, silent, wedded look." They sat across from each other—he facing the street and she looking vaguely at the other people, all of them eating, some talking, some silent.

He looked as if he were yearning for his newspaper, but even if he had one, he could hardly start reading it now. She looked as if she wanted him to say something, but she clearly did not feel like starting the conversation herself.

I was in an excellent position to watch them, a silent observer at a nearby table. I am not a voyeur—but I can't resist other people's conversations. For the moment, I had put my book aside.

Suddenly he looked up and said, "Mrs. Blowfield."

She asked, "What?"

"Mrs. Blowfield," he repeated in a tone of wonder.

"Who is Mrs. Blowfield?"

"Mrs. Blowfield. My grammar school teacher."

"Your grammar school teacher? What about her?"

"My grammar school teacher. She just walked by. Right here on the street."

"No kidding," said his wife. "No kidding. Your grammar school teacher?"

"Yes, my grammar school teacher. Mrs. Blowfield." His face looked dreamy, reverential.

"Imagine," said his wife in a fading voice.

"Mrs. Blowfield," he reiterated. "Mrs. Blowfield."

"Yes," she said. "I guess that was a surprise."

"Mrs. Blowfield," he repeated yet again. The wife was now clearly becoming bored or even annoyed. She could understand that seeing Mrs. Blowfield was important to her husband, but why, for God's sake, go on so, and why keep repeating her name?

At first the husband did not notice his wife's impatience.

"Mrs. Blowfield," he said, "that was Mrs. Blowfield. Grammar school teacher."

Now she tried to change the subject. "Gee, the service is slow tonight."

He did not respond, but said one more time, "Mrs. Blowfield."

She shot him an irritated look, which he must have recognized. He no longer said "Mrs. Blowfield." Now he thought it.

And he also thought that his wife could be a little more understanding; here was something important to him. He had seen Mrs. Blowfield after all these years and told his wife about it. She was always after him to share. Well, when he did, she got mad.

Meanwhile, she continued to simmer. How could he say "Mrs. Blowfield" ten times without saying anything more? What was the matter with him? He could be such a bore.

Well, of course, I can't swear that is what they thought. But it looked that way from my observation post. And it seemed to me that if they had such thoughts, neither of them could possibly be blamed: marriage had failed them both.

Or maybe our human, isolated condition had failed them: this little episode felt important to him, but how could she really be expected to "share" the experience, in itself so trivial, so personal, so utterly "unsharable"?

1999

A Conversation About Conversation

The older man at the table next to me in my favorite West Portal coffee shop was looking at the "Relationships" section of the *Chronicle* and occasionally let out a sigh. He obviously wanted to talk. Being done with my own newspaper, I looked at him encouragingly.

"You know," he said in a surprisingly resonant tone, "these ladies nowadays just don't want to talk to me." His craggy face creased into a puzzled expression.

"Well," I answered, "do you talk to women your age?"

"Yeah, maybe a bit younger."

"And still no luck?"

"No, not really."

That surprised me, because I had always heard that an available single man in his sixties—which is what I guessed his age to be—was a rather desirable commodity. I was going to ask him about that when he continued.

"As I get older I feel no one's looking at me."

I felt a gust of understanding. This is certainly something my friends and I talk about occasionally. It's as if we remain visible to fewer and fewer people.

"I had a couple of dates last month," he continues ruefully, "with a very attractive gal, eh, woman. But she broke it off, said we didn't communicate."

That last word he spoke sarcastically.

"She kept saying she wanted to talk. Well, that's what I wanted, too. I talked to her all the time."

"What did you talk about?" I asked with some curiosity.

"Oh, I told her about myself, my work, you know, and all that sort of stuff. I was in textiles all my life."

"What sort of thing did she talk about?"

"You know, the usual stuff."

"Was she retired, or did she still work?"

"She was still working. An accountant, downtown."

"Did she have children?" I asked.

"To tell you the truth, we only met a few times, and I never did find out if she had kids. I do know she was a widow, though."

"What did her husband die of?"

"How would I know? He died a few years ago. Long before I met her."

He frowned as if still trying to understand what had happened. He hadn't asked me a single question, not even if I had similar experiences.

"Do you try to listen to these women?" I asked bluntly.

He looked at me irritably.

"They aren't interested in anyone, just themselves. I told this one about my divorce, and she kept yawning."

I wanted to say something, to venture a diagnosis, to propose a remedy, but he was clearly feeling frustrated with our conversation and got up to go. He must have thought I was a bad listener.

1997

Related Aphorisms

Conversation is ultimately an attempt at overcoming solitude. Unfortunately, it often increases it.

The lies we tell reveal a truth about ourselves.

One sign of a deranged person is that he or she cannot hear anything in the spirit in which it was intended.

Many conversations are non-consensual.

So Many Writers, So Few Readers: At the Intersection of Art and Life

So Many Writers, So Few Readers

The other night I found myself at a poetry reading. Thirty or forty people, most of them young, in the obligatory uniform of those who attend such gatherings—corduroys, jeans, scruffy flannel shirts—listened more or less attentively as the readers on the platform either droned or ranted. Somewhat unfair of me, of course: perhaps it is getting harder for *me* to keep my mind on what is being said, but there was a uniformity about the lines the poets were reading, a hard-driving insistence that something valuable was being said, yet the significance of it all wasn't quite there. Lurid, fragmented images flickered briefly in the darkened room; but they were quickly snuffed out by the torrent of words streaming into all corners of the mind.

I wondered whether anybody was listening, whether anybody *could* listen. After all, here was I, interested in poetry, though not a fan of much modern poetry, barely able to stay conscious. Were *they*? I looked around, at the young, rapt woman, with her long, beautiful hands on her designer jeans; an older, long-haired woman, clearly a veteran of the drug wars of the sixties; a nervous young boy with a loose-leaf binder undoubtedly containing *his* poems.

Poetry readings are occasions for people to get together, to participate in something they think important, to look each other over, and perhaps to dream about themselves as poets, up there on the stage. It seems to me that they are *not* occasions to hear good poems or opportunities to discover new poetry, for there is something in the tone, the accents, the very sound of present-day poetry that militates against that. Whether refined or blustery, academic or populist, contemporary poetry is obscure and eccentric, and it is difficult to read and virtually impossible to follow when only heard.

But there are so many readings that a poet once called the phenomenon "po business," on the model of "show business." Name poets tour college campuses, and would-be student poets attend the readings. The attitude on the part of the readers ranges from *noblesse oblige* to genuine interest in presenting their work, while the audience is earnest and good-humored in the best American way. Everyone wins, except poetry, and that is nobody's fault really, only an indication of the thinness of the genre in its contemporary form. It is an eerie situation—so many people gathered for a purpose that doesn't truly capture and hold them. Every now and then one yearns for poetry that leaps out and seizes the listener, biting through its own constricting net—Auden, say, intoning

Follow poet, follow right.
To the bottom of the night

or Ginsberg, declaring,

I saw you, Walt Whitman, childless, lonely old grubber, poking among the meats in the refrigerator and eyeing the grocery boys...

Instead one hears the anemic tone of someone saying something like "the burning parrot's desk," or "the incomprehensible spider in his Sunday mood," or worse, a collection of words hurled across the room without, as they used to say, rhyme or reason.

I sometimes think, living in San Francisco—where my foot doctor lists on the emergency telephone numbers he gives out, along with the police and the fire departments, the box offices for the symphony and the opera—that there are more poets than readers of poetry and, by extension, more writers than readers. Is poetry now mainly for the people who write it?

2006

GETTING PUBLISHED IN THE UNITED STATES

A few years ago, a friend of mine got it into his head to start editing a short story magazine. His novel was going badly, he had just gotten a divorce, and he was at loose ends generally. Since he had a modest private income, he did not really have to work.

He was warned on all sides against this foolish venture. Editing a magazine is even more dangerous than opening a restaurant, he was told, and he kept saying he agreed, but he went ahead anyway. He placed an ad in a literary magazine for submissions, and soon he had a first issue to take to the printer.

His friends and relatives subscribed, and he tried to sell the other copies to bookstores, which didn't want them, and then he tried to give copies away to these same bookstores, but they still did not want them. They had so many little magazines.

At long last he was rid of all his copies, and then he waited. He didn't know for what exactly, but he waited.

To make a melancholy story a bit shorter: nothing happened. Or actually only one thing happened: he got an enormous number of submissions. Short stories started rolling in from all over the country, even though the circulation of the magazine had been limited to the San Francisco area. He never received fewer than twenty stories a day, although he did not advertise again. The magazine lasted a few years, and it never broke even, but he always had plenty of material.

I spent one summer in New York trying out the life of a literary agent. I had a friend's manuscript with me; eventually it became a best-seller. One day, in a literary agent's office, I was staring at dozens of huge cartons filled with large brown envelopes standing incongruously amid the chic furniture. At just that moment, a brawny man with another large crate walked in. "Messenger!" he roared. The agent explained wearily that most manuscripts nowadays come in by messenger service.

To a large extent, the agent's role has come to be to screen the publisher from too many unwanted manuscripts. The agent will reject 90 percent of what's submitted to her (most agents are women) and then the publisher will reject 90 percent of what the agent submits.

The young idealistic literary agent goes into the business hoping that she can find good writing. She often does—too much.

For that is the peculiar reality my friend the short-story editor found also: most of the work is pretty good. It's not brilliant, but it is competent and often interesting. In all his years as editor, he printed hundreds of perfectly good, workmanlike stories.

I cannot believe that the situation is as competitive elsewhere as it is in the United States. Freelance writing belongs to the most hazardous professions. "Send us anything of yours you want to," said the lady at the *Los Angeles Times*, after she printed my third article. I was ecstatic; I felt I had found my niche. But the friendly lady moved or the paper had a shakeup, and my next submission was greeted with the same interest as another smog alert in the Los Angeles Basin.

I'm not complaining. I manage to place my material some of the time. Of course, it's frequently lost and sometimes cut when it is printed. "Our magazine is a magazine for editors, not writers or readers," an editor told me.

None of which is to say that genius won't out. Sure, there is the story of the young man who killed himself after being rejected by dozens of publishers and whose bereaved mother then found a publisher to bring out his book. For that novel, *A Confederacy of Dunces*, John Kennedy Toole was posthumously awarded the Pulitzer Prize. And in New York publishing circles one editor was famous for being "the man who turned down *The Catcher in the Rye*." But even these two cases prove that genius will out.

And those who don't have genius? Well, they keep writing—and hoping.

1980

Everybody's Creative Urge

It used to be that people I met, after hearing I teach English at San Francisco State University, would tell me that they were not "good at English" or "had trouble with grammar."

No more. Nowadays, people are likely to say that they write, or have written short stories, or are working on a novel.

It's odd that in an age when people watch lots of television and prefer to talk endlessly on the telephone, there are so many still who want to write.

Or at least want to be writers.

These people are not necessarily big readers, and I'm not sure that they want to say something—but it's clear enough that they want to have said something, that they want to have written something.

But no, that's not fair; that's only part of it. They want to reveal themselves, they want more of themselves to show. They want to be seen, to be made more real than their ordinary lives can possibly allow. And who doesn't?

They are everywhere.

Could I please read this volume of poems, judge it, and perhaps get it published?

Could I look over this film script—and do I know any agents?

Would I have time to read a novel and see if it needs a second draft?

In the San Francisco Bay Area especially, writers lurk around every scenic corner.

"I just read Robert Bly's translations of Neruda's poems," sighs the waitress at Fisherman's Wharf. She is a tall, friendly young woman with a slight, bookish stoop to her shoulders. "Since you teach and write I thought you might want to look at what *I've* written. Of course, it's not as good as Neruda or Bly . . . but I think it *is* poetry."

I think, somewhat morosely, why should a literature professor be irritated that so many people are trying to produce literature?

"Now that I have my word processor," says the tall, balding man, "I go from my job at the bank straight to my novel. It's in the style of Kundera's *The Unbearable Lightness of Being.* The bank is just not enough for me, and I'm afraid I'm not enough for it either."

We are having drinks at a large garden party, and I watch him make much of the Swedish meatballs. "Not by bread alone," he smiles, likeably enough. I drift over to another guest, a businessman who wouldn't dream of setting pen to paper. His secretary does that. I happen to know she is working on a big book.

Again I fall victim to "ego-imperialism." I am now flat on my back in the hospital—having an X-ray taken. The technician seems excited. "It says here you teach. I think I've heard of you. I have a play I'd like you to see." He is casually arranging a leaden shield around my vital organs. The pain is in my back. What can it be? I worry.

"The play has real possibilities. I ended up publishing it myself. Just couldn't wait for an agent to make up his mind."

"I wish I knew a producer," I say hypocritically. "Or at least a director . . . Or even just someone who goes to the theatre."

But to be flat on your back is to be at a disadvantage in the humor department. You're not taken seriously. You've lost stature.

His rimless glasses blink on his round, benign face. "Hold still," he says, "Again . . . Now relax for a few minutes and then we'll do some more . . . The problem with plays is that there are so many floating around and not enough people who are serious about theatre. But at least plays differ from each other. Seen one X-ray, you've seen them all."

"Hey, wait a minute," I sputter. "The shield fell off. It hasn't been on me for the last couple of pictures."

"Oh, well, you're too old to want children anyway," he jokes and casually puts the shield back over me. "Do you teach drama too? What plays do you teach? You know, I have been writing for ten years."

A ten-year investment is no small thing, I think, and as I put my clothes back on he slips me a slender, self-published volume. "I just happen to have a copy with me," he smiles broadly, one literary man to another.

I drive home thinking that many a man my age has started a family all over again. True, I don't intend to, but still . . . Meanwhile, my back is hurting, and I think sourly about the human hunger for acclaim, recognition, applause. Is there anyone who doesn't want to be a celebrity?

But when I get home, the pain gradually lifts. A feeling of relieved well-being sets in, and I begin leafing through the awkwardly printed pages of the play, with its opinions and feelings, its shouts and musings, its characters and spectacles. Someone stands revealed; something has been created.

And this is really the other side, isn't it? We all need, somehow, to be able to show a little more of what we are and escape the anonymity which, living as we do, in this odd place and time, is our lot. Suddenly, in my pain-free euphoria, I find a certain beauty in so many trying to create something of meaning. And just as good, maybe better, is that they—we—in asking to be seen, might learn to do some seeing, learn to recognize in others and develop in ourselves that fuller life we all crave.

1990

THE POETRY-READING SCENE

It started in the late fifties and early sixties, when Beat poets like Allen Ginsberg and Gregory Corso and Lawrence Ferlinghetti frequently read their work in San Francisco coffeehouses to the accompaniment of jazz. Sometimes it was hard to see the connection between the poetry and the music, but never mind: these poets infused life into the formal, boring poetry readings, which usually had been poorly attended. And they created a dynamic, vibrant happening.

Soon enough many of the Beat poets became celebrities and went out on the reading and lecture circuit, mainly on university campuses throughout the country. But whatever informality had existed was lost in the public dimensions of these readings. Mass meetings assumed an almost political character, especially during the Vietnam years, sometimes with the atmosphere of a revivalist meeting.

In the seventies and early eighties, the better-known poets commanded great audiences, while the unknowns got no bookings—or had to make do with their friends. Some poets combined their readings with meetings on other subjects: Robert Bly drew in many thousands with his talks on "male consciousness" and how much men need a "wild man" inner self.

But the urge for a certain intimacy remained. The audience wanted to be close to the readers. Some years ago, a new, smaller format for readings has sprung up. Writers started reading in small bookstores, even when they didn't have a new book out. It's still mainly a West Coast phenomenon. Almost every evening in the San Francisco Bay Area, some poet is reading amidst wine and cheese and stacks of his own books. These have become social events. "I go for the poetry," one woman in the audience told me, "but even more for the company."

The poets are sometimes totally unknown. The storeowner calculates that any way he can draw people into his store is useful.

Some time ago I counted thirty poets reading in San Francisco in the same evening.

But lately we have had yet another turn in this phenomenon. Just as the comedians have an open-microphone night, where anyone can get up and perform a comic routine in a nightclub, so there are now poets who can read *unannounced.* If Thursday is "open-mike" night for poetry at a given bookstore, there are now likely to be a good number of poets, manuscripts in hand, waiting eagerly on Thursday night to read. The styles vary from witty-academic to booming post-Beat. The personalities range from wispy to truck-driver loud. This explosion of poetry is hard to believe. Where are the readers?

Or better, in this instance: where are the hearers? These unscheduled poets seem mainly to read to each other on such nights. When poets read only to each other, they may end up reading to themselves.

But even when there is an audience for poetry readings, wherever they are held and whatever kind they are, all these performances are now beginning to display a touch of nostalgia. Where have all the bardic poets gone? Readings suited the roaring of a young Allen Ginsberg far better than the quiet tones of a Robert Hass or Denise Levertov. Most present-day American poets are not bards; their poetry is best when it's read silently. Intricate word games and understated language are rarely understood by an audience. Such poetry is meant to be seen and not heard.

Under the pressure of being on stage, quieter poets sometimes try to boom like Allen Ginsberg or chant like Robert Bly, and attempt to take on the voice of the bard. It's as if declamation itself will make them more bardic, but the audience is not necessarily swept away. These attempts frequently highlight the gap between the readers' own subdued style and the poetry of larger sound. At such times, the restlessness in the audience is palpable.

Perhaps it's not surprising that the real craving for poetry in the United States is to be found outside of the poetry scene. Despite the activity I have here described, most Americans are relatively indifferent to "real" poets, but they admire, especially the young, the rock 'n roll lyrics made by the famous rock bands or the rap verses of different groups. The hearers of those lyrics are entranced—they memorize the song, sing it to friends, use it to express an emotion they cannot formulate themselves. For most Americans, true poetry is where poetry-lovers don't think it is.

1988

Have You Had a Standing Ovation Today?

An intense narcissism pervades the air at San Francisco Bay Area concerts and plays. We love our art and culture, but we love even more being the sort of people who love art and culture.

It seems hard for some in the audience to sit still while the performance is going on. They seem to crackle with tension to get into the act themselves.

More and more, theater-goers will laugh loudly or guffaw or even cheer any chance they get. It's a "statement." The audience declares its beliefs and signals its views to others in the audience.

Such people are so aware of being aware that they crave to be heard. It's this self-conscious, self-approving quality that gives the shrieks and whistles their edge.

At plays and at the opera, audiences will literally leap at the chance to give a standing ovation. If the actors have not muffed their lines or flagrantly trampled on all meaning, these people will come to their feet as if in prayer.

After a while, those who are still sitting down feel as people do at religious services when the leader of the flock intones, "Please rise." Sooner or later, they must rise.

Some of this activity is natural enough. Audiences want release from the tension of inactivity. Anyone who has had to sit still for a long time wants to move around, to scratch, to talk.

One reason for the volley of coughs, the salvo of retching that marks any pause between movements of a symphony, is simply that here are noises that can legitimately be made; they are allowed, and so people make them.

But the most important function of the cheering and clapping is that it takes attention away from the performer and directs it to where some in the audience feel it belongs—themselves.

Spectators now become performers; they are in the limelight, showing themselves knowledgeable, displaying their wit to others in the audience. They applaud their own discernment.

This sort of dramatic approbation is itself performance. In the final applause, the audience plays its starring role.

This brief period of glory, heightened and stimulated by the atmosphere of drama and song, is exciting. Since it's necessarily transitory, the clappers make the most of their display.

The same phenomenon occurs at lectures. Some in the audience long for the question period. They want their moment of fame. Never mind the question that requires a real answer. No, more important to show the others in the audience that you know the speaker's material as well as or better than the speaker, and can even take it in a direction he or she has neglected.

But some speakers answer at length and outshine the questioners. What then?

Well, then make a speech yourself. Give your own talk—barely disguised as a question. That way you reduce the speaker to nodding agreement or fatigued demurral.

Perhaps then, only then, can the rest of the audience see that you, sitting there so patiently, deserve the kudos and bravos so inexplicably bestowed on the front of the hall—that you should have been the speaker, the singer, the performer.

The least you can do for yourself is give yourself a standing ovation.

1980

HAS THE PREDICTED ANTI-INTELLECTUAL
FUTURE COME TO BE?

When I was in college in the fifties, many of my professors felt that America was a profoundly anti-intellectual country, and a good many things in that time seemed to bear out that assertion. Books did not sell well and were rarely discussed, and many Americans clearly had no love for ideas. Even before Richard Hofstadter published his famous book on anti-intellectualism in America, the intellectual future of the country appeared bleak.

And looking around us now, we can only conclude that much of what was feared then is true now: the level of our public entertainment is dismal, and the everyday discourse of the country is low. Political campaigns are conducted with slogans and sound bites. Intelligent, thoughtful conversations do not appear to flourish, and you can certainly spend days without hearing a book or an idea referred to. Yahooism is on the rise, and television is even more the "vast wasteland" than it was in 1960 when the term was coined. Intellectualism is largely confined to the academy, and almost every academic will confirm that it does not always thrive even in the academy. Few will disagree that the general coarsening of American culture is evident everywhere.

And yet, it has to be said that the dire predictions of that time were not wholly right—and may even have been largely wrong. After all, many more books are sold nowadays; many more students go to universities; many more intellectual magazines are published. Some important ones founded in the sixties, like the *New York Review of Books*, are not the struggling "little" magazines they once were; they are thriving corporate giants. Furthermore, many intellectuals appear on television, are interviewed at length, quoted in newspapers, and appear to be respected more than intellectuals were in the fifties and sixties.

So what have we here? Is it a case of those predictions being false after all? No, I don't think so. I don't think it's a matter of either/or, but both/and. We are, as a country, less intellectual and more so. We are coarser AND more refined. We are more intellectual in some way, less in others. We subject proposals and laws, for example, to more thoughtful, historically based review, but we do so in a climate, a surrounding context, of Yahooism and know-nothingness.

Another way to put it is that our intellectual standards have dropped but our respect for intellectuals has grown. We may not listen to the latter but we defer to them.

The reason may be that some conviction of thoughtfulness, some faith in intellectualism, is missing more than ever. We grant respect to the intellectual without having made intellectual processes a value. In large part, we have commodified our intellectuals: they are not people we emulate but "talking heads" we can be diverted by. Similarly, the magazines we display or even read with reverence do not change us and will not influence us. Universities, too, get ever more respect, but they are emblems of prestige, not places of learning or opportunities for profound personal change. They are icons: they help set a mood, they define a status, they signal an ambiance. We appreciate them. But we do not feel we really need them.

2001

REVISITING CULTURAL LITERACY

The debate over what every American citizen should know used to rage in the eighties but doesn't anymore. It has all but disappeared.

Just to refresh my memory, I had a look at the first edition of *The Dictionary of Cultural Literacy: What Every American Needs to Know*, by E. D. Hirsch, Joseph Kett, and James Trefil. It came out in 1988 with some fanfare, although subsequent revisions have not received much notice.

True literacy, the authors claim, comprises taken-for-granted background information, broadly shared knowledge. Accordingly, the authors propose lists of names and terms from twenty-three categories of knowledge. To recognize most is to be, in the authors' eyes, a culturally literate American.

The inclusions and exclusions are, of course, open to argument. Why, for instance, Rasputin but not Rastafarian? Why Lech Walesa but not Alice Walker? Why transcendentalism but not Transcendental Meditation? Why Joseph Smith—the founder of the Mormon Church—but not Bessie Smith?

These oddities detract somewhat from this reference book, with its crisp entries and fine introduction; but, more important, they raise the larger question: what are the gaps that should be filled in?

The crisis is still real. A recent study found that only 12 percent of Americans could locate Iraq on a map and that most Americans cannot find England, France, Japan, and South Africa.

When journalists report such findings, they frequently wonder how a country that spends so much on education can get so little. When college teachers of the old school discuss the remedy for this seeming ignorance, they usually advocate more required courses.

But everything seems to depend on who prescribes the cure. Political philosophers favor Rousseau and Plato. Scientists prescribe more science. Historians are aghast that students do not know Napoleon was defeated at Waterloo. The cure in all cases is more of what the specialist happens to teach.

But these advocates are often themselves illiterate in some major field outside of their own. Many years ago, C. P. Snow, the English novelist and scientist, identified the humanities and sciences as "two cultures" and argued that neither knew much about the other. He pleaded for bridging the gap—which hasn't happened, of course.

And herein lies the difficulty with the cultural literacy idea. Many educated people are unwittingly narrow. I recently asked a brilliant academic if she had been to the symphony lately. "Oh, I have a tin ear," she said cheerfully. Now would she argue as strenuously for a familiarity with Beethoven's Ninth Symphony as she does for Shakespeare's *Hamlet*? Would she even recognize the Ninth?

We are all specialized by our interests, our inclinations, our training—and our values. Not only are we knowledgeable in some fields and ignorant in others, we also unquestioningly assume, as Hirsch and his coauthors do, the importance of some over others. People who can't tell John Lennon from Elton John and have never listened to rock 'n roll could be accused of cultural illiteracy just as those who can't name an important twentieth-century poet could be.

Cultural elitists claim that this sort of argument denies that some things are more valuable than others. But that's just the point: no one can really say, with objective certainty, what those "more valuable" things are. The Beatles' music is retrospectively viewed as art, and earnest studies of Bob Dylan appear on the shelves and in college curricula. Many of the artifacts of popular culture are suddenly admired. Perhaps every age redefines just what high culture is, but the makers of the *Dictionary* seem unaware of that.

Clearly what lay behind the cultural literacy debate of the eighties was the longing for a more unified culture. But now the hope for it may be gone—or, in these more fundamentalist times, it is looked for elsewhere, not in shared knowledge but in shared values that originate in a shared faith.

The Dictionary of Cultural Literacy: What Every American Needs to Know
by E. D. Hirsch, Joseph Kett, and James Trefil
Houghton Mifflin, 619 pages

2005

CONFERENCE-GOING

Some years ago, I was invited to speak at a conference at the University of Minnesota. The subject of the two-day event was to be Translation, and there would be papers on the art of translation as well as translators reading from their translations in many languages.

Formal speeches included such subjects as the mistranslations of the work of Hans Christian Andersen, the difficulties of translating Russian Romantic poets into English, and my own lecture on the problems and pleasures of translating modern Dutch poetry.

A sizeable audience came out to hear these rather theoretical talks, and a somewhat lesser number came for the readings of Danish, Swedish, Russian, Finnish and Dutch work in English translation. A yet smaller group had registered for the workshops with individual translators who would advise the registrants on their own translations. The final event consisted of a panel discussion, in which a certain amount of controversy was expected and even solicited.

One thing struck me about this conference, as it has about other conferences I have attended. While the event was undeniably a success, each participant delineated his own subject without necessarily being engaged by anyone else's. That is to say, the witty and interesting talk on the role of the editor in publishing translations actually had no clear connection to the lecture on Isak Dinesen's own English versions of her work, and wasn't really supposed to.

In part this is due to the fact that conferences in the humanities are often modeled on conferences in the sciences, though they are of an entirely different nature. A scientist reports his latest findings to others working in similar fields. He tells of what his research has led him to and (ideally) provides others in his area with ideas and insights about how *they* should progress. It doesn't always work that way, of course, because sometimes scientists, too, talk right past each other and expect those who do not talk at all to share their interests. But on the whole, they talk to those people who can benefit from and actually *use* the speakers' discoveries.

It's different in the humanities. We often trade insights, not information. We exchange opinions, not facts. Even the talk on the role of the editor did not tell us much that was new. My own definitions of equivalency between translated poem and original, or my views on translating modern poetry, were not the sort of material that would actually change anyone's mind—they were perceptions, insights, attitudes.

Which is not to say that they aren't useful. They are. But what further struck me as the conference progressed was that my finely honed, proudly held, carefully formulated views on these matters were never mentioned, even in the panel discussions the next day, whereas my one-liners, witticisms and asides were. I had said in passing that the language of many translation theorists sometimes seemed to be a clear case of "physics envy," and in a discussion of language I had told the anecdote of a friend having a French student living in her house who thought the most beautiful word in English was "Listerine."

These witticisms came back to haunt me the next day. They were quoted and requoted, almost to my embarrassment. It was as if I had said nothing else. And then suddenly it occurred to me: these are the things we *all* remember; that is why people want to see talk shows, and why David Letterman is a star. We like to be amused and we like our messages quick and punchy. Others do; I do.

In fact, what one gets out of such a conference is different from what one is *supposed* to get out of it. The one-liners are little nuggets taken away from such an event. So are other things: the people one meets, the contacts one makes, the exchanges after the formal program is over. A heady, almost party-like mood prevails. I supposed you could speak of a kind of Conference Culture. And if all that has the effect of rekindling our enthusiasm for our work, well and good—even if we continue to speak a little bit past each other.

1987

POLITICAL CONVENTIONS AND
THE NEW JOURNALISM

During a political season, it might be worth recalling that previous conventions, aside from the obvious television coverage they invariably got, have been immortalized by such writers as Norman Mailer, who in 1960 wrote his famous account of John Kennedy's conquest of the convention and called it "Superman Comes to the Supermarket."

Mailer's account was electrifying. Instead of concentrating solely on the politics of the convention, he fleshed out the cast of characters, dramatized the clash of forces. Politics, he suggested, was a pastime anyway, like baseball or smoking, something to distract us from the painful business of living. Throughout, he expressed his own perceptions, feelings, and biases, especially in his lavish praise for the as-yet-unsung JFK. In that article, Mailer can be said to have initiated the so-called New Journalism, a genre of reportage that is supported, adorned, and embroidered with the writer's own feelings.

The rest is history—or at least the history of writing and reading in America. Mailer went on to do it again and again, although perhaps not as well as in his 1960 *Esquire* article; but the New Journalism flourished. James Baldwin had already published some of his most influential articles in the late fifties and the early sixties, one of them taking up a whole issue in *The New Yorker* magazine, and Norman Podhoretz—later to become the controversial editor of *Commentary*—had signaled the birth of the new genre in his *Harper's* magazine piece, "The Article as Art." It was Podhoretz's view that an art unselfconsciously practiced, unaware of itself as art, was likely to be, paradoxically, the most successful art.

Perhaps no one advanced the New Journalism more than Tom Wolfe, the brilliant raconteur of the follies of the sixties and seventies, a shrewd observer of the mores and manners (and the lack of them) of his time and place. From *Radical Chic* to *The Right Stuff*, from the antics of Ken Kesey to the everyday figures of the "Me Generation," he observed and described and sketched, sometimes in acid, while thrusting himself into the action he described, as he once thrust himself onto Ken Kesey's psychedelic bus.

But I doubt that any convention in the early years of the twenty-first century will be so immortalized. It's not that the personalities are so different from those of other times, but rather that this approach has become so widely accepted and assimilated that it is nowadays practiced on anything and does not seem to require, as it once did, the special event and the extraordinary occasion.

What has been the principal effect of this new style? Sometimes I think it will be felt mainly in the newspaper business as it is practiced on a day-to-day basis: the personal, flip, anecdotal style of, say, an article on prostitution in the community, the eccentric, casual reportage of someone who doesn't take the events he is reporting too seriously—for that matter, the proliferation of human interest stories in newspapers that once were the epitome of stodginess and respectability, even, unbelievably, *The New York Times.* And since the genre is now often practiced with the sort of self-consciousness that heretofore characterized only literature, it just may be that its best days are over anyway. No reason to mourn, then, that upcoming political events will probably not get the Mailer/Wolfe New Journalism treatment.

1990

The Poetry of Everyday Life

A funny kind of everyday poetry is flourishing. People who wouldn't be caught dead reading a poem are putting bumper stickers on their car that say pithy, witty things or make oblique points. T-shirts proclaim weighty slogans or utter cryptic aphorisms; everybody has something to say and is willing to say it in public. Even anonymous graffiti are public statements privately made—in fact, it could be argued that the author's satisfaction in being unknown gives these graffiti a certain daring and recklessness.

A good many messages nowadays contain puns. Someone's bumper sticker that asserts a driver's right to "bear arms" is lampooned by another bumper sticker that asserts the driver's right to "arm bears." Word play flourishes on T-shirts, in newspaper headlines, TV programs, advertising slogans, shop names, products, fashions—you name it. I don't know who said that the pun is the lowest form of humor, but that commonly expressed opinion seems widely ignored these days.

If you scan the daily paper, you may read that "Quake Findings Shake Up Experts," "Tobacco Prices Go Up in Smoke," "The Picture Is Brighter for Cable TV," "Panel Clears Additives But Won't Pass the Salt," "Try To Ban X-Ray Cookie Crumbles," and "Safety Is a Buzz Word for Chain Saws." An article about the anger of the Chinese people is called "Seeing Red," while a feature about a successful publisher of a bioengineering newsletter is titled "Ambitious Young Man in Genes." Even such somber matters as how to protect your house against a fire are not exempt. A recent title reads, "A Hot Topic: Fire-Proofing Your Home."

A handgun control group implores, somewhat counterproductively, "Stop the Piece Movement," and a government pamphlet proclaims that "Salt Shakes Up Some of Us." Products range from "Gunne Sax"

162

dresses to "Clo's Line," the Clover milk products you can see advertised on highway billboards—unless of course, glaucoma has "Robbed You Blind."

I used to drive by a hotel with a sign that urged "Have Your Next Affair Here." This city has a fine coffee and dessert place called "Just Desserts," a nice double pun. The waiting room for expectant fathers at a local hospital is the "Heirport," not to be confused with "Hairport," a barber shop.

Beauty and barber shops are especially inventive in this new genre, featuring such jaunty names as "Shear Madness," "Mane Concern," "Hairloom," "Razor's Edge," "The Clip Joint," "The March Hair," "Cut & Dry," "The Upper Cut," and "The Smart Set." A tape production service is named "Video Free America," an ice-cream store, "The Big Scoop," and a coffee house, "Sacred Grounds." I can have a picture framed at "Frame of Mind," a Xerox copy made at "Copyright," and a chair recaned at "Citizen Cane."

Need I go on?

Perhaps for us these days, puns have replaced the witty repartees and elegant turns of phrase of other ages. Our wit smacks less of the drawing room, is more democratic and everyday. And our growing absorption in television and other spectator pastimes has lessened our opportunity for creating or observing conversational sparkle. But our desire for imaginative verbal play persists, and the pun allows it easy expression.

Just to recognize a pun is gratifying because doing so requires not only a measure of wit but also a certain knowledge. "Razor's Edge" is a clever name for a hairdresser in part because of the recognizable literary and religious allusion. Since puns apply one context to another, they yield some of the pleasures of poetry. In poetry too the familiar is often expressed in startlingly new and unfamiliar terms—or the other way around. For that matter, the poets of many ages relied heavily on lusty and relentless wordplay.

Finally, a pleasant effect of some puns is that they satisfy a small communal impulse. After all, a funny sign on a shop in full public view invites a smile shared by others. The poetry of everyday life may be modest, but it's not without redeeming social significance.

1983

RELATED APHORISMS

Many people resent their well-deserved obscurity.

Violent *and* Peaceful: American Idiosyncrasies

FROM THE TRIVIAL TO THE PROFOUND: AMERICAN HABITS AND STYLES I'LL NEVER GET USED TO

Although I have spent over two-thirds of my life in the United States, I continue to be jarred and surprised by certain things I can't help but notice. I'll choose three at random. From the trivial, to the important, to the crucial, they first struck me, a sixteen-year-old Dutch refugee from Curaçao, when I arrived to attend an American college.

The first is the least significant but still has the power to annoy.

I have no idea to what extent people in other countries have taken on this habit, but many American moviegoers buy huge tubs of popcorn and crunch away for the first half-hour of the show. They start eating a few minutes before the film starts, and they seem to go into a kind of trance, their expression bovine and serene. Obviously no thought is given to the effect of this crunching sound on others, despite the warnings on the screen against talking or otherwise disturbing the other patrons. Like any sanctioned, legitimate noise in public, it is not heard as noise.

To this day, fifty years after my arrival, I find this habit incomprehensible, as strange as if at a dinner party, all the guests removed their shirts before eating.

The second habit is clearly a matter of style and infinitely more important. When you speak to them, Americans tend to look at you attentively, cheerfully, smilingly—but it is not entirely clear that they hear you. Especially when you say something about America, they almost always refer back to some preconceived notion of their own.

In the very Dutch culture I grew up with in Curaçao—all the more Dutch for being a colony, and so maybe twenty years behind the motherland—I remember my Dutch elders listening carefully, impassively nodding, sternly fixing their eyes upon me, and then commenting.

They would often disagree, or take a position ever so slightly different from mine, and that could be irritating; but at the very least I felt I was heard. Frequently in the United States, I have the feeling of getting more beaming goodwill than genuine attention.

Pleasurable as the smiling is, it betokens a good-natured but self-satisfied innocence. Is there a foreign policy implication here? *If I smile, you will be happy. If I bring you democracy, you should be pleased.*

The third matter seems to be more than a habit—a deep, unexamined feature of the culture.

I remember with startling clarity that when I first arrived in the United States, my college classmates, however pleasant or unassuming, appeared to have innumerable wants and needs for things—a new typewriter, different shoes for different occasions, turtleneck sweaters, a whole variety of foods I had never heard of. They were not overeaters, but they loved to talk about lobster, turkey, peach melba, cranberry sauce, or corn-on-the-cob. Sandwiches could be "open-faced," or regular; and they required lettuce, tomato, onion, pickles, mustard, mayonnaise.

True, I had just come from a wartime economy, but it seemed to me that even in the years I dimly remembered from my early childhood in the Netherlands before the war, a cheese sandwich consisted of bread and cheese. Period. Love it or leave it.

Here in the United States I was in the land of limitless desire, not only for food but also for gadgets and furnishings—copyholders for papers you were typing, magnetic clips, fountain pens that didn't leak, implements of all sorts. These were not perceived as wants, but needs—an attitude born less of materialism than a kind of easy assumption of opulence.

My background was austere. You had a pen, and you didn't lose it. If you were lucky enough to have a typewriter and a desk, you certainly didn't need a copyholder so that your precious papers could be upright.

The amazing "thinginess" of American culture has, of course, conquered the rest of the world. Gadgets are universally desired. What would globalization be without a "need" for things?

Nevertheless, deep down, I continue to yearn for fewer choices, fewer options, fewer things.

2005

A Nation in Short Pants

My friend H. has a doctor who wears the sort of top that leaves her midriff bare. She is young, much younger than H., which accounts for this attire, and H. knows this.

But to understand something is not to accept it. (Surely the French are wrong to say, "Tout comprendre, c'est tout pardonner"—to understand all is to forgive all.) H. realizes full well that young people dress differently, have their own styles, just the way we once did when we were young.

She also understands that to some extent the bare midriff irritates her as a further sign of her own aging—the dislocation we all feel as we grow older in an environment we don't quite recognize, a world in which some things have become ever more unfamiliar.

We all realize that gradually the distinction between regular grown-up clothes and play clothes has fallen away. First it was casual Fridays, and now the whole week seems to be casual. Even San Francisco's financial district boasts fewer three-piece suits for men and those smart, fetching but no-nonsense suits for women.

And we have all seen planeloads of airline passengers arriving in their bare legs, some hairy, some not. One of the finest moments on a recent David Letterman show occurred when the host looked at a fifty-year-old man in the audience wearing shorts, a T-shirt, and sneakers—as were almost all the men there—and snapped, "My God, what's the matter with you? You're dressed like a six-year-old!"

But back to the doctor. Is it only the fact that people dress differently nowadays that made H. uncomfortable? Is it only the dislocation of age?

I think not. I think that we will always crave a certain symbolic signaling of hierarchy, a modicum of authority, from those we wish to respect.

A tie, for instance, confers a certain authority. I've certainly known any number of incompetents who wore ties, that's not it; but other things being equal, the man with a tie gets a little more credit.

Ask yourself this: would you want the president of the United States to declare war while he is in T-shirt and jeans? Would you want your brain surgeon to bounce into the operating room in his Bermuda shorts? Is there not something to be gained from keeping a minimal decorum?

We don't like to say nowadays that something is improper. We use the more weasly word "inappropriate" instead. OK, I think it would be inappropriate for the pope to address the believers in St. Peter's Square in his ski clothes, and I don't think Madeleine Albright should ever confer with Yasser Arafat and Ehud Barak while wearing a tennis dress.

Similarly, I think H.'s doctor should cover up her midriff while talking to a patient.

2000

THE INFANTILIZATION OF AMERICA

Of all the holidays, Halloween is probably the greatest one for kids. I remember how, when my kids were little, they anticipated Halloween with the happiest keenness. How wonderful to go around in costume, knocking on people's doors, being given candy.

I liked the holiday too, mainly for their sakes, and enjoyed taking them around or, when they were a bit older, seeing them getting ready and leaving the house as rabbits or pirates or bullfighters. But I, with my Dutch-Jewish-Calvinist-Refugee background, always found something excessive in this holiday (maybe in all American holidays).

Why was there quite so much candy? Couldn't people try giving only one piece to each child instead of bags full? My kids would take along pillow-cases and fill them with chocolates, lollipops, milk duds, M&Ms, sugared apples.

And why did they want to eat it all that same night? My oldest son, now over forty, reminds me that long after he thought I had gone to sleep, I could hear him open candy wrappers and yell, "Haven't you had enough candy? Go to sleep now!"

Still, I could see it was fun for them. But now Halloween is for all of us. The great American slogan—"Everything that's worth doing is worth overdoing"—has once again proved accurate.

Last year at my bank, several tellers were in costume. One young man had a lush little flower garden on his head. Some customers said it was cute. In my mind I could hear one of my old Dutch schoolteachers snorting, "How can I trust my money to them? Even an old sock would be safer than that bank."

My part of San Francisco is by no means the hippest part of town, but behind the counter in the drug store, several larger-than-life bunnies padded around. I think I bought my toothpaste from a

171

large mouse in an otherwise respectable store on Taraval Street. Several mothers were accompanying their adorably outfitted children, but the mothers too were in costume.

On West Portal Avenue, an old man in a cowboy hat said "Trick or Treat" to no one in particular. Maybe for him it was a day like all others.

This may all be part of a larger trend toward infantilization. More and more cute little toys or stuffed animals are turning up in unlikely places.

At the oral surgeon I went to last year, after a gruesome procedure, I got a steep bill and a little stuffed lion. I did not have a child with me. And, yes, I was already, visibly, over sixty. I held the lion to my aching mouth all the way home.

I am not as much of a curmudgeon or killjoy as I sound. If fully grown people want to dress up for Halloween, why not?

Maybe we are working up toward a kind of Rio de Janeiro Carnival, where people are in disguise or half undressed for several days running.

But I have one major quibble: if this holiday is becoming one for adults as well as children, aren't we somehow making it less important for the kids? Won't children feel a little less special, and a little less like children, if the adults try to be as childlike as they are?

Shouldn't we be careful that we don't steal childhood from the children?

1999

Guantánamo: As American as Apple Pie, or as *Dr. Strangelove*

In a wonderful scene in Stanley Kubrick's film *Dr. Strangelove*, a bunch of good-natured, sloppily dressed, beer-drinking, *Playboy*-reading pilots are seen flying superbly made, sleek B-52 bombers loaded with deadly missiles targeting the Soviet Union.

That film came out forty years ago, but it has an odd bearing on our treatment of "unlawful combatants" in Guantánamo. Detailed accounts about that treatment have appeared in *Time*, *Newsweek*, the *New York Times*, and the *New Yorker*.

A classic American dichotomy seems to rule in Guantánamo: on the one hand, a kind of wacky improvisation; on the other, a well-oiled, highly regulated system. Odd human beings, slick technology.

Reading these various accounts, I get the impression that the interrogators are inept rather than deliberately cruel; it's *Animal House* landscaped with earnest procedures, efficient strategies, and terse advisories. Quirky, wild people making use of science, or at least the pseudo-science of pompous, verbose psychological operations.

You torment the victim—but don't cause "organ failure" or "impairment of bodily function." Then, a little scared, you rush him off to a doctor and give him the best medical care. After which, of course, a Cheney-like figure can say, "They get the finest medical care in the world. Much better than they had in Afghanistan."

And didn't a high government official claim that the prisoners eat very well, and that, after all, they're living in the tropics? I'm now waiting for him to say that they're really happy and having fun in the sun.

What apparently goes on in these interrogations bears a resemblance to fraternity initiations. It's hazing, and it's not meant to be all that awful. Sure, someone dies once in a while, but that was not the intention!

So here's what I imagine preceded the reported treatment of prisoners at "Gitmo" described recently by the media. It's hard to say which actions were inspired by the Army's "behavioral science consulting teams" and which by the interrogators themselves:

"Hey, let's try putting a bra on that guy."

"You're nuts, man. But go ahead."

"How about dogs? Arabs hate dogs."

"Dumb-ass. Not all these guys are Arabs."

"Oh, hell, what's the difference?"

"Let's make him bark like a dog."

"Let's have him dance with another prisoner."

"No, we'll ask Tracy to bring in a thong. I'll bet these guys have never seen one. Then we'll put it on someone's head."

Meanwhile, I picture solemn psychologists walking around with long faces and big clipboards. They take many notes and give sage counsel. This whole prisoner-and-war business is a major career opportunity. At the very least, having "served" in Guantánamo will look great on their résumé. They advise the interrogators but speak in generalities. My guess is that the interrogators are left free to fill in the blanks.

Perhaps, unlike the psychologists, the medical doctors who aid and abet these high jinks are first-rate and beautifully equipped. They ply their trade humanely, but when the injuries are mended, their patients pass back into the hands of the boys who are frisky and unpredictable.

"More beer, dude . . . Another interrogation coming."

* * *

We now know, a few years later, that these "techniques" were thought so successful that they were subsequently exported to Abu Ghraib. Once exposed, some of the goofballs went to jail, but the serious men with the clipboards, we have every reason to believe, are still thriving.

2005

NOTHING WILL BE DONE

By this time, the tragic school shootings at Columbine High School in Littleton, Colorado, have begun to fade. Only the families and friends are still aching with grief, and certainly the former will never find relief from it.

The debates continue, though. Gun control versus the right to bear arms. TV violence as cause or effect of the Violent Society. The Internet as neutral resource or seductive evil.

As I write this on the day after the shooting, we are in the memorial phase. Beautiful shrines of cards, messages, flowers, teddy bears and banners are springing up around Columbine High School. Students there and elsewhere are wearing buttons to express support for their fallen comrades. Surely the memorial is the art form of our time; unfortunately, we have frequent need for it.

On TV, I see students hugging each other in that slightly stylized way that is a feature of these memorials. There is much more hugging in our time than ever before, and yet there is also more violence. Something here goes against conventional wisdom, or at the very least against all New Age teaching.

Already on Day Two, various clerical people and grief counselors are beginning to say that "the healing must begin." Does anyone else in the country think the sheer rapidity with which this platitude is used is obscene? And does anyone else feel that these grief counselors are odious folk, mouthing their pieties, oozing their way across the battlefield, reiterating endlessly that "it's OK" to feel what you're feeling?

They are everywhere, like lawyers in the wake of a potentially lucrative accident, and ultimately represent nothing more than our inability to do something genuinely helpful for the victims and their survivors. The victims are dead, senselessly so, or seriously wounded. Their families will never recover; their friends are unlikely to be sustained by this rather lugubrious crowd clinging to them and urging them to "talk it out."

Grief counseling in our society takes the place of doing what is necessary to prevent such tragedies. Much easier to deploy a brigade of therapists than to do something real about the ready availability of guns and weaponry to angry, disaffected kids. That takes true awareness and true effort. That takes doing what, by and large, the society opposes.

Yes, the debates will rage, and there may even be some gun control legislation, but it will be so watered down in the end that it won't matter. We need more than gun control anyway. We need disarmament. And that, as everyone knows, won't happen. Nothing will be done.

And then there is TV violence, the thousands of murders the kids watch every year; its impact is obviously pernicious, but both the entertainment industry and the majority of Americans (who like violent shows) will oppose doing anything about that. So nothing will be done.

As for the equally violent "interactive" computer games, with their kinesthetically exciting but emotionally deadening effect, no one will stop making those. The profit is too great. So nothing will be done.

And the Internet where you can get tutored in making pipe bombs, well, it might be possible to censor some nude female flesh, but instruments of mass destruction, no, we can't infringe on your right to put those out there. We love weapons of mass destruction, except when Saddam Hussein has them.

So, in other words, nothing will be done.

But, as I said, the talk will go on for a while. It—along with grief counseling—makes us feel that something is being done. Actually, it covers up nicely that nothing will be done.

1999

Those 'Superficial' Americans

When Europeans discuss Americans, they sooner or later talk about how "superficial" they are.

"Sure, they smile a lot," says a Dutch friend, "but aren't you tired of living in a country where people are superficial?" She had lived in America for a while, so she could state firmly, "Friendships with Americans just don't have any depth."

I'm in a pretty good position to judge. Until I was almost seventeen, I lived in a thoroughly Dutch environment. But my whole adult life has been spent in America.

Here's how I see it: Americans are neither more nor less superficial than any other people, but Americans do affect a certain style which makes it easy for others to see them that way.

An American will smile warmly and bubble at people—say, the visiting Europeans—and warble out, "This is so great. It was wonderful meeting you. We should get together soon."

The visitor thinks this invitation is literally meant. When nothing comes of it, she or he concludes that the American did not mean it, or forgot it, or just simply was being, well, superficial.

Actually, it meant none of these. The American was saying, in a particularly gushy way, "I like you. It was nice to sit and talk to you here. Maybe we'll meet again some time."

In other words, it was a warm feeling, which the American expressed in a remark to be taken generally, not specifically.

The European thinks, *If he invites me, why doesn't he go through with it?*

Each mistakes the other's style.

I know this style and, having lived here so long, understand it. But I still don't like it very much. I have occasionally said to good American friends, "Don't gush so. If you think everything is 'wonderful,' then nothing really is. You lessen your credibility by being so excessive."

Usually they look at me as if I just don't understand. What's wrong with being friendly?

I suppose what it comes down to is that Americans like to have things go well; they smile and want to make nice.

They do not expect to be taken literally; what they say is just verbal mood music designed to brighten and heighten things. Nothing more, nothing less. This is why living in America tends to be easy. Americans enjoy making things possible; they do not want to stand in your way. They want you to feel good.

Small talk flourishes because everyone is intent on making things flow smoothly. No one is going to listen too closely to the talk, the banter, the free and easy exchange of pleasantries.

Not so in Holland. You speak and someone is very likely to say, "How do you mean that?" Or "Well, no, I don't quite see it that way."

Good for debate, but not a great social quickener.

So as usual, there are at least two sides to the matter of American superficiality.

Meanwhile, I confess that one of the few conversation habits I never got used to here in the U.S. is the furrowed brow, the attentive smile, the warm little nods—and the person not hearing a word I'm saying. I think I prefer the stern, unsmiling Dutchman who, with arms folded, hears everything I say and takes issue with each and every word of it.

1998

GENERALIZATIONS ABOUT THEM AND US

In the early years of the twentieth century, people might sit in a Parisian sidewalk cafe and happily try to guess from which country the strolling passersby came. Those were the days when it was fine to talk about "national character" and to stereotype people according to the way in which their culture was perceived.

Now, of course, this is not a way we talk about other cultures. It's politically incorrect to do so, and we don't believe in such large scale characterizations of whole nations and groups.

Or do we? After all, we use the terms "cultural traits" quite as openly as people once did "national character," and we have no hesitation in discussing "cultural patterns," or saying, "That's the way they do it in their culture." So maybe the following remarks about Them and Us are less reckless and retrograde that they appear.

1) The Arab Middle Eastern world loves intrigue, often for its own sake: the goal seems secondary. The various parties in this intrigue shift all the time, because finally it doesn't matter who your allies are, as long as you can keep "intriguing." All that slyness and plotting leads . . . where exactly?

Syria, we are told, is working together with Iran in order to bolster the Iraqi insurgency. Sunni Iraqis collaborate with the Syrians in order to undermine the Shiites. But the Shiites in Iraq work with the Shiites in Iran against the Americans—and the Sunnis. Have we come full circle yet?

One reason conspiracy theories are so popular in the Arab world is that there are so many conspiracies. And one reason why these conspiracy theories often seem to change is that the conspiracies themselves may well shift often in the shifting sands of the Middle East.

2) The U.S. proclivity, on the other hand, is a lust for planning multiple contingencies and producing exciting scenarios. We are never so happy as when we can turn the world into high-tech video games: "They do this, and we do that. . . . Look at the screen. . . . Zap!" Handshakes all around the "Situation Room" or, gasp, the "War Room." Understated, manly compliments. "Nice work, General!" Or sometimes even, "Heck of a job!"

The ultimate aim is security or victory, sure, but the pleasure is in the many forms of 'gaming' and warfare. We live in a culture of preadolescent boys lasting into manhood and even dotage.

Long before 9/11, we were obsessed with thrillers, spy movies, gadgets, espionage, and game playing. That horrible day—often compared to a ghastly film—merely crystallized what had already obtained, the proliferation of images we watch and attempt to defend against and manipulate.

The Cold War before then had supplied an abundance of pictures. Not that there weren't plenty of real enemies—of course there were. But we loved the struggle, we enjoyed the plans and counterplans. Careers were made, money flowed, but best of all was the gaming, the multiple reports, always filed, almost always forgotten. Rather than read an old report, start the fun all over again and write a new one.

Meanwhile, you could be important enough to turn your life into a kind of movie. And you could create names and acronyms, and these would be respectfully repeated. Remember "Mutually Assured Destruction," "MAD"?

The lines between warfare and its media portrayals blurred. You could be a warrior by going into a room and fiddling with buttons and looking at a screen. Afterwards, your colleagues might literally applaud your playing. What could be better?

These two cultural styles do not, of course, sum up their respective cultures. But they do reveal something our leaders do not often see, and they lay bare a significant side of the present-day clash between the two.

2005

"Why Do They Hate Us?": A Personal View

When I first came to this country 50 years ago, the contrast between the niceness of Americans and a certain public boastfulness was the first thing I noticed. I was almost 17, a freshman at Brandeis University, from Curaçao in the Netherlands West Indies.

The university president addressed the student body by saying, "Here at Brandeis, we believe in excellence. Nothing less than that. And excellent is what we are."

I was astonished. The Dutch culture in which I had been raised did not permit you to say that your school (or you, or your country) was the best. You were not supposed to praise yourself. Which did not mean, of course, that Dutch officialdom did not praise itself or its country. But it was limited praise for specific accomplishments or distinctive cultural traits. "The Dutch are the best bridge builders in the world," proclaimed my high school teacher.

You never heard that Holland was the greatest country on the planet, or that the Dutch way of life was superior to all others.

I happen to think that the United States *is* the greatest country in the world, and I might even say so to people; but I think I shouldn't say it often, and certainly not to foreigners.

One of the things we have slipped into as a culture is a kind of unwitting boastfulness that actually doesn't go with the generally restrained demeanor of many Americans. In this society, we're almost required to sing our own praises and call attention to ourselves. If we don't, we get overlooked.

For some reason, what in private life is done discreetly, or even indiscreetly, is in public always trumpeted loudly. Any candidate for office will have to declare sooner or later that America is the greatest, our democracy the finest, our way of life the best, and our freedom the envy of all people everywhere.

Politicians frequently say this to one and all, and when they do, it often comes out sounding like this: "America is great because of the greatness of the American people. And because the people are great they have created this great system of freedom and justice. That's what it's all about."

It is the sort of garbled bragging that foreigners dislike about us, and for good reason. Then when they actually meet Americans, they're pleasantly surprised by how relatively modest and unassuming we turn out to be in person.

Most cultures boast, of course, and it makes them look arrogant from time to time. But we in the United States have raised the volume, and we perennially boast with a sort of vast inclusiveness, praising ourselves not for this or that accomplishment but for what we have and what we are. Because we seem unaware of doing so, we also create the impression of ignorance, a sort of blindness, a self-deluded innocence. When this innocence is linked to great power, it is seen as all the more obnoxious.

2002

VIOLENT AND PEACEFUL

As I walked down West Portal Avenue with my European guests, they remarked once again how polite American drivers are and how well-disciplined our traffic is. On the busy shopping street, drivers stopped courteously at every stop sign, waiting for even the slowest pedestrians to cross. If a car stopped at the curb to let someone out, there was not the slightest sign of impatience from the car in back.

My guests, a Dutchman and his Dutch-Australian wife, have experienced traffic in many countries. But we do not need the word of outsiders to know that, compared to any country, our driving habits are civilized and peaceful.

Yet the evening before we had been talking about how violent America is. Again, most Americans would agree.

How is it we can be both?

While our atrocious murder and violence rate is more important than our courteous driving, both are culturally significant. One way of putting it is that this violent culture of ours has its relatively non-violent side. Another way is that there are always many cultures in one culture.

Recently I saw a TV program which showed some inner-city kids spending a summer on a kibbutz in Israel.

When they were still trying to get adjusted to life on the communal farm, one of them complained about people in the community dining room who bumped into you and didn't even say "Excuse me." That kid must have seen a lot of impolite behavior growing up in Bedford-Stuyvesant. But the point is that he was not used to that particular kind of kibbutz brusqueness, and he was understandably annoyed.

Same thing with our violence and gentle-driving culture. Our murder rates tower over those of almost all other countries, but our accident statistics are, by contrast, moderate, the envy of many other countries.

Are these two cultures fixed? Is there nothing we can do to nudge the violence downward, in the direction of the driving?

Of course, something can be done. Cultures are not immutable; they change all the time, slowly, gradually, the way fashions do.

Decreasing the violence on TV—which, when proposed, immediately makes some people say that we need to deal with the "root causes" of violence and not the images of violence—is a beginning.

The images are part of the culture of violence. They may not cause it, but they are the air that violent people breathe.

It's in the nature of a culture that it teaches by example, not by exhortation.

Kids learn to drive courteously—yes, compared to other countries they do—by seeing thousands of people around them drive courteously, people they like and people they dislike, people they imitate and people they don't.

The less they see people reaching for a gun—whether on TV or on the streets—the less likely it is that *they* will.

If we can have a culture of driving courtesy, we can also have a culture of lessened violence. The two live side by side, but the peaceful existence of one gives hope for modifying the violence of the other.

1999

Related Aphorisms

The merging of "I feel" and "I think" in American speech has undermined the value of each.

Places on the Map and in the Mind: A Personal Geography

HERE AND ELSEWHERE

Social Codes: Helsinki and San Francisco

I have been thinking a lot about social codes lately—Finnish social codes, American social codes. When people ask me, as they usually do, how I like Finland, they seem almost surprised that I like it as much as I do. But I don't usually tell them about my bad days, when I feel misunderstood in small ways—or seem myself to misunderstand what is around me.

I say small ways, because for me, life in Helsinki does not differ all that much from life in my own home city, San Francisco. Yes, of course the weather is altogether different, and California is full of people who say, "Have a nice day." But those differences are obvious, and anyone who comes to Finland knows them in advance. Besides, you'd be surprised at the number of people in Helsinki who say to a foreigner, in English, "Have a nice day."

Finns often ask me anxiously if I don't find Finnish people rude. I do not. I have seldom met so many friendly, kind people anywhere, from my colleagues at the university to the person on the street whom I ask where I can get the bus.

But despite that kindness, there is a problem. The person giving me directions is helpful but oddly restrained. With a tense smile, a pained look, he will tell me the bare minimum, and he will point to the place with a vague, ineffectual gesture. After I thank him, he can't leave quickly enough and seems to melt into the snow. (I say he and him, because Finnish women appear more expressive in their direction-giving, though if they can't speak English they will often say, "No, no," as if warding off an improper suggestion, and flee.)

This is certainly not rudeness but an unwillingness to thrust oneself forward even for a moment. And there, I think, lies a huge difference between Finland and California, where such directions are often given as if the person relished the occasion and enjoyed the moment on center stage, a brief but instant stardom. Almost too much information is given out, certainly not too little.

This Finnish "shyness," and I'm sure that's what it is, often strikes me as a kind of withholding, a joy almost in giving out as little as possible. And it accounts for the occasional disorientation a foreigner may feel in this otherwise so pleasant and well-run society.

This shyness has many manifestations. An American friend of mine was sitting in his office at a university in central Finland when an assistant knocked on his door and asked, "Would you like some white wine?" He answered, "No, thank you, I have to teach a class in ten minutes."

Later on when he found out that it had been her birthday, he felt really embarrassed. Had he known, he certainly would've joined her for a drink to mark the occasion.

I told a Finnish friend this story and he said, "Well, why would they be drinking wine if they weren't celebrating something? He should have known."

Yes, maybe; but I maintain that the different code is the culprit, not the Finns or the Americans. In America, the assistant would have come in, all bright and chirpy and said "Hey, it's my birthday today— want some white wine?"

Obviously neither way is right or wrong. And it certainly is a small matter. But life is considerably easier if you know the code and share it.

Take the business of asking questions. When I meet people socially, I am often disappointed by how few questions they ask once we get beyond how I like Finland or why I'm here. I realize that the American style of question-asking can be perfunctory. In Finland, though, it seems as if often there is very little interest.

But I am beginning to see that this is not so. The same thing that keeps people from thrusting themselves forward keeps them from wanting to "intrude." To show curiosity is to be aggressive, while in America *not* to show it is to be lacking in social graces. The result is that American people often seem interested when they are not. They ask questions, but do they really want to hear the answers?

If Finnish reserve results from politeness, so does its opposite in America, an instant intimacy—which then, as so many have pointed out, doesn't go very far or very deep. No doubt there is more to Finnish restraint than mere politeness, and the restraint is sometimes problematic even to Finns themselves, but at least I know that it's not lack of interest.

Which helps a little in the matter of social codes, though these remain such an unquestioned part of oneself that any unexpected difference can be unsettling.

1990

LOOKING AT FINLAND

Now that I've been away from Finland for a while, I once again have occasion to think about Finnish and American ways. Actually, despite being half a world apart, San Francisco and Helsinki probably have more in common than not; but I'm more intrigued by the dissimilarities than the similarities, the small social differences.

Americans constantly ask foreigners, "How do you like it here?" They're even asking me now that I'm back how I like the United States. Finns also put that question to foreigners, but just as often, if not more often, they ask, "*Why* are you here?"—as if there must be some specific reason why any foreigner would want to come to such a remote place. Of course, there often is; but actually, in my almost two years in Finland, I met any number of Americans who settled in Finland just for the love of the country.

Very often, when Finnish people go beyond that question, they're quite eager to talk about the things one does or does not like in Finland. But when I say what these are, they're frequently astonished; they would prefer it if I confirmed the list they have in their own minds. If they dislike their own countrymen's supposed inexpressiveness, they are quite eager to hear me say so too; but should I come up with something that they themselves don't mind, they often fall silent. When I mention that Finns often put up with small, unnecessary inconveniences, like many apartments without outside bell-buzzers, they often look at me blankly, uncomprehendingly. What difference does it make, they seem to ask, if your apartment does not have a buzzer? You can always meet your guest in front of the apartment house or in the downstairs hallway.

When I mentioned this to a Finnish friend who spent years in the United States, he said, "Look at the inconveniences you put up with in San Francisco; it takes twenty minutes for a taxi to come to the house." He's right; but we don't take it for granted. We complain about the

194

taxis, or the unions that won't allow for more taxis, or the foreigners who drive these taxis and don't know their way around.

Ultimately, of course, one complains about what one is not used to. For example, I find explanations or instructions hard to come by in Finland. All the way from traffic directions to how to file a form, there is often a vagueness. The thing that strikes me in the United States is how astonishingly procedure-oriented we are. You go to the Department of Motor Vehicles and fill out a variety of forms for, let us say, your driver's license renewal. Each step of the way is explained, either by simple clear directions on the wall, or a form you pick up as you come in, or both.

As you go through each line, all sorts of small things are done to guarantee the streamlining of the procedure. The clerk directs you to take a thumbprint, and he also provides you with tissues to wipe your hand off, while strategically underneath you stands a trash can where the tissue is supposed to be dropped. In a mass society, people need to be handled, to be moved. In Finland, it is often the individual helpfulness of bureaucrats that got me through, not the logic of the procedure.

Terms like rudeness and politeness, or inexpressiveness and expressiveness, are often too blurry to suit individual occasions. For example, when you give a speech in America, people come up afterwards to chat. This has never happened to me in Finland. It's not a lack of appreciation but Finns not wanting to intrude, a constraint Americans are not burdened by. Finnish people think you want to be left alone.

But I see a another reason: Americans come up for a moment to become as conspicuous as they feel they have a right to be. Something in Americans makes them feel that they should be up there giving the speech; that's probably why so many Americans ask questions following a talk. My impression of Finns is that they love anonymity as much as Americans love publicity.

1991

AMERICAN AND FINNISH BODY LANGUAGE

Every two years, the University of Helsinki hosts the North American Studies Conference, which rotates yearly between Helsinki and Tampere. In the halls of the building where I have my office, there were suddenly a great number of distinguished-looking men and women with name tags. Some of them would stand around the lobby, waiting for the next session to begin; others would have coffee in the student cafeteria or the faculty dining room.

In America, academics are known as a quiet and staid lot. They have the reputation of being sober and dour. Exceptions are, of course, ever with us, but on the whole the stereotype is oddly true.

But in the halls of Helsinki University these American academics always stood out. Waving to friends across the room, half-shouting to people at another table, smiling broadly to acknowledge a joke or a witticism, they seemed more animated than any group I had recently seen in Finland.

The point is obvious: Americans (and Canadians) have more body language, at least of the overt kind, than Finns. But what is less obvious, I think, is that body language is "advancing," is becoming ever more prominent in the American part of the world, mainly thanks to television.

People on TV or radio are always told to punch out their speech, to stress every third or fourth word, lest they come across as flat and dull. The rest of us, though not media figures, have been affected by this. What's more, our children were raised on television cartoons, and there the animation of the figures, the exaggerated voices and the violent gyrations, are necessitated by the genre. The cartoons imitate the kids, and the kids imitate the cartoons—the end result is more frantic movement.

And there are other factors. Cultures different from the Anglo-Saxon have always influenced America, but they are nowadays perceived as mainstream. Italians and Greeks, Latin Americans and Blacks—they have both greater visibility and sharper prominence in the United States than they did before, and their body language, from the expressive Mediterranean shrug to the whole-body gesticulation of many Blacks, is being freely assimilated.

Whatever the reason, body language is gaining. Among the young, it used to be an occasional accompaniment of speech, while now it's an indispensable adjunct. Two or three American twenty-year-olds, talking about last night's events, will *reenact* the story: "And then she was, like, 'Wow, I can't believe this.'" The speaker acts out how the other person responded: his eyes are rolling, his face is mugging and clowning. The indirect mode of relating something seems to have vanished among young Americans: perhaps because of television, conversations now *perform* what has happened or is happening; they show rather than tell.

As I looked at my Finnish students, I was beginning to see an occasional American mannerism making its appearance. These are the livelier students, or the ones who have spent a year in America. I was and am ambivalent about it: on the one hand, I applaud the greater animation, but on the other, I want to say: "Stop here, don't go too far. You may end up looking like a cartoon."
1991

Drugs, Laws and The Netherlands' Culture of Talk

Just before my last trip to Amsterdam for a two-month residency at the Dutch government's Translators' House, the big revelation in the local newspapers had been that some well-known drug dealers deducted their pit-bull terriers and guns as legitimate business expenses and that the tax authorities allowed the deduction. Though both pit bulls and firearms are illegal in the Netherlands, the tax people agreed that a business expense was a business expense.

But are drugs legal? Well, that's more difficult to determine. The rule of thumb seems to be that trafficking of drugs is not legal, while possession of small quantities of soft drugs for personal use *is*—and though this distinction seems clear enough, the fact is that some commerce is quietly allowed, "gedogen," as the Dutch say, i.e., tolerated, though not happily so.

It has not worked all that well, but, on the other hand, the U.S.'s War on Drugs hasn't either. Partly, Holland fell victim to its own enlightenment: when it became known as being soft on drugs, with Hash Cafes sporting marijuana leaves in their windows, as they often do, drugs (and users) from the rest of the world flowed in. But that, too, is not the whole story, which is rather inconclusive. Drug use hasn't risen alarmingly, but collateral crime has, and nowadays there are rumors of a substantial mafia not only in the drug business but in prostitution, weapons, and stolen goods. The police do what they can but are not set up for massive warfare against a sophisticated enemy; the court system is lenient, and public opinion, especially influential press opinion—far more liberal than its American counterpart—remains skeptical of police and politicians.

While Holland was never the utopia depicted in Jonathan Blank's documentary of a few years ago, *Sex, Drugs and Democracy*—which made it seem as if victimless crimes never had any consequences—there is a progressive current in the Netherlands that can make an outsider envious. Holland's legalized and well-regulated abortion and prostitution, as well as euthanasia for those who are terminally, painfully ill, are legendary and respected worldwide.

How did it happen? What makes it possible? "I think the difference with the U.S. is that ours is a talking culture; everything can be discussed, considered, weighed, and usually is," says Joost de Wit, for decades the director of an institute that promoted Dutch culture abroad. "No one is ridiculed for suggesting a new approach, even if it is not enacted. Dutch officials are praised for raising questions, not dismissed as troublemakers."

True, sometimes you feel as if the whole country is a kind of university; "debates" abound, meetings are everywhere. As in the academy, this sometimes leads to muddled thinking and uncertain policies, but it beats the alternative: thoughtlessness or ranting. Of course, it occasionally also leads to some unintentional humor: for a while, two Dutch trade unions of prostitutes battled each other for the right to represent Dutch sex-workers. But I think they talked out their differences.

1991

THE END OF NOSTALGIA

Throughout their long and painful history in America, many blacks have longed for Africa as the place where everyone is like them, where they would finally be at home again. While the stories that tourists and journalists have brought back are not always encouraging, none is as bitterly disappointed as Keith Richburg's *Out of America*.

Richburg was African bureau chief for the *Washington Post* and was headquartered in Nairobi, Kenya, from 1991 to 1994. What he saw during that period—in Kenya, in Rwanda, in Liberia, in Somalia, in Nigeria, in Zimbabwe—made him not only realize his essential Americanness but also feel glad of it. The idealization of Africa he too had felt during his student years in the late seventies changed abruptly with his actual experience of the African scene. Among the most moving passages in this book are those that express Richburg's despair at thinking that he could have been one of the mistreated wretches he sees everywhere in Africa, had it not been for the accident of his ancestors being forcibly shipped to the New World. The horror of this thought, the anguish of that ambivalence, vibrate throughout this book, for how can any black person ever appear to rejoice in the enslavement of his or her ancestors? And how can any African American who has suffered from the sense of alienation that Richburg and other American blacks feel still be happy that he is not one of those living in the motherland?

No one could, if the African situation were not so ghastly. But it is. With the exception of South Africa—and here Richburg holds his breath, for he realizes how much depended on one great man—the cruelties of tribalism, the corruption of the leadership, the contempt for human rights of Africa's rulers, hold sway. Why the situation is as bad as it is, a few decades after the demise of colonialism, Richburg cannot explain. He will not for a moment, however, accept the usual explanations, whether offered by black Africans or white liberals, that Africa's plight is the legacy of colonialism and the post-colonial pressures of the Cold War. It is a question that haunts the book, and only once does Richburg come close to answering it. He recalls asking Yoweri Museveni, the president of Uganda, why post-colonial East Asia has developed so vigorously and Africa has not. After some hemming and hawing, Museveni answers, "Discipline," and contrasts Uganda's Asians with its Africans. It is an answer that Richburg clearly endorses, but one would have liked an explanation for it. What is it in the variety of African cultures that militates against the sort of "discipline" required for success as the modern world defines it? After all, Africans have again and again shown their capacity for hard work: why then is "discipline" lacking?

Not only does *Out of America* assail the weakness of the rationalizations for Africa's underdevelopment, it is equally forceful in attacking them when they are made about the American ghetto. This is a brave and painful stand for a black man to take, but what is lacking, once again, is some explanation of why both cultures should suffer from the same weaknesses. Interestingly, Robert Kaplan, in his influential February 1994 *Atlantic Monthly* article "The Coming Anarchy," had made this equation of American ghetto and African shantytown, but backed away from it in his book *The Ends of the Earth*, published two years later. Few dare to embark on the kind of cultural generalization that seems required, though notable exceptions like Lawrence E. Harrison (*Underdevelopment is a State of Mind*) do occur.

My own hunch is that the problem lies not in the weakness of one culture but in the weakness engendered by the collision of one culture with another: in the United States it is black culture against the overarching white; in Africa it may well be native culture in conflict with the overarching demands of an alien, Westernized global community.

Richburg is justifiably incensed when he observes noted American leaders praising African dictators—Jesse Jackson's lavish praise for Ibrahim Babangida of Nigeria; the fawning applause for Sierra Leone's dictator Valentine Strasser at a summit of African and African American leaders in Gabon; former Virginia Governor Wilder's soft-pedaling on African violation of human rights. It is a kind of double standard and an indulgence in nostalgia that angers Richburg.

Richburg tends to underestimate the cultural squeeze in which the black world finds itself—that is one perspective *Out of America* doesn't give. Another is that while he rightly condemns the excuses Africans have made for the gradual destruction of their continent, he does not sufficiently consider the horrors certain forms of colonialism have wrought and what traces of it may linger in the collective memory of Africans. In some places, the Belgian Congo for example, colonialism was slavery by another name. If anything, Joseph Conrad's classic novella *Heart of Darkness* (1902) goes easy on the cruelties perpetrated there.

On the whole, though, *Out of America* is an important exercise in truth-telling. The book is important not only for its portrait of a continent but also for its author's self-scrutiny. Having witnessed bodies floating in a river, the mutilations inflicted on the weak, the swagger of children brandishing automatic weapons, the posturing of the "Big Man," whatever his name may happen to be—and despite his own physical resemblance to both victims and perpetrators—Richburg can only lament: "In America, I may feel like an alien, but in Africa, I *am* an alien."

Out of America: A Black Man Confronts Africa
by Keith Richburg
Harvest/HBJ Book, 266 pages

1998

PLANNERS AND SEARCHERS

William Easterly's provocative book, *The White Man's Burden: Why the West's Efforts to Aid the Rest Have Done So Much Ill and So Little Good*, puts the failure of foreign aid down to a gigantic act of non-listening, of imposing grand schemes on hapless, desperate countries. Easterly, a professor of economics at New York University, was for sixteen years a senior research economist at the World Bank. In his latest book, he sets himself against his former employers, as well as the International Monetary Fund, and by extension against such utopians as the economist Jeffrey Sachs, for being Planners, who impose grandly conceived solutions, which the recipients can't or won't implement and for which the donors are not held accountable. (That the most grandiose form of Planning, large-scale military intervention, is equally futile should not surprise anyone.)

When there are successes, these usually result from limited undertakings. Aid organizations can score with such projects as Food for Education in Bangladesh, a stipend for parents who send their children to school, or the Rural Roads Program in Peru; but these do not flow from grandiose schemes. More commonly, successes in the massive foreign aid programs of the last fifty years derive from Searchers, people who devise small programs with limited goals—vaccination schemes or sanitation improvements—which often originate locally with people searching for remedies. Since the world's poorest have the least clout, the need for Searchers is all the greater.

To illustrate one such Searcher, Easterly tells the story first told by John Stackhouse, in his book *Out of Poverty and Into Something More Comfortable*, of a Ugandan chemist, George Mpango, who, to combat undernourishment, developed a high-protein biscuit—no thanks to the aid community, which sent instruments to the chemist's lab he didn't ask for and didn't want, "since donors give us what they have, not what we need." Worse still is that aid organizations often reject local initiatives, such as helping to fund a university in Ghana founded by an American-educated entrepreneur. It's almost as if the aid agencies feel they know best, condescension apparently still clinging to these efforts as tenaciously as it did when Kipling coined the phrase that gives this book its title.

The snapshot of the Ugandan chemist is one of many scattered throughout the book, sketches of successes and heartbreaks. Easterly is keenly aware of the tragedy of world poverty and clearly upset by the inability of so many to engage it. Most of the countries that have received massive amounts of foreign aid are now poorer than ever, though of course AIDS and wars and bad governments have contributed to making that so.

The White Man's Burden is almost a reference work of solutions and dilemmas, histories and prospects. Easterly touches on many subjects, ranging from the complexities of aid bureaucracies to the political contradictions of recent Western policies to the relative success of Asian economies in the last few decades. His book is filled with charts and graphs but still written in the same engaging, detail-rich style that characterized his earlier *The Elusive Quest for Growth*. Among his many details is the news that sometimes corporations do better than NGOs or Western government agencies. Thus the Shell Foundation has fought the catastrophe of African indoor smoke by thinking "like Searchers" and helping to set up small enterprises to produce affordable smoke-reducing stoves that will actually be used by people who need them. This from a charitable foundation created by Shell Oil.

Not that oil ever appears to be a blessing for an otherwise poor country. Easterly explains that oil revenues ensure that the well-connected, privileged fight harder against redistribution than they otherwise would. I should think there are other reasons as well for the curse of oil, for instance, that in oil-rich countries the incentives for economic diversification lessen, and that poor people inevitably suffer from the presence of vast amounts of money, which their lack of skills keep them from sharing. But it's fascinating to hear Easterly make the point that oil revenues and large amounts of foreign aid work about the same way and bring neither democratization nor prosperity. Equally fascinating—and downright counterintuitive—is his contention that poor, developing countries have a better chance at democracy and development than those burdened with great natural resources. This too points up the need for limited, manageable help.

Limited solutions for specific problems are, of course, good and sensible, but Easterly doesn't fully address why, in Africa at least, even those frequently fail: a cultural clash, as I see it, between donors and recipients, with the latter's loyalty often to tribe over community, to family over country. Nationhood seems irrelevant. Postcolonial Africa's nations were artificially created and are now forced to live in—and compete with—a world of nation states. They have been dragged into globalized economies where they perform poorly, while some of their people are mesmerized by images of life in Europe and America. No wonder many of them try to rush the shores of Europe rather than build up their impoverished homelands, a movement of people that Easterly's otherwise excellent book does not take fully into account in its description of what has gone wrong with aid in particular and with the relations in general between the West and the Rest.

The White Man's Burden: Why the West's Efforts to Aid the Rest Have Done So Much Ill and So Little Good
by William Easterly
The Penguin Press, 417 pages

2006

"Turning It Over to the UN"

The United Nations has to do so many things that it can't possibly do all of them well. But we need to take a closer look at what we mean when we say, perhaps too glibly, "Turn it over to the United Nations."

I recently read Linda Polman's book *We Did Nothing*, with its provocative subtitle, *Why the Truth Doesn't Always Come Out When the UN Goes In*.

A few months ago, I spoke to the author in Amsterdam. She is a tall, attractive, animated woman, who has been traveling for thirty years and writing for fifteen. Her first book was a hilarious, heartbreaking account of a two-week boat trip on the Congo River from Kinshasa to Kisangani in Zaire.

I asked her about her greatest complaint regarding various UN "blue helmet" (noncombatant) peacekeeping missions. She admitted that some UN missions have been reasonably successful, but she felt the organization wasn't strong enough to enforce peace. "Blue helmet operations have succeeded in Haiti in 1994 and more recently in Sierra Leone, but unarmed peacekeepers can't do anything against armed violence by insurgents or armies."

While any future Iraq operation would probably differ from past UN peacekeeping missions, it's still instructive to hear her warnings— and read her book, published in Dutch by Atlas/Amsterdam in 1997 and in English translation by Penguin/Viking UK in 2003 (and now out in an updated edition). An American publication, if it comes, should be required reading for diplomats, UN delegates, politicians, think-tankers, aid-givers, and anybody who thinks about these subjects.

Polman feels that the dirty little secret about the UN is that its member states want it weak. In order to be effective, the UN must be strengthened, and that is precisely what the member states, including the United States, do not want.

"The member states," she told me, "are misusing the organization."

And the public misperceives the United Nations. "We see it, sometimes, as powerful. In reality, the UN is powerless."

The peacekeeping missions she describes in her book are perfect examples. Whether in Somalia, Haiti, or Rwanda, the blue helmets are frequently hapless, surrounded by a bewildered populace. Polman writes with a passionate precision that would be rare for the sort of journalist who observes the worst and then goes home. She lived in a container in Somalia until long after the Americans had left in the wake of Black Hawk Down. She spent two years in Haiti. Her time in Rwanda was the most harrowing, and also provides the greatest example of the ineffectualness of the United Nations.

Imagine a few hundred thousand people standing in a space the size of three football fields. It's 1995, the refugee camp at Kibeho. To lie down is to get trampled. They have been standing for sixty hours. Their lips are white with thirst. Every once in a while a few of them get shot by the soldiers who guard them. Thousands are shot or clubbed or trampled.

On the other side of the barbed wire onto which some of the refugees are squeezed or ripped to shreds are eighty peacekeepers, Zambian UN blue helmets. Were it not for the wise and brave leadership of their captain, Francis Sikaonga, more refugees would have come to grief, and perhaps the UN "Zambat" would have been overrun.

This is one year after the genocide in which a million Rwanda Tutsis were slaughtered. Now the shoe is on the other foot. The Tutsi soldiers show little mercy to the Hutus who have been herded onto those fields. Mixed in with the refugees are the fleeing Hutu soldiers who committed many of the murders. Some of the ones standing in that field, victims now, were murderers then. So maybe the Tutsi soldiers now show more mercy than their victims did before.

Polman's magnificent description renders the futility of asking what side we should take. The UN isn't allowed to take sides anyway; it operates on the principle of nonintervention. And even if it could stop the occasional killings of these wretched people in that field, it could not, with eighty men, oppose a few thousand soldiers.

When the order comes for the refugees to move elsewhere, the most heartrending scenes are those of children being thrown over the barbed wire fence, wounded, disfigured, mortally ill children, whose parents think the Zambian peacekeepers can help them. The scenes are eerily reminiscent of death marches in Nazi Germany in 1945, when the concentration camps were hastily evacuated before the advancing Soviet Army.

After the fifth day, most of the refugees are in place, though "not one is standing. The Hutus have become one with their possessions in a hideous, wet rubbish tip that stretches to the end of the world."

It's a hideous ending to a hideous story. Perhaps one glimmer of light is that despite the powerlessness of the United Nations, more refugees would have died had it not been for eighty blue-helmeted men from Zambia.

We Did Nothing: Why the Truth Doesn't Always Come Out When the UN Goes In
by Linda Polman
Penguin Books, 256 pages

2004

Do Muslims Communicate Differently?

At the age of six, Youssef Azghari came to the Netherlands, where his Moroccan father was one of hundreds of thousands of guest workers who wound up staying. Their children comprise a generation marked by radical extremism at one end of the spectrum and flawless integration at the other. Azghari, now thirty-four, is a lecturer in communication and sociology at a Dutch college.

His recent book, *Cultuurbepaalde communicatie* (*Culturally Determined Communication*), not yet translated from the Dutch, draws on his own experience with Moroccans in the Netherlands as well as scholarly analysis—and can tell us much about both the culture clash we see everywhere in Western Europe and the societies in the Muslim world we so eagerly seek to change.

In the Netherlands, the 2004 murder of Dutch filmmaker Theo van Gogh has painfully refocused the struggle to assimilate a substantial Muslim minority.

Before Van Gogh's murder came the assassination of the Dutch populist and anti-immigration politician Pim Fortuyn. And before that came September 11, 2001, which had considerable impact on Holland. The last four years have seen a sharp reversal of that country's widely admired love of tolerance.

Azghari clearly hopes to replace both unquestioning tolerance and wholesale rejection with understanding on both sides. In the process, he offers a fascinating look at what the West doesn't quite grasp in Muslim cultures, and vice versa.

He draws a sharp contrast between the two cultures but knows that there are gradations in between. As he sees it, the Netherlands—the West, really—is a "content-directed" society, by which he means that its societies care more for the content of the message than the form in which it's delivered.

Equality, honesty, acceptance, tolerance, and clarity are values such societies espouse. Even children are urged to think for themselves. Freedom of expression, individualism, and democracy are prized above everything.

The East, which Azghari takes to include the Muslim world as well as much of Asia, is "form-directed." Its societies value the package more than the message, he argues. The way something is said trumps individual expression.

Obedience, loyalty, respect, empathy, and discretion are supreme values. The naked truth is unseemly, for truth is less consequential than the manner in which it is revealed.

Children learn to respect their elders, and citizens learn to fear the state. Such societies ultimately favor a hierarchy, a reigning ideology—and a strong leader. Loyalty counts for more than self, and sacrifice is venerated.

While such observations about West and East are not new, and may well be oversimplified, there is special value in hearing them from someone with such intimate experience of both cultures. And there may be special merit in applying these ideas to the judgments made in the West about the Muslim world and our interventions in the Middle East.

Take, for instance, the idea you sometimes hear from our soldiers in Iraq, that Iraqis "can't be trusted," or "lie" to you.

Azghari argues that several factors can be misinterpreted by Westerners when Arabs are reporting actualities: (1) a certain "poeticizing" tendency, embellishing what is otherwise bald and unpleasant, (2) a desire to spare listeners by telling them what will please them, and (3) an emphasis on intentions rather than results. This lack of factuality has often been observed and derided by Westerners.

While we do not have to take this somewhat over-schematized view as literally as Azghari suggests, it could help clarify for us the world we are now in conflict with.

At least it could temper our optimistic predictions about its democratic future, for despite Turkey and Mali, Muslim societies have shown no great affinity for democracy, and Arab cultures, despite Lebanon, especially so. Equality and democracy are simply lesser values for them.

Add to that the radicalization Azghari notes in second-generation Muslims in Western Europe, and you can predict both more terrorism in the West and a tumultuous, undemocratic future in Iraq.

Cultuurbepaalde communicatie (Culturally Determined Communication)
by Youssef Azghari
Uitgeverij H. Nelissen, 181 pages
2006

THEFT AND SURVIVAL

Books about Islam just keep on coming, and one can only wonder who reads them. The specialist, inevitably; the general reader, maybe. But do our policy makers? Our national debates are conducted—and policies formulated—on the basis of slogans, half-truths, distortions and lies.

Still, knowledge is essential, a point *The Great Theft: Wrestling Islam from the Extremists* underscores. The author, Khaled Abou El Fadl, is a law professor at UCLA who has published ten books on Islam. His specialty is Islamic jurisprudence; but while his book is detailed and occasionally dry, it lucidly answers major questions of Westerners about Islam. Additionally, it implores Muslim moderates to restore Islam to the traditions of inquiry and tolerance that have been stolen from them by extremists—or puritans, as Abou El Fadl prefers to call them—and urges the West to view that schism as comparable to the violent Reformation that once shook Christianity.

The Great Theft explains the origins of modern extremism, its roots in the eighteenth-century reformist Wahhabi movement, and its arguments with mainstream Islam. Both mysticism and rationalism, Abd al-Wahhab preached, as well as intellectualism and sectarianism, had undermined Islam; only a literal return to the Prophet's words, literally interpreted, could restore Islam to itself. Thanks in part to Saudi Arabia's vigorous export of this radical movement, the puritans have eradicated Islam's rich history and now dominate the way the religion is viewed. But, says Abou El Fadl, Islam finds itself in a great "transformative moment"—though the majority moderates have been overshadowed by extremism, they can, with knowledge and understanding, still take Islam back.

One manifestation of extremism is, of course, the notion of *jihad*. Even the non-scholar is familiar with the term's two major interpretations: one, that it is essentially a struggle with oneself for a kind of moral self-improvement; the other, that it is a fight to the death against all infidels. Citing Qur'anic chapter and verse, and drawing on Islamic scholarship, Abou El Fadl demonstrates that the latter is a radical misinterpretation of the Prophet and what he stood for. Known to us from Osama bin Laden's various proclamations, this version is especially appealing to those who wish to forge a new identity by defining themselves as heroic followers of the true path.

Similarly, the author argues that it is a puritan perversion of Islam and the Qur'an to treat women as, say, the Taliban did—that in fact Prophet and text plead for a humane and rational treatment of all people, with human worth and dignity transcending all other considerations. He does so with much passion and scholarly exegesis but is most persuasive when he lays bare the sadistic motives beneath the precepts of the puritans.

Still, the uncomfortable question lingers: why, if the Qur'an stresses equality, cooperation, mutual support, and so forth, is the situation of women what it is in so many Muslim families in so many countries?

Which leads to my one complaint about this otherwise fine, instructive book. It extols the path of moderation, portrayed as the core of Islam, but, despite many reasons given, does not quite manage to say why the theft of Islam was so thorough. Maybe fanaticism always beats out moderation, but in the case of Islam the moderates seem particularly weak. It's fascinating to hear Abou El Fadl explain why Saudi Arabia dare not become more moderate—because as guardian of the holy places it "must define orthodoxy in the Muslim world"—but he does not account fully for the disarray, religious and cultural, of so many more moderate Muslim countries.

These are not matters that *Embracing the Infidel: Stories of Muslim Migrants on the Journey West* deals with. Despite its title, the book is not concerned with the nature of Islam. The author, Behzad Yaghmaian, an Iranian American professor of economics, tells the stories of Muslim migrants, who for one reason or another, have left their homelands. His book is a gripping tale of hardship, adventure, and yearning; of hopes raised and dashed; and of troubled and sometimes heroic adaptations to refugee camps in Bulgaria, tent cities in Greece, slum ghettos in Turkey, and, for the luckier ones, fugitive existences in Paris and London. Whether from the Islamic Republic of Iran or Saddam

Hussein's Iraq or post-Taliban Afghanistan, the migrants are bent on survival and a better life in the West.

Their obsession with visas, petitions, passports, documents, and borders reminds me of European Jews before and after the outbreak of World War II. I remember the same rumors about countries that don't send illegal border-crossers back, but actually do (Switzerland, then; Greece, now); the same obstacles, both natural and human—hideous mountain ranges, treacherous people smugglers, predatory and brutal border guards.

But traumatic though the situation of these wanderers is, and though they flee horrendous conditions, their fate if they must return home is not as inevitable as it was for European Jews. Many present-day migrants are not classic "political refugees." Is a woman escaping an oppressive Muslim father a political refugee? Does having your family in Afghanistan wiped out by American bombs earn you political asylum?

One of many strengths of this book is to show how blurry such categories are and what strangely mixed motives impel these brave, complicated people. A masterful storyteller, Yaghmaian reveals many layers to the refugees' personalities and histories, and some to his own. He wins their trust, not because he wants to write a book, but because he becomes deeply enmeshed in their lives.

Difficult as things are for the migrants, they can only become worse: the West now deems Afghanistan and Iraq "safe" to return to, while the fear of terrorism has further tightened Western entry requirements. More will ultimately have to go home.

Perhaps the only silver lining a detached observer might find is that the continued presence of such strong-minded, independent people in their homelands might make more likely the realization of the dream, cherished by the likes of Abou El Fadl, for a more moderate Islamic world.

The Great Theft: Wrestling Islam from the Extremists
by Khaled Abou El Fadl
Harper San Francisco; 320 pages

Embracing the Infidel: Stories of Muslim Migrants on the Journey West
by Behzad Yaghmaian
Delacorte Press/Bantam Dell Books; 368 pages

2006

On the Death of Khomeini: Living with Iran

Now that the Ayatollah Khoumeini is dead, it is time to have a backward look at America's fascination and revulsion with his bewildering country.

What stirs in us when we hear of Iran?

It was, during the hostage crisis, and for a while after, the country America loved to hate. It remains a place we are enduringly aware of. Why?

Iran and the United States represent two kinds of nations, and I submit that the uncomfortable awareness we have of Iran and the ambivalence we may feel toward it result from two important impulses in us that these two countries embody, those of tribalism and individualism.

The differences we have with Iran are greater and farther reaching, the conflicts deeper and more basic, than those we have with the countries from which we are divided by mere ideology.

Iran is that phenomenon not unusual in history: a country with the unity, or the zeal for unity, equal to that of a tribe or a family. Despite the existence of dissidents in Iran, its values are communal, its beliefs uniform, its style monistic. Fervid religion and a fundamental sense of its own moral superiority give it the strength to bear almost any hardship and endure almost any pain. Whatever its sorrow and its glory, the country experiences them together.

America, on the other hand, is a loosely joined collection of single individuals, divorced from family and community, and wedded only to the freedom to develop. A profound experiment in pluralism allows all these individuals to live together in relative harmony and to work out their destinies undisturbed by the interference of others. We call it peace and freedom—others may regard it as unfettered license and loneliness. We believe in people's right to live as they please and to worship as they want to, if they want to: "tribalists" regard that as mere self-indulgence

214

and heresy. Our proudest notions of democracy, though based on a veneration of law higher than individuals, are anathema to those who worship the tribe. They have no room for democracy, no space for individual initiative, and no particular drive to self-fulfillment.

When the family or tribe is further directed by a messianic fervor, be it religious or nationalistic, when the "holy fascism," as it has been called, is created, it cannot help but despise what seems to it to be mere hedonism or godless pursuit of self-indulgent pleasure. *We* become the Great Satan, while *they* seem to us the great fanatics, gripped by a communal lust for blood or self-sacrifice.

This clash of style, substance, and character is far greater than our ideologically based quarrels with the Soviets and the Communists generally. When Henry Kissinger flew from Pakistan to China to play the China card against Russia, when we all hailed Nixon's "opening" to China in 1972, we wasted no time in becoming China's friend. Within a few months, references by politicians to "Red China" were replaced by polite calls to establish better relations with the "People's Republic of China." And so we did. The quarrel was soon forgotten, the long, painful breach healed. There were more similarities between us than anyone had reckoned.

I doubt that we could ever find such similarities with Iran—or with any country that has deliberately abandoned its secular, Western, individualistic leanings, to return to a single-minded tribal family. We see in them a rampant medievalism—their religion excessive and fanatic, their holy crusades a shuddering remnant of what we in America left behind in a painful European past. And they see in us the sinfulness of personal indulgence and private luxury, a quagmire of hedonism without principle or God.

The conflict is all the more agonizing in that it mirrors a schism inside of us. We all have two disparate needs: to be ourselves, to develop our individual personalities and beings; and, on the other hand, to feel the closeness of community, the comforts of communal thought and action. Sometimes these two can be reconciled and joined: even the pluralistic society can be thrilled to recognize that The Pride Is Back. But mostly, these two needs assert themselves separately and contradictorily: to strike out on one's own inevitably means leaving the family behind, while to join the family, really to commit oneself to it, requires the sacrifice of personal desires.

Most of us have experienced the unbearable conflict engendered by these two contradictory impulses, and our high divorce rates attest to what our society has had to pay in pain for the intractability of these conflicting personal urges. For better or for worse, our own society leans toward the quest for personal freedom, which makes the ecstasy of communal togetherness—as anyone who has ever joined a cult can affirm—a rare and exceptional delight that the pluralistic, tolerant, liberal Jeffersonian society usually does not offer.

If these two impulses do not co-exist harmoniously within the human psyche, how then do we expect them to in the world at large— and how can we expect to live comfortably with Iran? Is it any wonder that something stirs uncomfortably in us at the mere mention of Iran?

1989

WORLD OF IMMIGRANTS

AN INTERNAL DEBATE BETWEEN TWO CULTURES

In a conversation I recently had with Richard Rodriguez, he talked about his love of duality and mythic oppositions. "I see the world in images, archetypes," he told me. "But I also see paradoxes. Mexico is old and pessimistic, but the average age is fifteen. Meanwhile, the United States is hopeful and young, but we experience the graying of America." His own father, he continued, is formal, sober, very Mexican, but he came to America to seek an easier, less careworn life.

Richard Rodriguez's *Days of Obligation: An Argument with My Mexican Father* is a meditation on being an American born of Mexican parents in California. Rodriguez's perceptions are so far-reaching that his autobiographical base inevitably broadens into a study of Mexicanness and Americanness, of Mexico and America as concepts, as ideas, as mythic entities.

The argument with his Mexican father referred to in the book's subtitle is Rodriguez's inner argument, for he sees two essential tendencies in himself and indeed in California: an American, innocent, Protestant buoyancy, posed against a Spanish, experienced, Catholic cynicism. Although his father is comfortably assimilated in Sacramento, California, Rodriguez continues to see in his gravity and decorum the Mexican heritage that alternately weighs on his son and gives him a sense of the world as it truly is.

Rodriguez apprehends his dualities in precise yet poetic prose. One of his almost allegorical vignettes describes the waitress in a twenty-four hour restaurant, divorced, newly blond (her painted eyebrows "are jet-black migraines"), anti-maternal; when she cleans the table, she wipes off its littered past, making it new. She represents the possibilities as well as the loosening and unraveling of America. Her opposite number in Mexico is indoors, at home, sustained by the family. Children in the latter kind of household are the confirmation of the past. The men are father or son, defending and defended by the others. That world is feminine, private, while the Anglo world is adventurous, raucous, and public.

It is into this tempting "Protestant" world that the Mexicans in the United States are thrust. Away from the voluptuous, motherly Church, away from the memory of Mexico, they taste the pleasure of independence and assertiveness, anarchy and renewal. The slow conversion to American ways is painful for the older generation, and momentous for the younger. More concretely, many become attracted to Evangelicalism. "Two teenagers from Latin America tell me they converted to evangelical Protestantism because American Protestants came to their villages in suits and ties," Rodriguez reports. "The evangelical appearance advertises an end to failure."

This attraction occurs among both Mexicans in America and Latinos in Latin America. Rodriguez describes the amazing growth of Evangelicalism in that part of the world most of us think of as solidly Roman Catholic. Evidently there, too, the appeal of the Protestant way is that it gives a sense of opportunity, restores to the individual a belief in actively working not only toward his salvation but also toward his prosperity. It's an old story, but here played out in a new setting, and very much in our own time. One consequence of this development is that the American influence in those parts of the world is growing, though at the expense of a certain psychological and cultural depth.

Rodriguez persistently causes our usual perspectives to shift. It's not the Indians who were engulfed by the Spaniards but, he argues, the other way around. Mexico has absorbed the conquistadors, assimilated them. "Spanish is now an Indian language. Mexico City has become the metropolitan see of the Spanish-speaking world." And he upsets the now-fashionable belief in retaining one's ethnicity within a multicultural society by championing a new melting pot; after all, "Mexico City is the capital of modernity, for in the sixteenth century… Mexico initiated the task of the twenty-first century—the renewal of the old, the known world, through miscegenation. Mexico carries the idea of a round world to its biological conclusion." It's a vision, at once sensible and radical, of the future against the grain of our separatist times.

This view of the Indianization of Spanish culture is consonant with recent thinking about the development of cultures away from the homeland. The Dutch sociologist Rob Kroes, for instance, in his book *De leegte van Amerika: een massacultuur in de wereld* (Amsterdam,

1992), has argued that transplanted cultures often develop the way Creole languages do—away from the mother tongue, they assimilate alien elements quickly, and hospitably take on newer and more variegated features, becoming as they do so markedly different from the original language.

In California, too, Rodriguez argues, it is not exactly the Anglos who swamped the Spanish. White Protestants accepted Spanish customs in order to celebrate their distance from their own past, for "[v]estiges of Spanish colonial served to remind Protestants that they were no longer part of the East." Such revision of commonly held notions is most startling when Rodriguez interprets *machismo*: whatever Americans mean by it, Mexicans find it akin to *gravitas*, located in the sober, care-taking male, brave, chivalrous, silent. Since Rodriguez's father—a formal, sensitive man—is the incarnation of that kind of *machismo*, the argument with him is ultimately unequal, for the tragic view of life propounded by the father is now lived by the son.

By including early in his book a moving account of the ravages that surround him, Rodriguez, a gay man in AIDS-ridden San Francisco, shows how he has mellowed since his first autobiography, *Hunger of Memory* (1982). *Days of Obligation* is gentler than *Hunger of Memory*, which turned at times into a polemic against affirmative action. Not that Rodriguez has fully changed his mind on that score, for he still believes that a common culture is necessary and that "diversity is a liquid noun...and stands for nothing." Yet in this book he depicts the history of his ambivalence—from that of the obedient boy infatuated with his best friend's defiance, to the grown man who, when visiting Tijuana, returns to sleep in San Diego every night, a brown man fearful of being drowned in a sea of brown faces—and shows how he overcomes the pain of that ambivalence, not by yielding to one side or the other but by accepting the existence of both. Fascinated by duality and paradox, he is no longer their victim.

One built-in limitation of Rodriguez's approach to these matters is that dualities are true in a poetic way—that is, they are valid from a certain emotional perspective only. Americans may well distrust "Mexican shading," and it may be that "we say yes when we mean yes," but for Americans, it seems to me, this is a manner, an aspiration, perhaps an ideal. Although we are unsubtle and value straightforwardness, our very innocence can cause hypocrisy. The problem with dualities is that their counter side can often be asserted with equal vigor. The danger of thinking in mythic entities is that they suddenly seem to be everywhere and make everything appear freighted with symbolic significance, blurring the line between fine observation and mere free association. Rodriguez's disquisition on *adobe* ("Adobe is mud shaped by human intention"), juxtaposed with a list of road signs (WEDDINGS ANYTIME/ANYPLACE), falls over the edge of sense or into the realm of semiotic play, at least to my mind.

But this weakness is probably indivisible from the chief strength of the book, which lies in the pleasure of its poetic prose and the beauty of its aphorisms. I cite several of these, almost at random:

> Femininity is defined by the son as motherhood. Only a culture so cruel to the wife could sustain such a sentimental regard for the *mamacita*.

> Information in an authoritarian society is power. In Mexico, power accumulates as information is withheld.

> Once upon a time, the homosexual appropriated to himself a mystical province, that of taste. Taste, which is, after all, the insecurity of the middle class, became the homosexual's licentiate to challenge the rule of nature.

> In Mexico, one is most oneself in private. The very existence of *tu* must undermine the realm of *usted*. In America, one is most oneself in public.

> History and Eden are irreconcilable ideas.

> The attention L.A. lavishes on a single face is as generous a metaphor as I can find for the love of God.

These help turn *Days of Obligation* into a poetic artifact and Richard Rodriguez into a young Octavio Paz, a true poet of the Americas.

Days of Obligation: An Argument with My Mexican Father
by Richard Rodriguez
Penguin, 256 pages

1994

ASSIMILATION AND ETHNICITY:
IDENTITY AND FAMILY

It's almost commonplace that the cultural ideal of immigrant assimilation into American culture, the "melting pot," has lately been replaced by the retention of ethnicity, the "salad bowl." How have minority writers perceived this phenomenon?

In 1959, when he was twenty-six, the American Jewish writer Philip Roth published a magnificent short story, "Eli, the Fanatic," in his first book, *Goodbye, Columbus.* Set in the time right after World War II, the story portrays a young, nervous suburban lawyer who is given the job by his fellow American Jews of removing a newly created religious school of Holocaust survivors from the fashionable suburb in which the assimilated, middle-class Jews have finally been allowed to settle. Eli accepts the job, hoping that he can work out a compromise by getting the Talmudic Jews to shed some of their embarrassing garb, or at least have their religious teacher wear the business suit that Eli gave him. Identifying ever more with them—that is, becoming ever more embroiled in the question of his own identity as a Jew—Eli ends up wearing the long, black Talmudic coat that the religious teacher has significantly left on his doorstep and, so dressed, walks through the primarily Christian suburb for all to see.

The question that Roth poses, of course, is whether assimilation into the majority culture is not betrayal—whether in fact the honest embracing of ethnic identity isn't more honorable. In this, the story prefigures the debate that took place in the sixties: shouldn't minorities retain their ethnicity proudly, rather than "becoming American" as quickly as possible?

Yet the ideal of retaining one's ethnicity has a price: the pressures and conflicts of retaining the old culture can be just as difficult as the overeagerness to embrace the new.

Among those who have found both assimilation and ethnicity painful is Maxine Hong Kingston. Her book about growing up Chinese in California, *The Woman Warrior*, came out in 1976 when yet another wave of Asian immigration into the United States—from Hong Kong, from Vietnam, from Cambodia—was underway.

She portrays herself as both hampered and nourished by her background. Her parents are not only Chinese, but they remain villagers forever. Their lack of straightforwardness, their endless proverbs about the uselessness of daughters ("raising children for strangers"), their subtle, unspoken threat to return to China where she might be "sold" into marriage—are all enormous constraints to the ease the girl naturally wants to feel in the new culture.

Like the other Chinese, her parents call the Americans "ghosts" and "barbarians" who lack substance and show bad manners by doing such uncouth things as looking people straight in the eye, which in China is done only when searching out liars. (Significantly, the word for "good manners" in Chinese is the same as "traditions.") The Chinese born in America are "half-ghosts," and, not surprisingly, the children in this family develop a whole array of neurotic strategies for escaping visiting relatives, like making little nests for themselves in closets or underneath stairs. Self-hatred is almost inevitable. In one harrowing scene, Kingston tries unsuccessfully to beat a Chinese schoolmate into speaking; out of Chinese reticence, the girl has never spoken in school.

Still, the rich culture from which Kingston stems sustains her also. Her mother tells her stories that become indelibly part of the writer's identity. Recording the story of her adulterous aunt, the woman who cannot be talked about, who must forever remain invisible, Kingston reveals her intimacy with the world of the Chinese village. Like her mother, she knows its view of adultery ("extravagance"), food, politeness, how women must walk ("pigeon-toed"), though it is knowledge that serves her ill in her American setting: "Even now China wraps double binds around my feet."

But some find an easier balance between ethnicity and assimilation. The Mexican American family in Arturo Islas's beautiful book of autobiographical stories, *The Rain God* (1984), lives in a community composed equally of Anglos and Hispanics. Their small desert town, like hundreds of communities in Texas, New Mexico, Arizona, and

California, may offer some resistance to the rapid advancement of recently arrived Mexicans, but none to this well-off, ambitious, fluent-in-English family.

No cultural issue is involved when one of the men is shown to be mortifyingly in love with his wife's best friend while he endures the renewal ceremony of his own marriage vows. It is passion rather than setting that ravages this family and ultimately takes so many to the Rain God, the ancient Indian deity in whose realm all streams and rivers end. But the family's loyalty to each other is unquestioned, even when rocked by infidelity, religious defection, and homosexuality. The story of Felix, the happy-natured father who, in pursuit of a young soldier, finds death in his beloved canyon, is eclipsed only by the dignified response of the family to protect his memory and his name.

The next generation is shakier, especially the sensitive young family chronicler, clearly modeled on the author. He is the individualist, the loner, the seeker rather than the doer, who moves to San Francisco, away from *la familia*. He embodies the book's cultural conflict: namely, that between an individualistic, atomistic society, which promises freedom but often delivers loneliness, and a warmer community, which offers the comforts of an extended family but stifles personal fulfillment—roughly the clash between Anglo American and Latin American values.

When the children of immigrants are writers, such conflicts can be a source of the creativity from which books are made. Certainly these minority writers are more concerned with the possibilities and ambivalences of their dual heritage than with the desirability of choosing one over the other, for they almost invariably show how *both* worlds live compellingly inside their characters and themselves.

Goodbye, Columbus and Five Short Stories
by Philip Roth
Vintage, 298 pages

The Woman Warrior: Memoirs of a Girlhood Among Ghosts
by Maxine Hong Kingston
Vintage, 224 pages

The Rain God
by Arturo Islas
Harper Perennial, 180 pages
1989

DID THE YEAR 2002 END THE GREAT DUTCH SOCIAL EXPERIMENT?

When the first Dutch politician in three hundred years to be assassinated lay dead last spring, people in the Netherlands were saying that everything had changed.

But the huge popularity of the murdered Pim Fortuyn was itself a sign that everything had changed. He was a photogenic, well-spoken, flamboyantly gay man who openly questioned his government's policies on immigration and derided the Establishment's condescension toward ordinary people. He never disguised his homosexuality and even joked about it. Nevertheless, Fortuyn had started to draw huge crowds and win local elections.

Attacked by the Dutch ruling coalition as a right-winger, a Dutch Le Pen, a homegrown Haider, Fortuyn was none of these. He was a populist with an occasionally confusing message but a style of saying things and asking questions that was challenging, forceful, and frequently colorful.

He asked, for example, whether a huge Muslim population, often originating in isolated North African villages, could live within the norms of a tolerant, secular, democratic society when powerful Muslim religious leaders attacked homosexuals as deserving of the death penalty.

And he raised the question heretofore posed publicly only by right-wingers, but privately by millions of Dutch people, whether the Netherlands was "full." Can a tiny country with sixteen million inhabitants support more immigrants, more asylum seekers, more migrants from former colonies? Is such growth possible? Is it culturally sustainable? The non-Dutch inhabitants now number close to two million, roughly 12 percent of the total population.

"He said what we thought," many people said after the death of their hero. The established parties had failed to notice the growing alarm of the population about minority crime or the abuse of the dole (more than half of the immigrant community is supported by the state). They spoke their abstract, politically correct language, retreated to their safe enclaves, and thought of crime as a statistic. The respectable newspapers too did not want to look reactionary; after all, Holland was famously a liberal, tolerant society.

Pim Fortuyn did not live to see any of his questions answered—or even posed by elected politicians. After his death, though, his party of loosely affiliated, hastily assembled candidates became the second largest bloc elected to the Parliament in The Hague.

Their performance in power was a huge disappointment—they were aggressive, but mainly toward each other. Their ineptitude and quarrelsomeness caused the collapse of the coalition government in which they served. And in a new election, they were soundly defeated.

Still, Fortuyn's accomplishment is that these days everything can be talked about. Political correctness is dead. Immigrants are now required to learn the Dutch language and made to study the ways of a secular, tolerant society, in which laws and institutions are supreme and all religions equally protected.

How successful those legal mandates will be is an open question. The immigrants will have to want to integrate, and the Dutch will have to be more forthcoming about recognizing them as "fully Dutch." The outcome of both remains to be seen.

And now that the most recently held elections have returned the established parties to power, can we be sure these parties will not resume the policies of silence and political correctness they were widely accused of fostering?

Many questions are still unresolved. If the country has indeed swung to the right, what now of the legendarily tolerant marijuana laws, homosexual marriages, the semi-legalized assisted suicides? Are we to assume that they will endure now that everything else has changed?

Or is the great social experiment of the last fifty years over?

2003

DELAYED AND INAPPROPRIATE EUROPEAN ANGER: FIGHTING THE WRONG BATTLE

By widely reprinting the Danish cartoons of Muhammad, Europeans are finally taking a stand—but for the wrong reason, on the wrong issue, and probably at the wrong time.

Why now?

Divorce lawyers call it "the waffle iron syndrome." The couple is divorcing; everything is being quietly and amicably divided. She gets the house, he gets the cash; the books are clearly hers, but the CD collection goes to him.

It all proceeds this way for a while till she says, "I'll take the waffle iron. OK?"

He retorts, "You'll take what?"

And they have the biggest fight ever.

Even without a divorce, every couple has been there. Quiet and restraint and decorum prevail, grievances are ignored or swallowed, till somebody has a major tantrum—usually about the wrong thing.

For decades, Western European elites, governmental and otherwise, have been so quiet, so discreet, so politically correct, that until the upheavals of the last few years (the murder of Theo van Gogh in the Netherlands and the riots in France), no criticism of Muslim immigrants could be expressed in polite company. Those who did so were labeled racists or far-Rightists, or even neo-Nazis.

But then the dam burst, and now many polite Europeans are having a tantrum. Recent cartoon-inspired violence may worsen it.

It's hard to exaggerate the reproaches against politicians, journalists, educators, and other movers and shakers for having swept immigrant problems under the rug, for keeping silent in the face of problems with integration, or no integration at all. The scorn, ridicule and fury directed against those who should have spoken up but didn't, or hypocritically moved away from immigrant-heavy, crime-ridden city centers, or sent their kids to "good" schools, was not widely reported in the U.S. press. In Denmark, the Netherlands, Belgium, and Sweden, the reproaches continue to this day.

Now it's all out in the open. No More Silence; No More Political Correctness.

Suddenly, many Europeans find the complaints of Muslims about newspaper cartoons first published in Denmark's Jyllands Posten (for instance, of the Prophet as terrorist) unacceptable. The furious response by Muslims could harden those feelings.

As if to make up for lost time, and not content to let Danes and their Muslim immigrants work things out, newspapers in France, Germany, the Netherlands, Switzerland, Spain, and Italy have now reprinted the offending cartoons. You don't have to be a Muslim to see that as a clear case of provocation.

And certainly the wrong battle about the wrong issue.

People who passed over in silence the suggestion of some imams that homosexuals should be flung from the tops of tall buildings now take umbrage at Muslim rage about offensive cartoons. People who had allowed plays to be withdrawn because they offended Muslim sensibilities now decry Muslim inability to understand that freedom means freedom to insult. People who had said "immigrants just needed more time to adjust" are now beside themselves about Muslim fury at having their Prophet caricatured.

Yes, freedom of the press is an important value, to be sure, but you can't exactly blame Muslims for being angry. And while Europe does not have precisely the same definition of "hate-speech" we do, it's not as if that concept is unknown there. After all, Holocaust-denial is a crime in several European countries.

Besides, ask yourself if anti-Jewish caricatures would have been widely reprinted in major European newspapers. Democracies, we should know, must treat their minorities with kid gloves. The dominant culture is by definition sturdier than any number of minority cultures. For reasons that should be obvious, an American university can have a black studies program but not a white studies program. That's not a double standard.

The two sides, says the Dutch Moroccan scholar Youssef Azghari, "still don't know much about each other."

The burning of the Danish and Norwegian embassies in Damascus, and the riots and demonstrations elsewhere, make this harder—but, still, now is the time to learn, and for Europeans to show the understanding that in their time of silence and quietude they seemed to demonstrate so excessively.

No point going from one extreme to the other.

2006

Europe Emboldens Its Muslim Women

Recently, the Bangladeshi banker Muhammad Yunus won the Nobel Peace Prize for having pioneered the granting of small loans to new enterprises. Most of his clients are women. What is well known to lenders, foreign aid agencies, and donors generally, but less so to the general public, is that huge numbers of the Third World's small entrepreneurs are women.

A worldwide but underreported phenomenon is that, when given the chance, women are more enterprising, more flexible, and more adaptable than men in adjusting to new ways and rising in an environment that often remains alien to men. In the developing world, it's often women who support the family by running a small business or otherwise providing a stable income. Certainly they're the ones grasping new opportunities.

A similar pattern is at work among immigrants into developed countries. Take the case of Muslim women in Western Europe.

An essay on Moroccan women in the Netherlands makes the point that they're less likely to want to return to their homelands than Moroccan men. It's not hard to understand—by returning, they have more to lose.

One of the untold stories of the immigration turmoil in Western Europe is that such women, despite their lesser position in the family—maybe because of it—do better in Europe than Muslim men. Compared to their powerlessness and isolation back home, they have freedoms and opportunities undreamt of before.

The reason they're not much in the news is that most Muslim women in Europe are quietly functioning as homemakers or as workers in a variety of jobs outside the home.

And their daughters and granddaughters, the second and third generation born in Europe, tend to do better in school than their sons and grandsons. This has been consistently so, though there are danger signs on the horizon. A French high-school teacher told me that some girls are starting to model themselves after the boys and flirt with negative, rejectionist attitudes. But most Muslim girls, she conceded, continue to perform better.

One reason, says the Moroccan Dutch commentator Youssef Azghari, is that girls are more strictly brought up and closely watched. Doing homework, studying, and preparing for a profession comes more easily to them than to boys, who are allowed to hang out on the street till all hours.

Whether it's that boys are more indulged, or fall prey to gangs, or simply don't respond as well to hardships, is difficult to say; but, on the whole, girls adjust and even find European ways compatible with their own lives and see opportunities that boys do not.

Maybe it's that girls expect greater pressure and have learned to be so pliable—to juggle stern fathers and difficult brothers—that anything European society can throw at them is easy compared to what they've already learned to put up with at home, from their own culture, in their own circle.

Obviously, in their behavior and their beliefs, these are the moderate Muslims that native Europeans clamor and yearn for. Why, then, aren't they appreciated more?

Because they're largely unseen and make no waves.

Of course, there are famous Muslim women in Europe, such as Ayaan Hirsi Ali, the Somali-born former member of the Dutch Parliament, now at the American Enterprise Institute in Washington. Her books, her outspokenness against her former religion, her film script of *Submission*—the ill-fated documentary that in 2004 occasioned the murder of its director Theo van Gogh by a radicalized young Dutch-born Muslim—have been publicized all over the world, but her stridency and her rejection of Islam are not shared by most Muslim women in Western Europe.

Nor do most Muslim women sympathize with the other extreme—fanatical devotion to the faith, or fundamentalist radicalism.

When Muslim women are well known, it's usually not because they've thrown over their religion or, at the other extreme, joined a radical group, but because they achieve prominence in approved-of, conventional ways. Six Muslim women hold seats in the Dutch Parliament, as compared to three Muslim men.

Radical groups and furious rhetoric apparently have less appeal to women. A young man may fall into the hands of a radical gang or be dazzled by a fiery imam, in large part because of a certain attraction to an exotic, subversive style. Heavy-handed, high-flown, sternly patriarchal language heard in mosques and on satellite TV, whether as political pronouncement, sacred text, or bombastic invective, may cast the spell of righteous, moralistic exhortation over men, but sways fewer women who, after all, have had such language used against them by their fathers and brothers. Familiar as it is, they fear it.

Similarly, ghetto speech, street language, whether utilitarian or rap-like, induces no great admiration. And young women may be more sensitive to the rage it provokes in the respectable European classes around them. An example of this rage is manifest in the French philosopher Alain Finkielkraut's characterization of such speech as "simplistic, vicious pidgin, pathetically hostile to beauty and nuance."

In her novel, *Kiffe Kiffe Tomorrow*, the young Algerian-French writer Faiza Guene shows her imperviousness to these flights of extremist fancy. Instead, the young girl who is the main character appreciates her mother's energy, common sense, and persistence. The mother has a job and is learning to read and write French. Fortunately, the father has long since returned to North Africa to live with a younger woman.

The phenomenon of absent fathers may actually have helped many a young Muslim woman. Fatherlessness permits the new culture to be more accessible. The lessening pressure also makes competing with boys in school more respectable and, as the Dutch sociologist Abram de Swaan has pointed out, education changes the relation of young Muslim women to Muslim men. Small wonder ever more Muslim women graduate from European universities.

In the Netherlands and Belgium, a good many women of North African and Middle Eastern descent are succeeding as psychologists, social workers, and counselors, thereby demonstrating that, while more needs to be done on all sides, assimilation and success in the new society are both desirable and possible, and even now within reach.

2006

233

BEWILDERING COMPLEXITIES OF
INTEGRATING MUSLIMS INTO EUROPE

The debate about immigration in the U.S., whatever its complications, is relatively straightforward compared to that raging in Europe, where complexities of policy, attitude toward outsiders and the nature of immigrants' backgrounds dominate all discussions.

During a teaching stint at the University of Helsinki in the early nineties, I was at a dinner party where the inevitable subject of immigration came up. Finland had recently taken in two thousand Somalis and resisted admitting more. It discouraged immigration and has remained homogeneous to this day.

Sweden, on the other hand, was much easier about giving political asylum and had hundreds of thousands of Muslim immigrants already. Now it has more.

The academics around the table wished Finland would be more like Sweden in this regard. My comment that some day Finland might be spared many problems was treated with polite silence—as was a remark from the other extreme by another guest, that he wouldn't mind a million or two Russians "who'd liven things up in Finland" (at that time, it was widely rumored that hungry Russians would soon swarm across Finnish borders).

Finland vs. Sweden is only one of many contrasts in the way European countries have handled immigration. These days, the usual contrast is between Sweden and Denmark. Denmark has taken a hard line with its Muslims, restricting further immigration in part by clamping down on marriage between resident Muslims and the spouse they might send for in the home country. Sweden, on the other hand, remains almost aggressively lenient.

Sharp differences about integration and assimilation of immigrant and minority populations into Europe continue to exist.

There is the French model of integration—dented somewhat by last year's immigrant riots in the notorious ghetto-like suburbs—that everybody living in France should be French, period, while the British multicultural model attempts to avoid segregated suburban high-rises and encourages immigrants to retain their own culture. Of course, in practice the two models frequently overlap.

In fact, within France, many variations exist: Paris favors the "be French" model, while Marseilles—a Mediterranean city with vast experience of non-French residents—has gone in for a more multicultural system, less segregation, and greater flexibility in having Muslims play a significant role in the civic life of the city.

The Netherlands has tried both models, especially in housing. At certain times, urban planning produced ghettoization, at other times greater mingling. Despite many pronouncements, neither has worked well. The last five years—after the rise and fall of populist politician Pim Fortuyn and the murder of filmmaker Theo van Gogh—have ended the silence and quieted politically correct platitudes, and the country has almost swung the other way, towards overt anger, pessimism and despair. Moderate native and Muslim Dutch voices are now often going unheard.

As if these complications weren't enough, let it be noted that there are major differences between Muslim immigrant groups. Algerians in France, Moroccans in the Netherlands, Turks in Germany, Iraqis in Scandinavia may all be Muslim, but their cultural backgrounds differ. Add to that the hostility between minorities within minorities: recently the Dutch newspaper *NRC Handelsblad* reported on a group of Syrian Christians in the Dutch town of Enschede who were collectively accused of hooliganism. As it turned out, an unsympathetic Turkish Dutch Muslim city councilman was the main complainant about what most townspeople saw as an exemplary subgroup.

Any number of Muslim immigrants function well as Dutch citizens, but the country's attention appears focused on criminal Moroccan youth, especially in the big cities, and the potential for terrorism among seemingly assimilated but radicalized youngsters, often of school age.

In a country of sixteen million, over a million Muslims, mainly of Turkish and Moroccan descent, now dominate the debate. How best to integrate them? Do they even want to integrate? Can a large minority refuse to integrate?

In his meteoric career, the populist Pim Fortuyn proposed that no country could be truly multicultural without fragmenting. Pluralist, yes; multiculturalist, not really.

This may well contain the key to the present dilemma. Muslim groups, which see their culture as entirely the equal of the prevailing Dutch culture, may be on a collision course with the host country. Norms of free speech and the equality of women, the Dutch now say, are not negotiable. The dominant culture has to be respected and in some fashion submitted to by all the citizens. The fabled Dutch tolerance cannot yield to those who are intolerant of its major values.

This would seem to be the advice of a recent book, *While Europe Slept*, which dwells on the habitual looking away of liberal European elites, a silence it regards as continuing. The author, Bruce Bawer, claims that if Europe does not defend against its "Weimar Moment," it will be destroyed from within. The Weimar Republic, it should be recalled, failed to take a stand against Hitler's extremism before he came to power.

But, as Bawer also notes, not only will the European Establishments have to come down hard on extremist behavior and even thought, they will also have to guarantee full equality to their newly minted citizens. For the one thing all European countries have in common is that they never really conceived of the immigrants and their descendants as being truly, really, genuinely Dutch or French or Danish or Swedish. That is a major difference between these countries and the U.S.

Immigrants will have to accept the reigning norms—but European host countries need to offer true acceptance and equality. If, in fact, both sides don't change, all will indeed be lost.

2006

MUSLIMS IN EUROPE: YET ANOTHER DILEMMA—OR A PASSING PHASE?

Two incidents described in a recent issue of the Dutch newspaper *NRC Handelsblad* illustrate one of many dilemmas European society faces these days.

A young Muslim woman, Samira Dahri, a lecturer in economics at a private college in the Netherlands, refused to shake hands with her male associates on religious grounds. When she was dismissed from her job, she took the matter to court, charging that she was being intimidated. "I experience shaking hands," she alleged, "as an undesired form of intimacy, as sexual intimidation."

While the court upheld her dismissal, it would not go so far as to oblige students and staff always to shake hands.

A second incident took place at the Embassy of the Netherlands in Amman, Jordan.

A traveling Member of the Dutch Parliament, Harry van Bommel, said at an embassy lunch to a young Jordanian embassy employee, "You look sensational." She filed a charge with the Dutch ambassador about these "unwanted intimacies."

When the MP noticed that his remark went over badly, he apologized at once. Since then he has offered another, more formal public apology.

The noted Dutch Arabist Rob Ermers, author of a recent book on honor and revenge in the Middle East, analyzed the incident this way:

While it's not forbidden to compliment an Arab woman, the word "sensational" carries sexual overtones and is perhaps close enough to the word "sexual" to have imputed seductive qualities to her.

For her to pass over this, especially since others heard the comment, explains Ermers, might well create the appearance that she was responsive to a suggestive invitation, surely a dishonor to her.

Van Bommel's first apology, continues Ermers, was insufficient because uttered out of earshot of the others at the table. Only a public apology could clear her of having seemed receptive to any overture.

Ermers gives the MP high marks for cultural sensitivity in not reiterating or explaining his innocent intention. Van Bommel apparently realized that the facts were less important than the young woman's honor.

Admirable though Ermers' analysis is, it does not fully persuade me.

Why was this apparently prim young woman, so keenly aware of her honor, at a mixed lunch? And since she was, didn't she have some responsibility to yield to Dutch rather than Arab ways? After all, she was at the Dutch Embassy.

Though Ermers says that filing a complaint was her way of going public, it strikes me as a European (or American) and not exactly Arab thing to do.

As for the woman in the Netherlands who was fired for refusing to shake hands and who charged sexual intimidation, was she not using feminism's hard-won legal techniques to uphold a distinctly non-feminist way of life?

Are such terms and concepts as "hostile workplace" and "unwanted attentions," which would seem to have little legal weight in most Arab Muslim societies, now deployed against the societies that brought such concepts into being—and in favor of values inimical to them?

The paradox is dizzying: Western techniques at the service of non-Western principles, Western means to non-Western ends. And the dilemma for present-day Europe seems to be, can its legal system be used against itself?

But that may be putting the matter too starkly. These two legal challenges could be atypical, and, for that matter, such legalistic probes may be little more than specific responses to perceived general injustices against all Muslims. If so, then this might all be a passing phase, inevitably giving way to yet another passing phase in the larger drama of Muslims in contemporary Europe.

2007

Related Aphorisms

Culture is a mode of perception.

PLACES IN THE MIND

A FILM IN BERKELEY

Don't know why this memory came back to me so suddenly after many years, so vividly, though its vividness was selective: I can hardly remember the film but do recall the audience.

It was a documentary in a Berkeley movie house about Dutch Trotskyite Sal Santen, a rather slow-moving film with a curious way of withholding important details. The film focused a lot on Santen's mournful face and again and again scanned the railroad tracks traversed by Santen on his way to a reunion with the comrade who had somehow judged him a traitor. Large questions seemed to go unanswered, or at any rate I can't remember the questions or the answers. They had something to do with whether someone's hurt feelings should make a difference in matters political.

The audience was straining for some substance, partly, I guess, because of the difficulty of the subject and partly because the movie was not making it easy for them.

In the midst of this earnest, attentive crowd of about a hundred students and older Berkeley residents sat a young father with his two-year-old child. The child started to whimper, then to fuss, then to whine. The audience began to stir and shift nervously, especially since the whining was rapidly turning to loud wailing.

Much relief was evident when the young father took his child out into the lobby where the noise continued, though somewhat abated. But again the two of them came in, and a good many in the audience turned around, since the young child started screaming as soon as the harried father had sat down, somewhat discreetly, in a far corner of the hall.

By now the tension was palpable. Our enjoyment of the movie, or at the very least our concentration, was seriously jeopardized. Perhaps even more acute was the tension occasioned by a real conflict: the audience, good liberal Berkeleyites, one would gather, could hardly find fault with a young father obviously involved in child care. Aside from that, one glance at him showed a sensitive, vulnerable, though harried, male. For another half hour the audience put up with the waves of noise coming from the rear and strained its attention on poor Sal Santen and his problems. But suddenly the man in front of me half stood up and erupted: "*Out, out, get out.*" Immediately there was a chorus of supportive clapping and yelling, "*Take that child out of here.*" The harried father fled with his child into the night.

But not so fast. Berkeley wouldn't be Berkeley if there weren't some spirited high-level discussion. The young woman three seats over yelled, "*You guys are sure showing compassion,*" and there was a ripple of approval for that. A few others started hissing and there were even a few scattered, half-hearted boos. For a few minutes, the film was forgotten.

But peace returned and we could all get back to the movie. The little drama in the audience had provided a nice counterpoint to the events on the screen, for as little was resolved in the one as in the other: the unsatisfactoriness of all political attitudes stood revealed, as well as the final helplessness of political attitudes in the face of human and circumstantial complexity.

For that matter, remembering the human drama and not the film makes a similar point.

2006

CALIFORNIA: EXCESSIVE BUT COOL ABOUT IT

The other day my San Francisco neighborhood bakery had a sign posted in the window. "$300 Reward—Fifteen-Foot Python Lost Last Month. Don't try to pick him up. Just telephone." Rather casually, it gave the phone number to call if you happened to come across a large and deadly snake.

I couldn't imagine such an event in Helsinki, where even cats must be leashed outdoors. And if by some rare chance it happened, if some wild zoo animal, say, escaped, would the messages have been so casually worded? And could there be such a mellow response (or lack of response) to such a startling announcement?

Once the sign was taken down, I inquired at the bakery. Oh, the snake was not found, but since its mate was still in captivity, the owner was now waiting for her to go into heat and then lure the lost male snake to her.

Isn't that entrapment? I asked.

We laughed. Entrapment has long been a controversial law-enforcement issue. The most celebrated case under debate at that time was of the mayor of Washington, D.C., who for many years was rumored to be a cocaine user. The FBI enlisted a former girlfriend of the mayor to lure him into her hotel room and offer him some crack. He took it. The hidden videotapes were whirring and *presto!* the FBI roared in from the next room and arrested him. Only in America.

Many years ago, the American novelist Philip Roth remarked that satire had become impossible to write in a country where the reality so readily parodies itself. The writer's imaginings paled next to the grotesque actualities which American life so readily provides. In this proclivity for the outrageous, California is in the forefront—but it also has a capacity to be calmly accepting of its extremes.

The incident with the snake brings out that odd sense one has in California of being on the Frontier. The Wild West is never very far away. In a friend's neighborhood in the heart of Los Angeles, coyotes swoop down on sultry nights from nearby towering hills on unsuspecting, well-cared-for pets and devour them. The coyotes' hoarse bark can be heard for miles. What is one to do about it? "Oh, I just keep my cat in every night," said my friend.

Nature in this beautiful state has been eradicated, air-conditioned, freewayed out of existence—but remains untameably present. Neither frost nor blistering heat is tolerated, and yet the long seasonal drought allows sudden firestorms to demolish hundreds of houses overnight. "Climate-controlled" automobiles float through the scenery, but the road to a popular sunbathing beach near San Francisco is again and again buried by landslides. "The road refuses to stay in place," one engineer said dryly.

The state is so large, so prosperous, and so well known that even foreign heads of state recite its proud statistic about being the fifth largest economy in the world. Mitterand came here to visit Silicon Valley, with its microchip and computer industry, and Gorbachev paid a respectful courtesy call. More recently, Tony Blair came. At the last moment Gorbachev canceled a visit to the right-wing Hoover Institution, which has one of the world's great collections of Russian materials and with which, of all people, Alexander Kerensky was associated until shortly before his death in 1970. Kerensky in California—why not?

For me, California's ambience stems less from its wealth, or its innovative industry, or even its Hollywood-induced reputation as the "dream factory," than from its access to a wilder, freer America. Hundreds of thousands of people are said to live in the rugged mountains, without benefit of a Social Security card, income taxes, or even an address. An educated guess about the number of Mexicans living illegally in Los Angeles alone is two million. California is the kind of America that much of America itself no longer quite is, a more unpredictable place, of a more anarchic time. Visiting Europeans sometimes sense the energy of the cowboy movies or, if they're older, the freedom of their childhood Indian books. American tourists likewise notice something different, an easy, glossy surface with a seductive, dangerous stirring underneath. For those of us who live here, it's oddly pleasurable to have that dimly-sensed inner anarchy occasionally reawakened—that common human need to feel, once in a while, that everything is possible.

But the thought of that python on the loose in my neighborhood is not reassuring.

1989

BAUDRILLARD'S *AMERICA*

I have a Dutch friend who doesn't like San Francisco, which reminds him too much of Amsterdam. What's his favorite American city? Dallas!

In his book *America*, Jean Baudrillard calls Las Vegas "sublime," which it probably has never been called before. As for Los Angeles, "The light everywhere reveals and illuminates the absence of architecture. This is what gives the city its beauty, this city that is so intimate and warm, whatever anyone says of it."

This absence of architecture, like the absence of an oppressive past, releases Americans into an unselfconscious freedom of space and action. Baudrillard calls it modernity.

The noted French philosopher—nowadays post-Marxian as well as post-modernist—doesn't look for Europeanness in America. Driving through the United States, he knows that the experience is not in getting out of the car and looking at sights, but in the driving itself. Tourist attractions don't interest him; he takes joy in the ordinary, the everyday. "Where the others spend their time in libraries, I spend mine in the deserts and on the roads."

He is fascinated by the phenomena of America, which, with its signs, gadgets, toys, emblems, and games, is a semiotician's paradise. Baudrillard takes loving notice of breakdancing, the New York Marathon, the way Americans smile, sunglasses, Burger Kings, freeways, the politeness of American drivers, the use of the word "into," and *Saturday Night Fever* in Porterville, California.

Sometimes the book is a poem to America, its beauty, its misunderstood grandeur. In Los Angeles, the freeways have become pure art: "Gigantic, spontaneous spectacle of automotive traffic. A total collective act, staged by the entire population, twenty-four hours a day. By virtue of the sheer size of the layout and the kind of complexity that binds this network of thoroughfares together, traffic rises here to the level of a dramatic attraction, acquires the status of symbolic organization."

Baudrillard doesn't so much interpret as contextualize American phenomena. Since Europeans look with nineteenth-century eyes at a twentieth-century continent—with vision colored by politics, ideology, and history—they are frequently blind to "the perpetual present of signs" and "the revolution of the American way of life" which is utopian and pragmatic.

The American way of life is above all characterized by an easy equality. "Just look at this girl who serves you in the guest-room; she does so *in total freedom*, with a smile, without prejudice or pretentiousness. . . . In America . . . . you are astonished by the almost natural way status is forgotten, by the ease and freedom of personal relations." But in America, what is natural is often, paradoxically, the imposition of artifice on the landscape, and this too Baudrillard admires extravagantly, noting happily "the challenge of all the artificial lights to the violence of the sun's rays." It is this that gives the book occasionally an odd, French-Decadent flavor—despite Baudrillard's strictures against viewing America with European sight—as if Flaubert or Huysmans were driving around the United States looking at supermarkets, watching TV in motel rooms, and gambling in air-conditioned desert casinos.

For Baudrillard the desert is a perfect symbol of the American experience, since he finds significance in surfaces—i.e., in the absence of "meaning" and interpretation. The desert is empty, silent, an extension of the human "capacity for absence." Not only are the towns intertwined with the desert, but the "endless, indifferent cities" are as wild and lacking in history as the desert. As in Los Angeles, "you are delivered from all depth there." This "challenge to profundity" is precisely what characterizes America as a whole—an absence of culture that is thrilling and the essence of modernity.

Baudrillard's writing is so fine, and on the whole so insightful, that one is tempted to accept as poetry what seems weak as analysis. But I have the following small reservations: at times there is so much poetic play, such *jouissance*, that the author runs off the track of sense. At other times he overinterprets. I doubt very much that the bank teller didn't want him to withdraw a large sum in cash because of an

American belief in the "fluidity" of money—the clerk was probably afraid that the professorial-looking foreigner would be robbed of all that cash. Most important, Baudrillard seems unaware of the growing Europeanization of America. Everywhere, even in the untrendy towns of the Midwest, people in coffee houses or sidewalk cafes are eating croissants or sipping wine. The American picnics Baudrillard so lovingly comments on might on closer inspection reveal long loaves of French bread and generous servings of *paté*. Especially in his beloved California, the "boutiquization"—as it has been called—of American culture flourishes. Had he seen it, Baudrillard would unquestionably have regarded it as an anti-modernist sign of a reactionary trend.

America
by Jean Baudrillard
Verso, 129 pages

1989

Columbus

Recently I gave a talk at a Latin American studies conference at a large southern California university campus. The setting for the conference was appropriate. In the brilliant sunshine, students of all races, colors, and creeds abounded; but especially the Latin American look, that blend of Indian and Spanish, was everywhere.

On a bulletin board nailed to a large oak tree, someone had written: "No more Columbus Day. Native American People Stand Up and Be Counted." It is not an isolated sentiment. Some years ago, the Berkeley City Council canceled its October 12th Columbus Day celebration and replaced it with Indigenous People's Day, while in San Francisco, a Columbus Day parade was disrupted by protestors.

The five-hundred-year celebration of Columbus's "discovery" of America had turned into a fiasco. In our current multicultural way of thinking, that word is politically incorrect, for it implies that there was nothing here on this continent, no people of any significance. Columbus's deed was not discovery but conquest, the rape of a continent by a stronger, more ruthless force.

It is a measure of the changes that have taken place in the last few years that this view is becoming ever more widespread. Not only are celebrations being canceled, but textbooks are being rewritten as history is drastically reinterpreted.

But not without a struggle. There are those who say that such revisionism is destructive to America's sense of itself as a Western society and that it violates a fundamental fact. In a recent pamphlet, Professor George Reisman states, "I consider Columbus to be the discoverer not because of any such absurd reason as a preference of Europeans over Asiatics (Leif Ericson was as much a European as Columbus), but because it was Columbus who opened the Western hemisphere to the civilization I have made my own. Columbus was the man who made it possible to bring to these shores *my ideas and values.*"

This spirited defense of Columbus as the bringer of Western values, which include freedom and the respect for human dignity, may be true in the abstract, but it violates one essential fact: Columbus also brought disease, slavery, and the fanatic imposition of one religion on all others. Not for nothing does the brilliant Caribbean writer Jamaica Kinkaid remember as one of her fondest school memories a picture of a disgraced Columbus dragged back to Spain in chains.

Another Caribbean writer, V. S. Naipaul, has argued that rather than evil, Columbus was banal, "looking less for America or Asia than for gold." He was petty, egocentric, colorless. Once having found "the Indies," he indulged, like the fictional Robinson Crusoe, in the "dream of total power."

But here on this beautiful campus in southern California, despite the militant sign on the bulletin board and despite the presence of so many of Latin America's children, there was no great evidence of either Columbus-bashing or consciousness-raising. Our conference covered such topics as the Indians of Nicaragua, the two cultures in Caribbean literature—my subject—and the feminist movement in Mexico; but there was scant interest from the students. They were lounging on the grass, glancing at their textbooks, listening to their transistor radios, talking, and loafing. Their presence has indeed made a difference in American culture, and their history as indigenous people might henceforth be respected—but ultimately, no dramatic turns can be expected, for North American culture will assimilate these changes in perception and presentation, even co-opt them, and, for better or worse, these students will be no different from so many European Americans before them.

That night, most of us conference participants, Anglo and Latin, ate at a Mexican restaurant nearby, where middle-class Mexican Americans celebrated a birthday party with Spanish speeches by the fifty-year-old celebrant's friends and English speeches by the younger generation. Afterwards, some of the guests asked us staid conference-goers to dance.

The guests behaved in every respect like European Americans. No matter how he was being seen now, Columbus had clearly won the day.

1992

LIVING BY THE WORD AND IN THE WORLD

When important novelists publish their essays, they sometimes run into a problem. There is an odd narcissism that lurks in the essay-writing mode. The writer watches herself so fondly, is so lovingly attuned to her psyche, that she shivers with delight at the panorama of her moods and perceptions. It's a problem that occasionally besets even fine essayists like Annie Dillard and Joan Didion. And it seems to lead Alice Walker into a kind of self-indulgence, allowing her to say such embarrassing things as that she had "written [*The Color Purple*] as a gift for the people."

The Color Purple remains Alice Walker's best work and her most controversial. It antagonized many black Americans when it came out some years ago. Mercilessly explicit in its portrait of the way a black man oppressed a black woman, the book seemed an attack against blacks and an appeal to a female audience, whether black or white.

The tendency to go against the black grain is again evident in the present collection. Her spiritual identification with American Indians and her Earth-consciousness are not bound to restore her popularity in the black community, yet she clearly also sees herself as an important black voice. Like the old blues singer who used to come to her rural Southern childhood home to sing and ask for food, like the poet Langston Hughes who lectured and read from his work at Sarah Lawrence when Alice Walker was a promising, much-encouraged student there, she is in the tradition of great black artists.

What she shares with most of them is an abiding aversion to the white man's role in history and his continuing dominance in the present. He is the conqueror, the enslaver, the oppressor of women—and now the despoiler of the environment. In the depiction of this figure she resembles the Romantic poet William Blake, who pictured this tyrannical old man as the embodiment of all that curbs and limits us. Here is how she imagines the rapist of her then eleven-year-old great-great-grandmother: "My image of him at the time—and over a period of years, and still—was of a small, white, naked, pale-eyed, oldish white man. Weak-looking: weak, near-sighted eyes, weak limbs. Ineffectual."

This is the figure that haunts the book, as it does the work of many recent black writers. Blake calls him Urizen, the Restrainer; Alice Walker uses the Sioux word for white man, Wasichu, "the fat taker." Opposed to him is an alternative consciousness, which, she claims, lodges in Third Worlders, American Indians, lesbians, and blacks, especially black women. They are the ones who worship rather than rape the land.

Such a coming together of a black point of view and an Indian consciousness could be fascinating, but unfortunately it's all too simply and crudely put. The Indians whose "light step upon the Earth" Walker admires extravagantly fought innumerable wars against each other, as she admits herself; but she cherishes their reverence for the land. And it is this, in essay after essay, that Walker perceives in—or projects on—all those she favors.

But can such thought ever be more than a mere critique of Western civilization, and by this time a pretty well-worn one? And is there not something sentimental in bunching all these groups together, only because they have all been victimized? "All indigenous peoples are by their attachment to Mother Earth and experience with Wasichus, Conquistadors and Afrikaners, one." Walker does not seem to realize that these days the Third World resists—for good reason—the sort of First World environmentalism she preaches.

If it's a critique at best, then at worst it becomes, however rhetorically accomplished, a kind of California-babble. "Locating the Indian" inside yourself is little better than the still-surviving sixties cliché of "centering yourself." "Alice is like a plant," she quotes a friend as saying about her, and indeed, in an essay called "Everything is a Human Being," she remarks that she was "in intense dialogue with the trees." What would the Nicaraguans, with whom she claims such kinship, make of this comment: "I always think of the place where I work as holy"?

All this is to affirm that Alice Walker's great strength is in fiction. It is also to wish that she had taken her own argument in favor of wholeness and complexity more seriously when she points out to blacks that "crucial to our development... is an acceptance of our actual as opposed to our mythical selves. We are the mestizos of North America. We are Black, yes, but we are 'white,' too, and we are red." For this is a more eloquent statement of our common and flawed humanity than the present collection of short pieces, with its facile divisions and glib distinctions, allows her to show.

Living by the Word
by Alice Walker
Harvest Books, 224 pages

1990

CHANGING PERSPECTIVES IN BLACK AND WHITE

Long before Herbert Marcuse and others made the word "co-optation" fashionable, the concept was well understood—and regarded as a specifically American talent. "If the Yanks can't beat it, they'll join it," an Australian once said to me, "and if they can't join it, they'll put it in a sandwich."

No minority group in America has experienced sporadic co-optation more than blacks. In our century they have occasionally become wildly fashionable. Looking back at the Harlem of the twenties, the black poet Langston Hughes wrote that "the Negro was in vogue." Whites would come to Harlem to cabarets, to places like the famous Cotton Club, to listen to jazz, to dance, to let themselves go—and to watch black people. Parties for socialites and literati were as highly prized in Harlem as they were on the Paris Left Bank of Hemingway and Fitzgerald, and the Jazz Age found a delicious exoticism in the African drumbeats that enlivened the musical scene. While Langston Hughes would sound the note of co-optation and write later on that "You've taken my blues and gone—/You sing 'em on Broadway/And you sing 'em in Hollywood Bowl, /And you mixed 'em up with symphonies/ And you fixed 'em/ So they don't sound like me . . . ." there is little doubt that he and most blacks welcomed this Harlem Renaissance at the time, were hopeful that it would lead to better times—and were proud of the range of black literary talent it revealed.

One such talent was Claude McKay, a Jamaican who came to America at twenty-one, a highly literate adventurer. His *Home to Harlem*, a big best-seller of 1928, presented a world that was nothing if not exotic. The cabarets, the all-night joints, the gambling halls; the drinking and drug-taking; the women who would fight for men and often support them; the primitive vitality of the book's protagonist—all these proved immensely appealing to white and black readers. Though some black critics feared that the book would only confirm white stereotypes of blacks, it remains a major work of black literature.

In most of his books, McKay was a great believer in blacks as life-affirming, immediate, vital, spontaneous—precisely what he felt white civilization was not. This belief has remained a major theme in black literature, down to the present, though it must be admitted that these same views coming from whites would be regarded as questionable and condescending. Perhaps the difference is that whites who remark on the "naturalness" of blacks, wittingly or unwittingly, describe a primitivism that seems a rung lower than the civilization whites have attained, while blacks describe a conscious rebellion against white civilization. The difference is great.

The Harlem Renaissance ended with the Depression, when, as Langston Hughes put it, "the white people had much less money to spend on themselves, and practically none to spend on Negroes . . ." Those black writers who emerged soon after, especially Richard Wright, did not celebrate the vitality of black people and turned more bitterly against a white world that seemed intent on keeping them in childlike servitude. Both in fiction and in autobiography, Wright rails against a white world from which he had been excluded. Though he was a best-selling author, Wright lived in bitterness and exile much of his life.

During the thirties and forties, blacks were very definitely not in vogue, literarily or otherwise. While black music has always been admired in America, from the blues and jazz to soul, black literature is a sometime thing. Wright was respected; and later on in the fifties, Ralph Ellison's *Invisible Man* (1952) was respected; but its hero rejects both the white and black world through which he journeys, and the novel can easily be read as an intensely pessimistic indictment of all humanity. Though the book was an instant classic, Ellison did not reach a truly black audience and did not appear to stir a white audience, and it remains to this day something of a university textbook. Somehow invisibility was the issue for black authors as well as their black subjects.

The late fifties and early sixties changed all that. Perhaps it was again a matter of fashion and ultimate co-optation. Certainly blacks were again "in vogue," but it was infinitely harder for whites to put the likes of James Baldwin and LeRoi Jones in a sandwich. Baldwin, perhaps more than any other black writer, started dissecting the relationship between white and black in the United States. In an early book, most of it written while he was still in his twenties, *Notes of a Native Son* (1955), essay after superb essay reflects on the subtle agonies not only of blacks but of whites who live with the self-imposed blindness and innocence that results from not recognizing the humanity of blacks. In his essay "Stranger in the Village," Baldwin recounts in moving detail how in the Swiss village where he lived for two years, he moves from the agonizing realization that "the most illiterate among them is related, in a way that I am not, to Dante, Shakespeare, Michelangelo, Aeschylus, da Vinci, Rembrandt, and Racine," to a recognition of his authentic relationship to western culture and the celebration of his identity as a black and an American. In the process of laying bare his own pain, he reveals the anguish of whites and credits them with finally realizing that "this world is white no longer."

In the sixties, a writer like LeRoi Jones could hardly contain his irritation with James Baldwin. "Part of every English sentence James Baldwin writes must be given over to telling a willing audience how sensitive and intelligent he is, in the face of terrible odds." In any number of ways, Jones makes the point that, in effect, black writers have allowed themselves to be co-opted, that they have addressed white audiences when they should have written for blacks. And it is this sixties militancy that set the tone for a while: from Jones himself—in 1965 he took the African name Imamu Amiri Baraka—to Ishmael Reed, to any number of younger authors. They wrote about blacks and were not particularly concerned with white psyches. But their anger often seemed to provide white radicals with the emotional fuel their own ideologies needed. In retrospect, one can't help but see that such famous remarks as those of the black leader H. Rap Brown—"The only politics relevant to black people today is the politics of revolution,"—were convenient to white radicals and a feature of the rhetorically picturesque landscape of the time. Were blacks co-opted once again after all?

In the seventies and eighties, things changed. Blacks were not and are not in vogue, and black writing cannot easily be used for political ends. Black writers are in fact addressing blacks, though not in the militant tones of the sixties. They are also addressing whites—and especially women. For the black writers of our own time are predominantly women—Alice Walker, Toni Morrison, Paule Marshall, to name but a few. There is a return to storytelling, a respect for the Southern past, and a reverence for the oral tradition. In Alice Walker's fine story "Everyday Use," the heroine is a mother whose daughter has become fashionably political up North and patronizes both her mother and her unsophisticated sister. She has discovered her blackness and visits her southern home with an eye to retrieving such items as a butter dish, a churn top, a quilt, as quaint *objets d'art*. Above all she can't stand that her mother would put such things to "everyday use."

Walker's sympathies with brave, enduring women is manifestly clear in *The Color Purple* (1982). Celie's survival is emblematic of the survival of black women who have been oppressed by whites as well as by black men. Both the novel and Steven Spielberg's film version were strongly criticized by black critics; but the book is secure as an American classic.

More demanding as a writer and equally gifted is Toni Morrison, whose *Song of Solomon* (1977) was widely praised, while such later novels as *Tar Baby* (1981) and *Beloved* (1987) were received with less enthusiasm. I admire especially an early book, *Sula* (1973), which is almost an allegory of the two ways of being black, the kind, self-effacing, God-fearing way and the unpredictable, selfish, and hedonistic way. Her two female characters both come to harm, neither is wholly admirable, and yet Morrison apparently finds no alternative to these two patterns.

Many black novels and stories have sketched two such paths, though frequently these represent more strictly than *Sula* the bourgeois and the vagabond, the "white" and the "black." It is, to an extent, a reflection of a genuine black dilemma: how to be black in a white world. Often such fiction shows the irreconcilable differences between the two paths and yet the need for their coming together—at the end of *Sula*, such a reconciliation comes in large part because the two main characters are both women. And it is this feminist element in present-day black fiction that seems least likely to be susceptible to co-optation, for it signifies a bond between black women that is wholly outside any uses the white community may have for it. These days it no longer matters whether "the Negro is in vogue."

1992

At Long Last, a Diagnosis: Humor and Satire

At Long Last—A Diagnosis

When I was a small boy and first contemplated that puzzling glass of water—was it half full or half empty?—I instantly felt that, naturally, it was half empty. How could anyone doubt that?

What I didn't know, at the age of five or six, was that I had all the symptoms of "Cheerfulness-, Happiness-, and Optimism-Impaired Syndrome," or CHOIS. That condition, only recently discovered and now fully described in an authoritative book by Drs. Willard Schnitzel, Joanna Drol and Carl Eigenwys, can now justly take its place alongside other recent analyses of what ails so many of us.

Alas, for me the diagnosis came in my advanced maturity. The large cloud hanging over my life would surely have lifted if I had had the Schnitzel/Drol/Eigenwys methods and meds available to me in earlier, unhappy stages of my life. Surely affirming that clouds do have silver linings and that maybe they are lovely when looked at in a certain way—or just taking daily anti-gloom medication—would have made a big difference.

And, perhaps more important, just knowing that I was ill, suffering from a common and pervasive syndrome shared by many, would have helped enormously.

I remember as an adolescent entering a roomful of chatting and laughing fourteen- and fifteen-year-olds. Few kids would talk to me, and the girls, after a few polite remarks, politely fled. At the time I thought the problem lay in my shyness, which made it difficult for me to think of what to say to those beautiful creatures. Or, worse yet, I thought my problem was an unattractive personality.

But now all is clear: I know I was suffering from CHOIS. This widely accepted medical condition is still not perfectly understood. "We can treat CHOIS," says Dr. Susan Candela, a psychologist at

Meadows University in Denver, "but we do not know why it exists. It seems to start in early childhood, possibly as the result of a chemical deficiency."

Other experts have taken strenuous exception to this suggestion and blame abusive or neglectful parents. Still others see a genetic cause. "This condition can reach back many generations," argues Dr. Jonah Smith of Smith/Data/Org, a research center for psychophysical phenomena in Roanoke, Virginia. "I wouldn't be surprised if Thomas Jefferson had CHOIS."

At any rate, if my condition had been recognized and treated, I would have flourished and would by now surely understand that the glass is half full.

I remember at the age of forty being shocked when someone told me I was a gloomy person and looked older than I was. I felt a total failure—angry, devastated, lonely. Without awareness of CHOIS, I simply did not have the tools to fight my situation. I did not know who I was.

Fortunately, though belatedly, I'm happy now. I meet twice a week with about thirty other CHOIS sufferers. Hearing their stories is like filling in the gaps in mine. These meetings are the high point of my week.

I have also started working for the nationwide CHOIS organization: we are in major cities of every state except Texas, and our aim is to have local chapters in small and large communities throughout the country. And we're considering a mass meeting in Madison Square Garden, where people will feel empowered to make a choice for CHOIS.

2005

Rappers No Longer What They Used To Be: A Fantasy

Among the little-noted cultural phenomena of our time is that rap, whether in its "gangsta" or other forms, is no longer confined to certain segments of the population.

"Why should rappers be only young and mainly black?" asked CarltonD, my former colleague in the English department and now several years retired. "You know what I'm saying?"

Some still call him Dr. Drummond, or even Professor, but CarltonD now scorns such titles and even raps about them. "They gave me the fancy name, but on the streets it ain't the same," he chants.

What streets was he referring to, I wondered, standing in his Quintara Street garden, surrounded by neat houses and backyards, looking out on harmless-looking, vacant streets.

"It's Taraval Street, mainly," he mused. "There used to be a hardware store, where there's now a Bakers of Paris. Do you know what that means?"

"Not sure."

"It means," he said with just a touch of exasperation, "they're trying to ghettoize it, make the street like West Portal, upscale." And he pulled up his oversized, baggy pants, perhaps in a hip-hop gesture.

Sometimes he gets together with my other colleagues Rudy and Frank, and they rap about times past. Arms flying, they sing about dean selection committees or budget cuts, "We were soldiers, in those trenches. It don't get worse than having a course cut, when they want your mouth to be shut." At this last sentiment, Frank, who was once a part-time administrator, jabs his thumb into the audience, now composed of one patient wife and myself.

263

Rap, we're always told, gives a voice to the voiceless. It seems that too long the plight of the old, the retired, and the relatively well-off has gone unheard. "They think they can warehouse us," sings CodpieceH, né Rudy, "Wait till we turn Assisted Living on its bad, sad head."

This new underground phenomenon appears to be catching on. Recently the California Teachers Association convention heard a number called, "Do you teach good or well?"

My three friends are hoping to perform in public soon. I suggest they try one of those retirement ceremonies at our university where farewell pieces of luggage are bestowed on deserving retirees.

I still have the tote bag I got, but I do not remember any musical accompaniment.

1998

THE HEARING

Senator: "Welcome, sir. We are convening here to rule on your confirmation. The Senate, as you know, must vote yea or nay on your nomination. We are fortunate to have before us a man of your distinction and experience. Now without further ado, let's get to the heart of the matter."

Nominee: "Thank you for those kind words, Senator. In the interest of brevity, I will forego an opening statement so that I can immediately answer your questions."

Senator: "You have been nominated as director general of a new agency. In your prior position as head of DIS, how did you assess its impact on our national security on the global scene?"

"That takes a bit of background. As head of DIS I first had to deconflict the MOU from the CIA and DOD. That required HiOps activity within IOD and the various QUIs that were out there. Following that lengthy process, DIS was in a position to energize its presence on the world scene as well as disseminate its resources at the service of a larger footprint. All those goals were accomplished, Senator."

"Then would you say you established a successful regional context for these efforts?"

"Absolutely."

"Why, then, did several organs of our government criticize DIS for its failures overseas, such as refusing to admit two years after the fact that the Soviet Union had collapsed?"

"That, Senator, was because we were lacking a cultural context, which of course explains why we need more HUMINTs and have asked Congress for a substantial further allocation."

"Agreed. I've just returned from an overseas visit to several classified nations and have myself questioned some of our brave men and women in the field and can categorically confirm that they all hunger for more HUMINTs. But some of them spoke of allocating those resources to RPP rather than the agency you would head, the RVDS. What's your position on that?"

"Senator, as head of RVDS I would first of all be an enabler, a defender, a champion of protective access. Then I would create a culture of risk-taking and excellence. And to be even more specific about it, I would stimulate an expeditionary mentality, which RPP has not always found it possible to do, given their constraints."

"Yes, those are good, solid plans. Let me turn once again to what some have called failures of planning and intelligence-gathering."

"Senator, having been in government at many levels for twenty-five years, I can only say that we established RVDS with the thought that we must move beyond the archeology of each weakness, the panorama, if you will, of every missionary incompleteness. Suffice it to say now that NNC kicked the classified matter—of which we can't speak here—back to the SYZ people who inevitably INKed it back. Then we drilled a hole and saw how deep it went. The whole matter was worked in a CIA channel as a precursor mode. I'm just giving you the narrative of what happened and how it developed."

"Would you say you had any doubts about the viability of the program?"

"No, Senator. I did not."

"Could you explain to us why that was?"

"Senator, when I first heard from NAD that such a program and such an agency were contemplated, our staff and other experts determined that the plan was viable. We checked with MRD, MIZ, and Q1800. They determined likewise. So I can only say with absolute conviction that there is no question about the viability of the program."

"That's convincing, sir. I am grateful to you for testifying before this committee and thank you for your many years of outstanding service to our country. You have my confidence and my vote. I will now yield the floor to my distinguished colleague from Delaware."

2006

Report from the Future:
Diplomacy and Listening

Since the puzzling lack of success of Karen Hughes, assistant secretary of state (and presidential advisor and confidante), during her trip to Muslim countries, the Bush administration has decided to send another envoy to the Middle East and beyond.

Our sources have learned of a meeting, in a rarely used conference room in the White House, of a small group of policymakers in early January 2006. They urged a more "down-to-earth" envoy, able to speak to the family and religious orientation of audiences, while also young enough to communicate on an almost equal footing with students.

"I'm going to look, study, and listen," announced the newly appointed director for special communications and media, Carlita Myerdale, who heads an advisory panel straddling the Departments of Defense and State. Until her appointment she was the editor and publisher of the suburban *East Texas Weekly*, and she remains a close friend of the Bush family.

Since the major media have not reported widely on Myerdale's recent swing through Muslim lands, here is a brief account of the highlights.

In Cairo, Egypt, Myerdale spoke at length about the underlying values of American policy in the Middle East. After a fifty-minute talk on America's role as a leader in promoting a morality-based foreign policy, she was asked by a member of the audience of academics and diplomats whether the shifting grounds of the rationale for the invasion of Iraq caused her any concern. "Rationale," she replied, "well, our foreign policy tries to be rational. But above all, the purpose of my trip is to look and listen."

She stressed at length the importance of listening for countries, as well as for people.

In Ankara, Turkey, her audience consisted of students, and Myerdale once again underscored the administration's commitment to families as well as education. In this predominantly secular Muslim country, recently roiled by a would-be Islamist movement, one student asked, "Is the United States becoming a theocracy?"

"Yes, indeed, we are a democracy," replied Myerdale, "but my purpose here is to observe, study, and hone my listening skills." Turkish students afterwards commented on her prolonged smiling.

In Islamabad, Pakistan, where she was asked about America's policies toward Israel, a visibly fatigued Ms. Myerdale replied that all people are against war and terrorism—Palestinians, Israelis, and Americans, especially families but single people too. Pressed again about the lack of evenhandedness in the American policy toward Israel and Palestine, she mentioned that she herself had children and quipped, "I think they're beginning to miss their mom." She further stressed that she was not a seasoned diplomat but one who is "able to listen and hear about the concerns of the people of the Middle East" and wants to hear these concerns expressed.

"Pakistan is not generally considered part of the Middle East," one testy diplomat observed.

"Thank you for sharing that," Myerdale replied. "I am happy to hear your concerns."

On her way home, she made a brief stop in Amman, Jordan, where she was asked about United States support for authoritarian regimes. Myerdale noted that "people at the State and Defense Departments work tirelessly, some of us putting in fourteen hours a day, trying to address these problems." She defended the image of the United States by arguing that "imagery has always been important to us."

She further urged her listeners to "join the international community."

Perhaps the only gaffe on this whole diplomatic journey occurred when she referred to "a hundred million Iraqis" having voted, but an aide later explained that she had meant "if you add up the voters in all the various recent Iraqi elections."

2005

A Portrait—and a Question

Last year only one book was printed in Bestaatnietstan, President Abouwe Loleawa's *Bliss: A Book of Columns and Aphorisms for the People*. His most famous saying is frequently cited as an example of great wit: "Men want to look—women want to be looked at."

Each school day in the capital Bontempu begins with a schoolchild reciting one of these sayings, and pupils who write and comment about them are graciously received at an award winners' ceremony in one of President Loleawa's palaces. When one teacher objected that this best-known witticism was "not suitable for children," the People's Correctness Service called on him, and he subsequently disappeared. His body parts were soon after delivered in neatly wrapped packages to his wife and eight children.

Loleawa prides himself on his skill as a writer and occasionally laments that there are so few serious readers in his country. His main palace boasts a good many superb first editions, but there are no public libraries in Bestaatnietstan.

Close associates have seen these treasures and have occasionally whispered about a superb collection of pornographic films in the palace. The president's brother, the country's minister of commerce, owns a chain of video stores, but he is an austere, religious man, who is rumored to look askance at excesses and so rents out pornography to members of the government's inner circle only.

The CIA has learned that President Loleawa supplements his diet with a cocktail of vitamin pills, Viagra, and marijuana, and American diplomats and visiting oilmen have occasionally noted a glittery look in his eyes. He has not been well since he came down with a mysterious disease some years ago—after extensive treatment in Paris and six months in Switzerland, he returned pale and drawn, and his face had a pockmarked look. From that day on he ordered himself called The Handsome One, but some older people preferred to call him The Good One, while still others favored the saltier No Sweat, since the president wore heavy clothing and an Astrakhan hat even in hot summer weather. A well-known underground song goes—and I translate—"Suit from Paris, Hat from Moscow—Where's the Man Himself?"

When the president came to power in a coup, the country seemed to be a bulwark against neighboring Bohabana, which was heavily supported by the Soviet Union. The Cold War over, Bestaatnietstan lost its American support and fell off the map—until oil was found. Now the president presides over a considerable fortune, though his country remains abysmally poor.

His Western advisors urged diversification on him, but so far the only other industry that has taken off is a well-regarded secret police academy. What happened was that during the slump in the country's fortunes, many policemen were dismissed and, with the president's blessing, they established the famous School for Correctness. Many countries now send their best and brightest to this school for training, and at the last graduation ceremony, the president called it "our second greatest national treasure," leaving the notables to guess at the first.

So far, so good. You recognize him.

President Abouwe Loleawa is a not far-fetched composite of people you've heard about. But now for the mystery: who would rather be hated and feared than loved? What is it about such men that makes them reject the love they could get from their people by, say, distributing the oil wealth, or using it for schools and housing and health care?

Surely Loleawa would get more fame, and maybe even more power, by being loved. As it is, he is constantly surrounded by bodyguards and policemen in and out of uniform. He cannot move around his country for fear of being killed. As a beloved figure he would have more freedom, more influence—and a certain fame all over the world. Why does he choose contempt over respect?

I ask the question in all seriousness.

2006

Related Aphorisms

For academics only: life offers many promotions, but
ultimately no tenure.

Conventional Wisdom, No; Common Sense, Yes: Political Notes

Has It Happened Here?

I came to this country as a college student in 1951 from the Caribbean island of Curaçao, where my family had ended up as refugees during World War II.

In the midst of exciting days surrounded by new students, a somewhat new language, a rather unfamiliar culture, I was dimly aware of a malevolent presence. Other students, more politically inclined than I was at the time, were watching the new medium of television in the evenings, and I heard enough to know that a kind of virus was abroad in the land. Senator Joseph McCarthy was making snarling, virulent assertions on the Senate floor, flailing wildly at imaginary enemies and intimidating some of the populace. Fascism, we felt, was raising its head in the United States. Our teachers were warning darkly that It Can Happen Here.

But suddenly, or not so suddenly, it was all gone. We had elections; my own favorite Adlai Stevenson lost, but the newly elected President Eisenhower was able to neutralize the McCarthyite threat. Yes, the Army-McCarthy hearings were a major factor in McCarthy's downfall, but also there seemed to be something in America that righted things when they got out of whack; some sort of inner check to balance mayhem and extremism.

I never thought Americans had much talent for fascism; they seemed too levelheaded, too open- and fair-minded. I realize this was not exactly a sophisticated political position but rather a strong feeling that never quite left me and is still not entirely gone.

Years later I observed a similar pattern. The Civil Rights movement looked hopeless when it started, the South so dead set against granting equality to black people. But the struggle gathered momentum, and then suddenly—or, again, not so suddenly for those who fought in it—was won, and blacks registered in motels in the South, ate in any and all restaurants, and white southerners seemed to accept that. By and large, America had once again righted itself.

During the student movement of the sixties, now a college professor, I took a dim view of students' "non-negotiable" demands, their imprisoning university deans in their offices, and the shrill, emotional calls against "the System." Though opposed to the war in Vietnam, I never saw it and university administrations as part of a similar oppressive system. I now followed politics with the keenest interest but was beginning to think of myself as rather conservative. Long after McCarthyism was dead, I even became a defender of Richard Nixon, whom I had not voted for: impeachment seemed too great a punishment for his petty crimes; the press was ganging up on him; Woodward and Bernstein hid their sources—was that fair?

I've always known that my adopted country has a leaning to hysteria. It's just that the hysteria never seemed to last.

But now I'm not so sure. Maybe It Has Happened Here. Unthinkable, unimaginable, un-American things are being done. Imprisonment of people not charged with a crime or denied access to a lawyer—sometimes American citizens, usually "enemy combatants." New definitions and redefinitions are the order of the day. Torture isn't allowed, but "extreme physical and psychological pressure" is. In other words, torture is redefined, which makes it permissible.

The philosopher Hannah Arendt saw as a central feature of totalitarianism the notion that "everything is possible." There are no constraints. When international treaties and our participation in the Geneva Conventions can be suspended, when the government can review your library records, then indeed almost everything seems possible, and we have to ask ourselves if the dangerous, blurry shores of some kind of totalitarianism, American-style, aren't distantly in sight.

2004

Conventional Wisdom, No; Common Sense, Yes: Why We Should Negotiate with Osama bin Laden and Other Notes

We are always told to think "outside the box," but of course few people do. Governments are often the worst culprits, evidently fearing scorn, disapproval, or at least bewilderment. When they do think creatively, they frequently earn plaudits. Remember Nixon going to China?

Here are a few unconventional thoughts on current issues. In all cases, I think they're sensible, though perhaps unusual.

1) **Bin Laden**. We should negotiate with Osama bin Laden!

"What? What is there to negotiate about? We have nothing to give each other."

Wrong. Negotiating is mainly talking—and talking in this instance would give him some of the stature he craves.

"Would it make him give up his goals—or us ours?"

No, but it might make Al Qaeda less violent. What, I ask you, could possibly be lost?

And while I'm on the subject of talking: we should, of course, also talk to Iran. On the highest levels.

Can anyone really say that the present tough-guy approach is better?

2) **Iraq**. We have to give up the meaningless, preconceived notion that if we withdraw from Iraq, all hell will break loose and "there'll be a bloodbath."

Such notions are reinforced by constant repetition. They are not in themselves valid.

Our departure may or may not provoke a bloodbath. Probably not, since we would remove one major irritant, ourselves.

Most likely, a number of militias will take over, each of them controlling their own turf. That may not be a desirable solution, but it is more desirable than the prospect of more American deaths.

3) **Post-9/11 remedies**. We should now admit that the various solutions that emerged after 9/11 or were offered by the 9/11 commission are worthless.

Creating the Department of Homeland Security was wasteful and unnecessary. That bureaucracy is as likely to get in the way of a rescue as to promote it. I point to the aftermath of Hurricane Katrina.

Similarly, the recommendation for a directorate of national intelligence merely ended up creating another layer of bureaucracy and igniting the inevitable turf wars. Is there any reason to believe that having two super agencies in charge of intelligence improves our security? And what does it gain a CIA director to have one more boss to report to?

This recommendation was rubbish from Day One and should be scrapped. At this writing, the evidence of the inevitable friction between the two directors is all around us.

4) **Forget structural solutions**. Whenever something goes wrong, a commission recommends a restructuring—either FEMA should be folded into the Department of Homeland Security or it should be removed from that department. . . . And so on.

Both have their advantages, but these are never as significant as personnel matters.

Anyone who has worked in any organization knows that a handful of extraordinary people is surrounded by a small army of, shall we say, ordinary workers. The competent people keep the organization going; the others have meetings and eat lunch.

There are enough people in most existing structures to manage a disaster as well as possible. Tinkering with the structure will accomplish nothing.

2006

The Democratic Party and the Culture Wars
(Co-authored with Mark Peattie)

So often the Democratic party is said to do best when it avoids extremes, in effect when it's not dominated by left-wing politics. But this desired centrist movement is ill defined, and because of that ambiguity, the Democratic party is faced with the difficulty of finding a voice and a vision. Tolerance on some of the volatile social issues of our day is commendable, but if the Democratic party gets unwittingly caught up in the culture wars, it will fall victim to them and will remain out of national office.

For many workers in Detroit or farmers in Nebraska—or even city sophisticates in San Francisco or Boston—news that kids are ordered to wear helmets on jungle gyms, or that California wanted to give drivers' licenses to illegal immigrants, or that two gay men in Massachusetts may get a chance to marry each other, evokes a sense of indignation. Actually, these matters are no business of theirs and have no impact on their lives, but, rightly or wrongly, they are appalled. They see it as part of a trend in this country, a growing slackness, a breakdown of standards, a weakness. When they feel that way, they're probably going to vote Republican.

Are you upset by misogynist lyrics in rap songs? Are you against senseless lawsuits, obsessions with political correctness, and, yes, do you have misgivings about gay marriage? These are cultural issues that ought not to be subject to left or right appropriation and certainly should not define progressive politics.

The fact is the Democratic party seems tormented by cultural issues that weaken its appeal for the majority of Americans, and the Republicans, without firing a shot, are the immediate beneficiaries.

We hold that chances of getting universal health care, or a more decent wage, or keeping a job would probably be much better under a Democratic administration, but people do not necessarily vote their own self-interest. Most vote their emotions even more than their self-interest.

Never mind that most Democrats are probably also relatively conservative on cultural issues. It's the Republicans who are seen as safeguarding common sense norms and traditional values.

It is time for the Democratic party to recognize and address this problem. It is time for Democrats to reserve the right to be politically liberal and culturally moderate.

Only by making a clear distinction between cultural issues—on which honest men and women can disagree—and the great Democratic tradition of political and economic liberalism will the Democratic party be able to bring back those Democrats who have deserted them in the past for the likes of Reagan and Bush. Once it does so, it can bind its energies to those core issues that are more than ever central to the public's well being: a truly equitable system of taxation; an end to the flow of jobs overseas; and health care for all.

The Democratic party is the party more likely to make good on all those issues. Who can deny the triumphs of the New Deal, the Fair Deal, and the other milestones of the Democratic tradition? And who cannot remember that President Clinton tried, however clumsily, to bring universal health care to all the people?

Our prescription is not for underscoring Clintonian centrism or electing a Bush Lite. On the contrary, the party should hit hard on all those political inequities that have grown worse in the last three decades and alarmingly worse in the last few years. But it cannot allow itself to fall victim to all those issues in which it is inevitably in the minority.

2004

WHERE THE RIGHT GOES WRONG

In the fall of 2000, a good friend was convinced that her small, working-class town would vote for Gore, not Bush. "After all," she said, "these are working people, with not much money. They know the Democratic party is better for the common people."

Don't bet on it, I thought. People don't vote their self-interest. More often, they vote their emotions.

Liberals rarely understand why there's such an emotional pull to the right in this country. All sorts of issues lend almost automatic support to the right. Crime? Of course—we're letting too many criminals go free. Of course—the values of this society create wrongdoing and wrongdoers.

Crime, immigration, education, political correctness—these are all issues that draw ordinary citizens toward the right. For every person who believes poverty causes crime, there are probably five who think laxity—whether personal or societal—does.

The whole grab bag of political correctness is almost universally disliked. Whether it's diversity training or sensitivity enhancement or any other psychobabble delineation, people largely (but privately) scoff at it.

Liberal solutions are distrusted. If you think allocating more funds for schools improves education or having more psychologists in prison mitigates criminal behavior, you're in the minority. And if liberal solutions are distrusted, liberals are seen as soft-headed or foolish.

Conservatives perceive liberals as taking all these assumptions on faith and not questioning their beliefs. But, of course, conservatives take a whole lot of things on faith too—and look away from a great many others.

Conservatives have an unquestioned belief in authority. They say they believe in the Constitution, but they tend to overlook those provisions protecting minorities. They dislike government but worship institutions. Their take on tradition is that it is inevitably good. They have a strong desire to comfort the rich and powerful. Success is seen as a mark of virtue. Traditional values are seldom questioned. Change is unwelcome. New ideas are derided.

And when it comes to power, conservatives can quickly become radicals. When that happens, the Right will sooner or later squander the enormous good will it has garnered. Instead of being bound by the laws they say they admire, conservatives may end up justifying power grabs that violate these laws.

Have we seen this under Bush Jr.? Whereas Reagan, Nixon, and even Bush Sr. moved toward the center, Bush Jr. and his people careened to the right and beyond. Before September 11 and after, they have acted like radicals and not conservatives. They have dismissed the rules conservatives have aspired to live by, the national structures and the international frameworks their predecessors had set in place, and they are in danger of elevating authority figures above the law.

Consciously or unconsciously, theirs has been a betrayal—and not least a betrayal of the Right.

2002

What Makes for Successful Political Speech?

Many politicians habitually employ the language of distance. Their rhetoric is abstract, detached, cliché-ridden. They sound patently insincere, even when they're not. People may end up voting for them, but that doesn't mean they like them.

When a more authentic politician comes along, the voters will quickly abandon the dull, evasive, gray babblers and turn with relief to someone who speaks directly. Quite understandably, ordinary citizens do not feel anyone who can't speak TO them can actually speak FOR them.

Most recently, President Clinton maintained his high popularity through thick and thin because he had this gift of authenticity.

As far as I can judge, Tony Blair has it. He sounds as if the answers he gives to questions are his. Like him or not, he appears genuine.

The most authentic politician I can recall was President Kennedy. He was funny, direct, and looked you in the eye. To see him was to be persuaded he had something to say to you. Of course he used speech writers, but he made those speeches sound as if they came from his own heart and head.

In the United States, "scripted" politicians are sometimes elected, but they are never liked. My foremost example is Al Gore. So careful were his handlers, so fearful was he of making a misstep, that he sounded constricted and false even when he was telling the truth. He could not be himself, so a lot of people concluded he had no self, that he was the perfect product of a "Washington culture."

Asked whether Social Security should rely on stock market investments, he was not able to say, "Look at the stock market. It's not doing well. Would you really want your retirement money there?"

Instead he came out with a lot of figures and statistics that put people to sleep.

After beauty consultant Naomi Wolf recommended to Gore that he wear natural "earth" colors and work on his body language, his suits looked better, but his gestures became even more studied and weird. I sometimes wonder if the inappropriately long kiss he gave Tipper at the Democratic National Convention in 2000 was not an attempt to "be natural."

Other American politicians come to mind: Walter Mondale, who sounded as if he had swallowed his briefing books and only imperfectly digested them; Dukakis, who was unable to say, in response to a hypothetical question, what he'd like to do to a man who raped Mrs. Dukakis. Many others.

Jimmy Carter sounds real now. But he used to seem hesitant, evasive, indirect, even while he promised us he would "never lie" to us.

All this is not to say that style matters and content does not. Of course what politicians say is important, but whether they're running for national office or want to represent a district in San Francisco, they should avoid prefabricated language and say what they think. Then they have a real chance of sounding genuine and being credible.

My readers will wonder, What about Bush?

His case is complicated. Because he so obviously believes the few formulas he endlessly reiterates, he manages to sound, to his followers at least, extraordinarily believable. Paradoxical, I know, but true, alas.

2002

LIES, LIES, LIES

In our impatient, sound-bite age, oddly unsophisticated and prissy, we often hear lies and liars condemned. Everybody is quick to point the finger, though few are eager to examine themselves and their own lies.

I too hate liars, but I have to admit that many sins are committed in the name of truth-telling. The other day in "Dear Abby" I read about a young husband who, before his marriage, had an affair with the mother of his wife-to-be. From the moment she heard about it, decades later, the wife could no longer bear to look at her mother. It does not take much imagination to see that she could probably no longer look at her husband also and that her marriage is in deep trouble. She may well lose the two people closest to her.

And why? Because someone in a moment of foolish truth-telling informed her of the affair. It seems to me that even if the wife had found out on her own, she would have been much better off being lied to than told the truth. Both husband and mother should have denied it all.

I realize this is not a classic case, and not a classic lie. But what lie is? Are there ever classic lies?

Take one of the most famous lies of all, the one Bill Clinton told. Of course, he concealed his relationship with Monica from his wife. Wouldn't you?

But the minute you say this, people respond, "Yes, but he lied to the whole country."

Sure he did—and so would I if I had been in his shoes.

Even aside from the fact that it wasn't the whole country's business, lying to the country was the right and proper thing to do. He had made a bad mistake, but he could only compound it infinitely by announcing, "Yes, I had sex with that woman. And what's more, she is an intern."

Nothing would have been gained, and he—and the country—would have looked foolish. That it came out by dribs and drabs is bad enough.

Now let's go to another politician's lie. It is now abundantly clear—to those who weren't clear about it all along—that George Bush twisted, exaggerated, distorted, and manipulated the threat coming from Saddam Hussein. He wanted to go to war with Iraq in the worst way—whether for revenge, oil, spleen, rearranging the Middle East, whatever—and he couldn't bear to have the facts stand in his way.

So why does that lie matter, and Clinton's not? Simple—because it affects millions of people, the lives of young men and women he sent "into harm's way," the credibility of the United States, and possibly the stability and security of the whole world.

At least one measure of a lie's wickedness is its effect. There are times to lie and times to speak the truth, but a lie can never be excused when it causes harm.

Of course, the people who excuse Bush's lies think the overall effect was well worth it. They use a similar argument.

While history will be the final judge, of course, let me just add that history has never been kind to those who have been utterly self-deluded. If you lie, at least have the grace to know you're doing it—those who don't, I believe, stand little chance of ever being exonerated.

2003

STALKERS AND TERRORISTS: THE
EMOTIONAL CONNECTION

"Remember, exactly five years ago, we walked to the ocean from your house on that beautiful evening? It was my greatest experience in years."

I scarcely remember the evening, don't know when it was, but remember enough to be sure that we didn't walk to the ocean and may just have talked about it.

My acquaintance was using the language of lovers. After all, lovers heighten their beginnings, suffuse them with possibilities and romance, and if they distort these a bit from the point of view of rosy hindsight, so be it, that's part of their intimacy.

Even parents and children heighten the past. It's a way of saying, "You're deeply important to me." These utterances "sacralize" the bond between them.

But here, the context was different: there was no bond to strengthen, certainly not a mutual one. Here the remark was meant to signal a strength of feeling; it sought to create, forcibly, a change in our cool and distant relations and make them warmer, more intense.

And it was a kind of emotional blackmail. Now I was supposed to answer in kind, with a similar emotionality. I could now be forced to feel the intensity. It's what linguists call a "performative" statement—it seeks through words to bring about a new situation, a reconstituted reality.

This exchange is, of course, intrinsically un-important, and I do not want to load it down with over-interpretation. But it is fascinating for the dynamic it shows. When that dynamic is played out, and its feelings are revealed, they are close to those involved in stalkers and stalking.

I'll go even further. Gestures of this sort, as I now see it, amount to a kind of emotional terrorism.

Terrorists, too, want to be recognized—and they too create a relationship that doesn't exist, or exists only in their minds. Feelings are for them the great facts they insist must be acknowledged. In the process, they forge—in both senses of the word—a relationship.

So the act of terror is a kind of clamor for attention, at the same time that it seeks to create what was there only on one side, in the attacker's psyche.

Terrorists, like stalkers, say in effect, "If you can't notice me this way, I'll see to it that you'll notice me that way!" Like stalkers, they suffer from being spurned and have now found a way to make themselves visible, inescapable, and emotionally ever-present. You can never again ignore them.

Whether impelled by love or rage, they cannot accept neglect or indifference. There is the same inflated experience of past grievances, the same desire for more connection than exists.

"This is a blow against those who launched the Crusades," say the Jihadists. Sure, but we don't remember the Crusades, barely know about them, and actually couldn't care less. Now, of course, we know; we've been jolted into recognition, aware at last.

The ends of terrorism are not strategic but emotional. Their aim is to redress a balance and create an indelible connection.

The inherent gesture is more than a criminal act, more than a statement, more than a message. Its aim is that of the spurned lover: see me, hear me, feel me; you will never escape me.

Terrorists will continue to stalk us, and give up only when stalkers give up: with the advent of a new passion.

2007

Human Behavior and Foreign Policy: A Parallel

Political scientists hate it when people compare human behavior to that of nations. But I feel otherwise. Occasionally, there are striking parallels.

Human beings have an extraordinary capacity to invest certain things with extraordinary importance. When you're in love, few other things matter. When you dislike someone, that dislike is not only with you much of the time, but you advance many reasons to bolster and enlarge it.

When you perceive your self-interest threatened, inevitably you dwell on the threat.

But then, explicably or inexplicably, you lose interest. Your beloved marries someone else (or you marry her). Or the person you dislike leaves town, or his presidential term is finally, thank God, over. Or you now define your self-interest as being threatened by someone else.

These concerns are suddenly forgotten, ignored, "demoted" as preoccupations.

All this we know well enough. It's part of what's laughingly called the human condition.

But, I submit to you, this is what happens in foreign affairs as well. Then it's not a laughing matter but almost a form of collective hysteria.

We went into Vietnam because "vital interests" were at stake. Communism had to be halted somewhere. Remember?

In the sixties and seventies lots of people (not just LBJ) claimed we had strategic interests there, insisted we did, and few even in the political science establishment said we didn't.

Even those who never believed in the domino theory felt that the fight against communism made Vietnam an important front line. And what happened? After we pulled out, it suddenly wasn't strategically important anymore. Over a decade before the fall of communism, we abandoned the fort—and weren't overrun.

Nothing much happened (except to the Vietnamese and, alas, the Cambodians).

Something similar will take place after Iraq, even though we do have strategic interests in the Middle East and we didn't in Vietnam.

Am I saying that there are no problems other than those we define as problems?

No, of course not.

I am saying that we consider some problems important, while others just like them are ignored. We consider some crucial and vital to our interests, and a few years later, with little change in the picture, we ignore them.

After we leave Iraq there may be all sorts of chaos there—though perhaps less than anticipated, since we probably are one of many militias and would then be gone—but things will not be much worse for us and probably the world. There will still be the need to buy oil (but the Iraqis will have the need to sell it)—and there will still be the problem of their possibly exporting terrorism.

It's likely that the victorious Shiites would eliminate Al Qaeda and establish an Iran-style government. How much terrorism does Iran export? It has an obnoxious regime, hostile to us, but there's no evidence whatsoever that they send their agents throughout the world.

A nuclear Iran is a problem, sure, but a nuclear Pakistan is a greater problem, for reasons that are obvious (proximity to the Taliban, presence of many radicals inside Pakistan, instability, etc).

But we define Iran's nuclear potential as a great danger, and we don't talk about Pakistan, because we are friendly with its leader—and hope for the best.

We elevate the status of one and drop consideration of the other. After the regime changes, or we lose interest, the problem is then "demoted" or ignored.

I'm not making some frivolous comment about "having a problem only if you think you do," but making a serious point, based on observation.

You can be sure that after we leave Iraq, you'll hear little about Iraq's "strategic importance."

New problems will then be invested with new significance.
2008

Where I Stand on Israel

My cousin in New York described my views on Israel to a friend as "pro-Palestinian." My brother thinks they're "far to the left, even of National Public Radio." I've also been told that my proposals, were they enacted, would weaken Israel.

On the contrary, I see them as a way of saving Israel.

My prescriptions are based on common sense. It is better for two states to live side by side as independent though angry neighbors than as hostile entities occasionally marauding into one another's territory. In order for such an accommodation to happen, the two states must both be viable. Even so, there may still be some terrorism—but it will be distinctly less. Extremist groups like Hamas will still strike out, but they will have less support. The proposals I make are for lessening hostilities and casualties, not eliminating them.

It is nonsense for Israel to expect the Palestinians to settle for a noncontiguous territory dotted with Israeli "settlements." There can be no solution if Israel does not abandon all settlements, legal and illegal, on the West Bank. Successive American governments have called the Israeli settlements illegal—unfortunately, our governments have done nothing to enforce their judgment.

(I would propose that some of these settlements serve as townships for returning Palestinian refugees, but that should be left to the rulers of the new Palestinian state.)

What former Prime Minister Ehud Barak offered President Yassir Arafat at Camp David and later at Taba in 2000 was not a viable Palestinian state. Under that plan, Palestinian towns and villages would be ringed by Israeli service roads.

Arafat was no statesman. Even though it was a bad deal, he should have accepted it—and then started pushing to have it changed, with the help of the European Union or the United Nations, or whoever. Instead, he just said "No."

It is to the credit of the Bush administration that it helped elevate Mahmoud Abbas to the presidency of Palestine. He is clearly a credible negotiating partner.

Meanwhile, the Bush administration has weakened its hand by its pointless war in Iraq. This invasion has accomplished nothing for the United States and nothing for Israel. Even if the U.S. government got its wish and a happily democratic Iraq arose from the ashes of Saddam's bestial regime, would such a democracy in an Islamic state be any friendlier toward Israel?

And because the United States is now preoccupied with Iraq, it cannot do in Israel what needs to be done: impose a settlement, preferably one that will make both sides unhappy, including provisions for a shared Jerusalem and a monetary swap for the Right of Return. The United States would also have to provide troops as buffers between the two neighboring states. But these troops are now in Iraq.

What I am suggesting does not differ overmuch from what any number of American Jewish groups have been recommending for years. From Rabbi Michael Lerner's Tikkun to the nationwide Brit Tzedek movement, these are commonplace prescriptions. To call them "left-wing" is a convenient evasion.

I say this to my relatives, and for that matter to the larger American Jewish community. Only such compromises will allow Israel to live. If, on the other hand, the Likud and its adherents—whether of the American or Israeli variety—persist, they will ultimately ensure the complete and utter destruction of the state of Israel. No force, no weaponry, no fortress-like embattlements will allow it to survive indefinitely.

2003

CHRISTMAS THOUGHTS ON PEACE AND WAR

What could be more fitting in the holiday season than some reflections on peace and war? Peace is always talked about, longed for, stated as a goal, aspired to as an ideal, and never more so than at the end of the year. But is it really understood? Do people know the causes of peace?

My own view is that people want peace, sure, but they want it so much on their own terms that, in effect, they don't really want it. Meaning that they're so intent on getting their own way they're far readier for war than they know—ready for hurt, anger, hostility.

Similarly, when nations cannot accept feeling thwarted, diplomacy fails and peace falters.

As evidence, here are a few perspectives based partly on the war in Iraq.

1) Despite the lust for planning, rehearsing, and "gaming" possible scenarios, and despite this having been a war of choice, the decision to go to war was emotional rather than rational. The president and his people just wanted to.

2) This war has failed, at least in part, because the "deciders" did not really know the enemy. And they did not want to learn. Their eagerness for war made them ignore all manner of expert advice. In international affairs, cultural ignorance, or innocence, or naiveté, is almost always punished.

3) However flimsy the reasons for going to any war, many people will support it. The joy in a good fight is so great, the expectation of a kind of emotional cleansing so strong, that many people will lose all scruples in the face of it.

4) Once a war is launched, its pleasures and excitements—at least initially—will inflame even peaceful people. That will change only when the war goes badly. *Then* peace becomes ardently desired.

5) How is peace created and maintained? By tolerating dissatisfactions and making endless attempts to adjust one's desires to the exigencies of other people's, or other countries', realities. Peace is often not a happy-making condition—in fact, peace often feels cowardly.

"Why have an army if you can't use it?" famously asked President Clinton's secretary of state, Madeleine Albright, of then–chief of staff General Colin Powell. (Contrary to their present anti-war utterances, a few years later both Albright and former UN ambassador Richard Holbrooke waffled when Bush started promoting his Iraq war.)

6) Diplomacy is widely misunderstood. It's not only a process of endless hairsplitting and the hammering out of agreements, which may or may not hold, but it also requires dissembling, flattery, ego building, and bribery. Henry Kissinger is alleged to have relayed the Israelis' great admiration for the Syrians, and vice-versa, when he created the Golan Heights agreement. That agreement has now held for over thirty five years.

In the public arena, as well as the personal, emotional bonds, ties, vanities, or embroilments often trump self-interest. For that reason alone, President Bush and Secretary of State Condoleezza Rice should answer the letters of Iran's President Ahmadinejad. Such a correspondence could create opportunities for forging these bonds.

Would wise, peace-loving leaders ignore such opportunities?
2006

RELATED APHORISMS

Tolerance thrives on indifference.

Fanaticism is emotional literal-mindedness.

Rage is the last refuge of the ineffectual.

The love of peace is complicated, the love of war simple.

Who are Heroes? Confronting the Holocaust and 9/11

COMING TO TERMS WITH THE HOLOCAUST

When World War II ended, I was ten years old. Before me lay the promise of adolescence; behind me was a horror so vast and incalculable that it warded off all comprehension.

If I thought about the war at all during my adolescence, it was with a kind of nameless shame. We Jews had been the victims of an unprecedented massacre. And our powerlessness was almost obscene.

True, there was cause for pride in my immediate family's escape from occupied Europe. Almost two years after the Nazi takeover, we fled Holland, making our way slowly across Western Europe. In December 1942 we left Portugal for South America.

But to think even about this victory over circumstance was to invite pain, for the thought of escape led irresistibly to the millions who had not escaped.

And it was easy in those years after the war to think about other things. We lived comfortably enough on the Dutch island of Curaçao, off the coast of Venezuela. I went to school there and had a normal schoolboy's interests.

When I came to an American college in 1951, the subject of the past rarely came up. Though I went to an essentially Jewish university (Brandeis), the Holocaust was mentioned in those years only in courses on fascism and other totalitarianisms. That suited my mood of avoidance perfectly.

During the ensuing years, as a young husband and father, a college teacher in San Francisco, an aspiring literary critic, I rarely dwelled on my past, except in moments and hours of unspeakable pain that welled up unbidden, inappropriate and unwelcome.

I was still preoccupied with family, career, the future, when my father settled in San Francisco in the seventies. But his own obsessive dwelling on the tragedy that struck his people and his family—he lost his parents and six brothers in the Holocaust—reached down inside of me to what had so long been shut away. After his death, it was as if I took over his mourning and his grief.

Not that I was a great believer in the personal benefits of "bearing witness." The events of those wartime years are so huge, so devastating, that to think about them and to feel them fully is certainly to be destroyed. They simply cannot be assimilated, and the psychological truism which holds that traumas must be faced and confronted before they can be healed withers in the face of their enormity.

My unwilling return to the past, quickened by my father's death, was accelerated by a trip to Israel. I did the tourist rounds of that sad and beautiful country but could not bring myself to visit Yad Vashem, the Holocaust Memorial in Jerusalem. It was difficult enough to face the shards and splinters that were everywhere: the account in the Jewish Historical Museum of the mother whose blood-curdling scream unsettled even the SS when they shot her children before her eyes; the living memories of the people I met who referred in unfinished sentences to parents, friends, relatives, "lost in the war," or "disappeared," or "never came back."

Some inevitable process of acutely painful personal reminiscence had begun. It was further prodded by a sympathetic editor who wanted me to write the story of my family's escape for the *Reader's Digest*. I set down the events of our flight as plainly as I could: how a young Dutch cop tipped us off before we were to be deported; how a farmer walked us across the border into Belgium; how we met my uncle—later to perish in Auschwitz—in Brussels; how we ended up in Besançon and crossed illegally into unoccupied France with a refugee-smuggler; how we lived almost euphorically in Nice in the summer of 1942 and scurried to Monaco when its prince declared that no one would come to harm there; how we were promptly arrested for deportation by the Vichy French police, who had swept into Monaco; how we were released, only because my mother's excellent French persuaded the officer in charge that he had overlooked a technicality; how we fled hysterically to Perpignan and scrambled for all sorts of papers and documents and visas for Spain; and how we finally sailed from Portugal to freedom in South America.

I could never understand where we got the documents that allowed us to flee to Spain three days before the Nazis swallowed up unoccupied France as well. Now, in a relentless pursuit for the article,

I was reminded by my older brother that a mysterious figure, a young Jewish Dutchman named Sally Noach, had given us the papers.

Noach was an extraordinary and heroic man. Somehow he was able to act as a kind of unofficial Dutch consul in Lyon and gave documents and all manner of papers to practically all comers. He even supplied documents to refugees of newly set-up internment camps and then persuaded the Vichy French authorities, who worked closely with the Gestapo, that they had mistakenly arrested non-Jews. Finally, Noach himself had to run for his life, escaping to Spain and then to England.

In hearing from family friends and reading about Sally Noach's life, I found some relief for the gloom that had swept over me. It had always seemed to me that our own escape to freedom had been accidental, a fluke, a combination of several strokes of luck. And of course it was. But I now saw that it was also due to the courage of that man—and the generosity of the cop who had warned us, and the ingenuity and persistence of my parents. Some effort, some initiative, could evidently, sometimes, ward off disaster.

But my gloom continued. Suddenly, belatedly, now in the early eighties a movie here, a TV documentary there, retold, discussed, analyzed, some bit of horror about the Holocaust. Surely I could not rejoice at *our* escape or permit myself any ease in thinking that *my* children would never experience a similar catastrophe, for the children I just happened to read about, in yet another magazine or newspaper article, on whom grisly medical experiments had been conducted and who were hanged in Hamburg just before the Allies came, were as deserving of life and happiness as I, a survivor, had been and as my children are. Nothing could lessen the pain of those children's deaths—no words spoken, no consolation uttered. And no hopeful lesson drawn from the courage of some could equal the despair I felt for those children's senseless suffering.

I knew their lives to have been as real as mine is, even if I could conveniently push aside that knowledge in the busy absorption of day-to-day living. And to compound the horror of that thought: if the children of others were as real as mine, what about the children who were dying right now, at the torturers' hands in so many countries? Was that to be accepted?

Yet from that thought came a circuitous comfort. Those children were here now, still—some of them—subject to our help. If somehow their suffering could be lessened, through some word or deed, through money, food, the writing of one letter or a thousand letters—from the easiest volunteer work to the ultimate sacrifice of one's own health and liberty and life—then something could still be wrested from the forces of chaos and evil. It was, after all, what Sally Noach had done. It was what Raoul Wallenberg had done on a much more massive scale. And it was what thousands had done—and are doing now.

That thought, more than any other, has the power to make the past a little less my enemy.

1985

A Second-Generation Holocaust Story

AMSTERDAM—There are still some survivors in this city, and then, of course, there are the children of survivors.

I heard the story of one of those children. Frank, now in his fifties, rarely talks about it himself; but I was told by his close friend about Frank's parents, who somehow made it through the war and narrowly escaped being deported to a concentration camp.

Frank's German-Jewish mother arrived in the Netherlands in the thirties. She had been a young opera singer in Germany, the country she considered hers until Hitler came to power. In the Netherlands she performed in cheap clubs to support herself and then married a Gentile Dutchman so she wouldn't be sent back to Germany by the Dutch.

It was not a happy marriage, but it saved her life. She stayed in the Netherlands, and when the Germans occupied that country in 1940, they left her alone because she was married to a non-Jew. Toward the end of the war, they changed their minds and grabbed wives of "Aryan" husbands too, but she had gone into hiding in a friend's cellar.

She fell ill after the war and became an invalid. The horrors she endured may have led to her disease—or not. She may just have been unlucky.

But this is Frank's story—a classic second-generation Holocaust story.

He has spent his adult life trying to create order out of the chaos and dreadful unhappiness of his childhood. His parents, like many survivors, brooded about the past and not much else.

Frank now lives in a tiny Amsterdam apartment but has somehow acquired a small house. For eight years he has been fixing it up. The friend who told me the story said he readily admits to wanting to create order and harmony by way of this new house. It can somehow stand as the opposite of everything he has known. The symbolism is clear even to him.

But of course, the house will never be ready. Nothing can be created to stand against the chaos he has known. Nothing like what happened can ever be set right.

Besides, if it somehow could, if he could ever really finish the house, he would feel much too guilty to live in it. The second generation has survivors' guilt as great as the first.

Why should the second-generation survivors have escaped that? Not only can't they create whole lives, they don't believe they deserve to.

That aspect of the story may or may not be clear to Frank.
2004

ON THE DEATH OF HELEN COLIJN

Recently I got word of the death of Helen Colijn in the Netherlands, and it made me think back to that time in the eighties when, for a year or two, I spoke to Helen regularly, visiting her in her small, oddly isolated house in the hills outside of Stanford University.

An editor at the *Reader's Digest* had suggested I talk to her about her story and that of the women who formed a vocal orchestra in a Japanese prison camp in Indonesia during World War II. I remember being slightly reluctant to talk to her. My own wartime experiences were then, as they are now, and will always be, undigested, and I did not really want to revisit that dreadful time, though I had myself thought about it, written about it, and of course read about it at great length.

But Helen's story took place at the other end of the earth and was a "good" story, a victory over adversity, of hope over unrelenting misery, and I wanted to write it. Besides, I became fascinated with a phenomenon present in many survivors, a growing obsession with what she lived through, an ever deeper absorption in what was terrible then but over time had become the central experience of her life.

The events were these: after the Dutch East Indies were overrun by the Japanese in early 1942, Helen and four hundred women and children—Dutch, Australian, British—were imprisoned until 1945. In one wretched camp after another, the prisoners, though starved and frequently mistreated by the guards, formed an orchestra of voices, humming symphonic music reconstructed by the musically gifted among them. Whether performing Dvorak or Schubert, they looked forward to the concerts, were sustained by them, and even got the guards to listen. By the end of the war, half of the singers had died.

The writer Renate Rubinstein, herself a survivor, once observed that as we get older we find it more difficult to push away our recollection of that time. Far from getting used to it, absorbing it, or assimilating it, we actually become ever more incapable of coming to terms with such horrors as concentration camps or the genocide of millions.

Afterwards, in the course of peacetime living, the war became Helen's pivotal experience. The desire to forget, which of course she felt at first, the rewards of a career in her new homeland America—the good things life could still offer—she saw as small and insignificant compared to the enormity of what she had been through.

When in 1980 Helen's sister Antoinette gave a copy of the camp choral arrangements to Stanford University, it opened the door for a series of reunions, performances, records and CDs. My article, "A Song of Survival," appeared in the Dutch, Belgian, Australian, and South African editions of the *Reader's Digest* in the late eighties. Helen's book, *Song of Survival: Women Interned*, came out in 1997, as did the film about these experiences, *Paradise Road*, starring Glenn Close. Helen was, of course, deeply involved in all these endeavors.

Inevitably, the mind stylizes crucial events, hones away what appears extraneous, sharpens certain occurrences. It's what memory does, and what, of course, the creation of art encourages. Her memory crystallized experience, and she then shaped it into something meaningful. Ultimately the two, experience and art, became one for her. It was either that, I suppose, or fall victim to her obsession and perish by the experience. In that sense, she triumphed over pain a second time, her stubborn defiance of misery making her reenact inside herself the transfiguration that had taken place in the camps.

It could only have been done by a hard-edged, sensitive spirit.
2006

Personal Observations on Paul Verhoeven's World War Two Film, *Black Book*

In late 1942 when I was seven, my family lived in southern France, then not yet occupied by the Nazis but run by the collaborationist Vichy regime. We had fled Holland months earlier, crossing borders illegally, in mortal peril of being arrested and deported by the Germans. Such crossings required documents, travel permits, valid passports, identity cards, endless "papers," most of which we did not have.

In unoccupied France, help was hard to come by, as was reliable information. Fortunately, my father heard about a man who worked in the Dutch consular office in Lyon. His name was Sally Noach.

Noach was a Dutch Jew, who, in an improvised act of resistance, volunteered his services to the honorary consul of the Netherlands, Maurice Jacquet. The latter, a defiant, brave French businessman, allowed Noach to pass out any document he wanted to.

To make the next jump from France to the relative safety of Spain, we needed an all-important document, which we hoped Noach would give us.

"But," said my father, "this gentleman won't do much unless he gets a present." And he proudly showed off a handsome black briefcase he had somehow procured on the black market.

My father may have grasped something important about Noach. He was an honorable man, who helped hundreds of refugees, a genuinely good man, but he had his opportunistic side and his motives were sometimes mixed.

This is one of the dramatically explosive points made in Paul Verhoeven's film *Black Book*—that those who joined the Resistance were not unmixed and in fact ranged all the way from heroic to craven, from selfless to exploitative, from patriotic to traitorous. And some did heroic things for a while, but later, unaccountably, turned.

Many of them were anti-Semitic, disdainful of their Jewish compatriots. The difference between those who were Dutch and those who were Dutch-Jewish is prominently revealed in the film.

It's the sort of observation that Dutch novelists made long before the public did. For close to twenty years, the myths about war and resistance promoted a myopic disregard for what really happened. In the decades after liberation in 1945, the Resistance was sacrosanct—the bravery of the freedom fighters unquestioned, except by Dutch writers like Willem Frederik Hermans and Harry Mulisch. The former had shown as early as 1958 in a novel called *The Dark Room of Damocles* that some in the Resistance were hard to separate from collaborators, their activities occasionally indistinguishable from those of delinquents, bent on mischief as much as on saving lives.

In the late sixties and seventies, the public caught up with the novelists, and a serious examination of the Resistance began to spell out the more nuanced view that many risked much—and indeed paid with their lives—while others were hell-raisers who merely escaped the boredom that afflicted them before the war.

Recently, a book about Dutch wartime bounty hunters revealed that some Dutch people betrayed Jews to the Nazis for as little as seven guilders and fifty cents, roughly the equivalent of twenty dollars today.

Verhoeven's new film gets this right by showing that many people profited from the Nazi occupation while passing themselves off after the war as having bravely resisted a brutal foe. He also gets it right that many in the Resistance—both Jewish and non-Jewish—paid the ultimate price for their bravery.

And he understands too that towards the end of the war—in 1944, when this film takes place—everyone, German or non-German, was positioning himself for postwar safety.

The flawed character of the Resistance fighters does not contradict in any way that the Nazis were evil. They were. Their cause was. Yet even in that evil camp, there were degrees of it—as in the case of the German "Sicherheitsdienst" officer the film's heroine becomes involved with.

What is so unsettling about *Black Book* is that it gradually dawns on the viewer that no one can be trusted. The good people may turn out to be bad, and the genuinely good ones are often mistaken for traitors. This appears to be the truth not only about the Dutch Resistance, but also about similar Resistance movements in the Nazi-occupied countries.

But could the Jewish heroine of Verhoeven's *Black Book* have done all she did—and live to tell the tale? Yes, she could, though of course it was rare. Most of the true heroes did not survive.

Verhoeven and scriptwriter Gerard Soeteman have been criticized for her portrayal, but again, the film shows a certain double-sidedness in her nature: she is brave and cunning, but also vain and seductive. She does not merely pretend to sing wholeheartedly for the Nazi officers she infiltrates—she savors the performance and has missed being on stage.

Carice van Houten as the Jewish Resistance fighter and spy Rachel Steinn is so compelling in her role precisely because she brings out that double-sidedness—which conforms to a major truth as we have slowly come to know it in the many decades since World War Two. She enjoyed her exploits and her bravery, while at the same time the losses she endured—her parents, her brother, her whole world—make credible the moving lines she speaks after war's end, "Will it never be over?" and later, in another context, "For us, the war is just beginning."

It's a thought familiar to most survivors, as well as a paraphrase of a memorable utterance in the work of yet another Dutch novelist, Marga Minco.

Rachel's complexity has much to do with what the Dutch historian Chris van der Heijden called the "gray past," the fact that, in contrast to the myths following the war, few people were wholly good or bad, white or black; the greatest number was gray. Most people cooperated with the occupying forces up to a point, and there were inevitably degrees of collaboration by most people in the occupied territories in Europe.

This simple fact of a spectrum of colors characterizing people's behavior is crucial to an understanding of what happened and to the acceptance of the past. Only when we know what truly took place can a kind of peace come to those who still remember. And even for those who do not remember, clarity about the events during the war and the Holocaust, as the historian Tony Judt has argued in his book *Postwar*, matters deeply to the health of Europe's future.

For that reason alone, I'm a little troubled by the film's sly allusions to the present. To hear the Nazis refer to Resistance fighters as "terrorists" and to see them practice "waterboarding" may give us a jolt of recognition, but the implicit comparison between then and now takes us away from that time and place. And we need, again and again, to be told and shown how it was then.

In that effort, films like *Black Book* serve as necessary reminders of important truths.

2007

September 11, 2001

As I walked to Taraval Street from my house late Tuesday afternoon, two American flags were out. (There would be many more on Wednesday.) In a bar a few blocks farther on, I could see five men intently watching TV in front of two pool tables. When I got to the restaurant where I thought I would have a quick dinner, the owner and her family were also watching TV. I remained the only diner for the next hour.

On the bus today, an uncharacteristic, almost thoughtful silence prevailed. People read the newspaper or kept quiet.

No one I talk to these days can speak of anything else. That mood some people have almost yearned for—of national unity, closeness, unanimity—is suddenly here. It manifests itself in the volunteering, the donating of blood, the spontaneous attendance at places of worship.

And yet, though the country seems to feel with one heart, it inevitably speaks with many voices. After all, opinions continue to differ radically about what should be done. Suggestions range all the way from "Bomb someone, anyone," on the one extreme, to "We must love everyone alike," on the other.

That is to say, no one can really know what should be done. To pursue the elusive terrorists—as if that hasn't been tried many times—risks a great many innocent civilian casualties. To do nothing is unacceptable.

This is what is so compelling about watching TV. The talking heads, the pundits, the terrorism experts, the former National Security advisers do not have a clue either. They sound as if they're agreeing with each other, and they have even accepted each other's language. Suddenly, for example, everyone is asserting, in almost the same words, that you do not need the sort of proof "you would need in a court of law" to convict the terrorists.

They all call for a strong response, and they all say we must be firm and determined and have a long-range plan.

But when it comes to specifics, to targets, to the nature of the retaliation—or even whether retaliation should be the most important ingredient of our response—they differ and, more important, their language gets fuzzy and abstract, and they just "vague out."

They sound decisive and clear, but they aren't. Even the ones who predicted a major terrorist attack on the United States got some of it wrong, since they connected that predicted event to the likely use of biological weapons.

It is hard to blame them. A certain logic has slipped away from attack and counterattack. At one time, terrorism seemed to have a purpose: it softened the victims, made them lose heart. This is different. Can the terrorists really think that now America will change its policies? Last Tuesday's assault seems motivated by revenge, the desire to inflict pain—nothing more.

In such a climate, few things are clear. No retaliation, no military action—certainly no missile shield—will bring the safety and security we all crave.

It's a pity. The emotional unity of the people, the outpouring of horror and grief, would seem to create an opportunity. But the question remains: an opportunity to do what?

2001

9/11 ONE YEAR LATER

For weeks I dreaded the commemoration of last year's September 11 terrorist attacks. I find myself ever more uncomfortable with the tone taken by the media, by officialdom, by pontificators everywhere. And by lots of ordinary people.

Most of my friends feel somewhat the same way, but there is one difference between us. They object to the war talk, the super-patriotism that has engulfed us, whereas I dislike a kind of gooeyness, a sentimentality that blocks out genuine thought and feeling.

I felt from the instant the attacks occurred that a military response in Afghanistan was justified. And if people want to wave a flag to show their solidarity with that war, fine.

But what I can't abide is a sort of wallowing, a surrender to a maudlin and muddled sentimentality.

For the victims, this was a tragedy. For their families too, of course. For the country, it was a major blow. For the rest of us, it was serious enough—but by no means an unparalleled catastrophe.

Forty thousand people die on the highways every year. How many people perish yearly as a consequence of handguns? Do you see any memorials? Are masses of people making pilgrimages to highways, holding hands and lighting candles?

"We too are victims now," someone said to me after it happened, almost smugly. It's a thought I've heard again and again during this last year.

If these people mean that we can now join the rest of the world, that like the Spaniards, we now have experienced terrorism first hand, or like the Irish, or like the citizens of India, then I am with them.

But most of the time it doesn't sound like that. It sounds like self-dramatization, self-pity, like an almost sensual submission to a desired state, like a happy embracing of a finally-achieved role.

An odd self-inflation is at work. The victims are mourned, true, but somehow this event is about us, our drama, our lamentable plight. Our world has changed; we suffer. And now, however grievously wounded, we must learn to "heal."

A noxious psychobabble has taken over. First we get all the pity we require; then various prayers and platitudes are spoken. Phrases and formulas fill the airwaves. Much advice is given, most of it syrupy and fatuous. Small children must be made to express their grief, and if they're not so inclined, then we'll put words in their mouths.

Certain terms are constantly invoked, like *family* and *closeness*, *mourning* and *closure*. The relentless, deadening language of pop psychology, ostensibly seeking to help, covers the dreadful event like a blanket and smothers whatever thought and useful reflection the citizenry might have—about how ordinary people can commit evil acts, how fanaticism comes about, how the same event can be perceived so differently by different cultures. Even the poignancy of suddenly lost lives is hardly sensed in the clamor that surrounds us.

"Great gobs of artificial, exploitative grief," Rob Morse of the *San Francisco Chronicle* called it. Definitely. But the media, those ghastly mirrors of ourselves, are not only manipulative but also manipulated. By us. Our own slack ways of thinking and feeling are probably as much to blame. We like not thinking. We enjoy the easy, prefabricated sentiment. And that seems to be our version of the Brave New World.

2002

WHO ARE HEROES? WHO ARE VICTIMS?

I've heard it said a number of times on radio and television that the three thousand or so people who perished at the World Trade Center are "heroes." Not content with mourning them, we apparently must elevate their status.

Where does this idea come from? Why is it not enough for us to say that they were sadly, tragically, absurdly killed in a dastardly attack? Why must we now claim that they were something they were palpably not?

The policemen and the firefighters, the chaplains and the volunteers—all those people who ran up the stairs of the Twin Towers on September 11—are clearly heroes. So are the office workers who stayed behind with an injured colleague. They risked their lives trying to rescue those who needed rescuing. All the plaudits that have gone their way are deserved.

But the people who were in the wrong place at the wrong time were simply victims. There is nothing heroic about showing up for work.

By blurring the two categories, by saying that they were all heroes, we dishonor the heroes and diminish their courage. In effect we say: it doesn't matter what you did—you're a hero.

And in fact, we dishonor the victims too, by making them something they're not, by not looking at them, by denying their reality as victims.

I'm not saying, of course, that there can't be quiet heroism. The teacher who goes to her job for forty years battling rowdy kids is perhaps heroic. The diplomat trying to create peace one more time, when all around him say to quit, is possibly heroic. Examples abound of heroism having nothing to do with running up flights of burning stairs.

But just turning up on the job doesn't qualify. We diminish those victims, distort their reality, falsify their experience, by calling them heroes. We should mourn them as innocent, defenseless bystanders—as victims. That doesn't make their loss any less.

Our society seems to have a need to inflate things, to make them bigger than they are. You shouldn't have a good day; you should have a great day. If I declare, with passion, that everyone here is wonderful or brave or heroic, people may see me as a warm, compassionate person. The consequence is that nobody takes what is said seriously, and that—the corollary—there is no need to say anything meaningful. Inflation has led to an ironic deflation.

Such inflation of feeling is not only false but sentimental. It pretends to feeling that isn't there. In the process, it blocks the real thing. Sentimentality always stands in the way of sentiment.

2002

RELATED APHORISMS

Nowadays we confer sainthood on victims.

Acts of Kindness: Good Deeds, Largely Unpunished

A Story for the Season

Observed right here in the West Portal District, at Starbucks, an unlikely place for miracles, however small. The time was closer to Ramadan than to Christmas, but I tell the story now because, like a haunting, beautiful melody, I can't get it out of my mind.

It was about 7:30 in the evening. The striking young Muslim woman had just walked in. She wore a headscarf, but the radiance of her face, an unselfconscious kindness, was immediately visible. I don't remember if she wore slacks or more traditional dress. I do recall that her bearing was somehow unusual and noticeable.

At the far end of the café sat an old man, about whom I remember little, except that he slouched down over a ragged newspaper.

As usual, I had a book with me and soon disappeared into it. Perhaps twenty minutes later, the old man walked over to me, his gait halting but his smile beaming with gratitude, surprise, disbelief.

"She bought me a cup of coffee," he said. "And I don't even know her."

I knew instantly to whom he referred, but he went on. "That Egyptian woman over there brought over a cup of coffee." He remained incredulous for several minutes, repeating the little story again and again.

Close to the doorway stood the Muslim woman, chatting on her cell phone.

The old man sat down at his table but now seemed taller. I do not remember anything more, other than my own feeling of intense and almost teary-eyed pleasure at what I had seen.

Shortly thereafter I left. The pleasure, and even wonder, continued, and I thought of Portia's lines in *The Merchant of Venice*:

"How far that little candle throws his beams!
So shines a good deed in a naughty world."

Long ago, my grandmother would rave or grow tearful over some minor act of kindness, or even politeness, and I would think, "How on earth can she think that's so important? Does she really think it was for *her*?"

But now, in my older years, I realize how crucial kindness is, and, what's more, it doesn't matter so much what the motive for it might be, or whether it was done for you, or for Ramadan, or Christmas, or God himself.

And tears, it seems to me, are appropriate, more so for the kindness received than for the pain suffered. I think older people cry less for themselves than for what the Roman poet Virgil called "lacrimae rerum," the tears of things.

For those tears, few remedies exist—short of small miracles of kindness.

2004

THE SEASON OF GIVING

There is little question in my mind that the frenzy of gift-giving that takes place around this time of year is wasteful and silly. Ask yourself how many of your friends really need anything—I mean need what you can actually give them, wrapped and beribboned.

We all have enough. Children have more toys than they know what to do with. Adults have an abundance of gadgets, doodads, clothing, furnishings. It would make more sense for us to start divesting ourselves of things than acquiring them.

But we're somehow in this ludicrous swim and, conformist creatures that we are, we must splash around or face a kind of drowning by disapproval. So, in the season of giving, the quest for the appropriate present begins.

Since I'm in this contrary mood, let me say what an inappropriate gift is. A truly inappropriate gift is one you buy in your own image, i.e., as if you were the recipient. The best way I can illustrate is from an experience of my own in the early eighties.

I was walking along in San Francisco's Marina district with my ex–mother-in-law Ida, and since it was just before the Christmas rush, Ida wanted to look around in a bookstore. There she saw Eddie Fisher's brand-new autobiography, *My Life and Loves*. "Oh, isn't that great," exclaimed Ida to one and all, "Eddie Fisher has written a book. And it's about his life. He must have had a fascinating life." One or two other patrons looked at us, but that's often the way it was in Ida's company, which Ida herself attributed to her vast charm.

I made a mental note, "Get Eddie Fisher's autobiography for Ida."

The big day came, and we all, three generations, sat around Ida's table. Ida and her husband, the dear sainted Larry, my ex-wife and her

323

husband, my ex–sisters-in-law with their husbands, their children, my children, and myself.

After the eating, the stories, the recitation of funny little incidents, the jokes Larry told, the improbable account of a typical Ida day—"All the doctors told me I was beautiful"—came the big moment: passing out the gifts, unwrapping them, oohing and aahing.

I gave Ida my present: Eddie Fisher's autobiography. Ida beamed with delight. She gave her daughters and their husbands similar-looking book-shaped presents, and then she gave her husband Larry and me also the same book-shaped gift.

We all thought we got books, but not exactly. We all received copies of Eddie Fisher's *My Life and Loves*.

I guess I'll open it one of these years and find out what really happened with Debbie Reynolds and Elizabeth Taylor.

1999

"Why Don't You . . . ?"

Whenever I tell my friends that I spend a certain amount of time with difficult people, and when I complain a little about how boring this can be, they almost invariably want to cure me of the practice. "Why don't you ask them to stop calling you?" they say. Or "Why don't you tell them that you're busy?" They offer these and other suggestions for ridding myself of the problem.

Well, fair enough. I complain, so they, in all kindness, try to help. They don't want me to be wasting time or to be unhappy. And also, they want me to stop griping.

This is a trait the well-known linguist Deborah Tannen attributes to men—they always want to remedy the woman's problem, want to prescribe a cure. Women, she says, want "rapport" talk, men favor "report" talk. They listen to you so they can give advice, not to exchange thoughts and feelings.

Well, I think Tannen is wrong. Both sexes are afflicted. Certainly among my friends, both men and women want to fix me, to cure me, of this habit.

They mean well, but what surprises me is that in their exasperation they sooner or later—usually it's sooner—ask, "What are you getting out of this?" Sometimes it's not even a question, just a declaration. "You must be getting something out of it."

I suppose I am, but wait a minute, what about altruism, doing the Christian thing, a good deed, that sort of thing? Don't difficult people need someone to talk to? Can't I be doing a good thing for its own sake, what Jews call a "mitzvah"?

Such is the sour ideology of our time: you can't perform a selfless act—for its own sake, because it does some good, because it relieves

325

a bit of pain. No, you have to have a selfish motive; you're "getting something out of it."

And yet we attribute great goodness and heroism to some brave people; we're quick to point to heroes who risk their lives for others. Could it be that anything less than risking your life in a burning building is not seen as meaningful?

Is it possible that a lesser good deed just doesn't count? Is the Good Samaritan just someone who is getting a kick out of doing his compassion thing? What's he getting out of it anyway?

And did his friends say, "Why didn't you just tell that crime victim you're busy?"

But in all fairness, the Good Samaritan did not complain about how difficult his rescue work was, and I do. So maybe I deserve what I get from my friends.

And, it should be added, my deeds are not wholly good; they are a compound of kindness and weakness. I am probably too timid to tell my bothersome charges to go away.

But I still don't think I should be cured of it—and I also don't think I'm doing it for my own benefit.

2001

Is a Good Deed Less Good
When Unkindly Done?

Every few months I visit a very old lady, who lives in a regal mansion in the Oakland hills. Her house is as imposing as she still is. Tall and stately, she walks slowly from room to room, pointing at the magnificent views of the East Bay and San Francisco. Every room contains the wealth of a lifetime's accumulated good taste.

Like most social occasions, this one is slightly ritualistic. She receives me graciously and offers me a cup of home-brewed tea and then rings for a servant (did you know that there were still house servants in our midst?), who brings the tea along with sugar and cream and a pot of hot water on a beautiful silver-plated tray.

She has always lived like that. Brought up by her grandfather, a three-term governor of Rhode Island, she has mingled all her life with rich and well-connected people. I have often questioned her about that part of her past and found what she had to say interesting and occasionally perceptive.

Years ago in New York, when I first met her at a gathering of Friends of the United Nations, she talked about these important people with a touch of irony, though she was also kind enough to recommend me to a friend of hers who helped me with a research project.

But that is only one reason why I see her. Another, more important one, is that she has few visitors and is, in her own way, painfully lonely.

She does not like to dwell on that. Nor is she inclined to talk about some of the things she has been able to accomplish in her many years of philanthropic work, though she frequently mentions her several trips to Africa at the service of a war against malaria. She speaks forthrightly of her struggles to set up foundations in the hopeful times immediately after independence came to most of the continent. She thinks she picked up malaria herself, but her doctors contend the condition is "semi-malarial."

This I've heard half a dozen times, but the repetitions don't bother me.

What does bother me, and irritate me, and weary me, is the subject she really wants to talk about, and does at inordinate, boastful length: her lovers. Every time I go over there, I have to hear about the handsome European count De Meskaleri—his intentions as mysterious as his country of origin (Greece, France, Italy?)—who wanted "desperately" to marry her, but that her parents opposed the match and that, later on, as the young bride of an American ambassador to Sweden, a certain Congolese priest threatened "to defrock himself"—which "would be suicide for him, Manfred,"— if she did not sleep with him.

Once or twice she has said to me that she did, though on another few occasions that she didn't. I tried to point out the contradiction to her, but she replied enigmatically, "What could I do, Manfred?"

Out of annoyance, I once asked what that Congolese priest was doing in Sweden, but her answer was evasive. In fact, I've asked her many such questions, because when she starts on this subject I get so irked that I need a way to let off steam.

And that leads me to ponder this: is a Good Deed diminished by one's angry mood? Do I simply not have the temperament to do good? Why would I expect such experiences as these to be pleasurable?

I can't imagine Mother Teresa thinking, "Get a job" when she's coming to the aid of a poor beggar, or looking around her at all the wretches sleeping on the floor of the Calcutta railway station and saying to herself, "These people are tedious beyond endurance."

Nor am I consoled by the notion of the great philosopher Kierkegaard, that we demonstrate our faith in God most when God would seem to be absent. Loving God when he demonstrates his presence is all too easy.

By the same reasoning, a good deed would be less good when it's easy— and better, more authentic, when it's hard.

Unfortunately, that logic doesn't persuade me.

2007

Love Conquers All—Including Despair

The invitation from the speakers' bureau read, "Say what you would say if you had only one more lecture to give." But some principle of superstition had always held me back from giving "The Last Lecture." Suppose immediately after delivering it I keeled over?

In 35 years of college teaching, there were quite a few things I wanted to say that I had never said to my classes. There was a time when, given this opportunity, I would have talked to the students about Life. I would have given them the summing up that the topic called for, and if that wisdom seemed bitter or cold, so be it.

In that gloomy year, I wanted to tell a roomful of eager students that boredom was a major motive in human affairs. I wanted to vent my discovery that serious issues seriously debated were often only games, and that people in public and private life hid their motives—from each other and themselves. Deception and self-delusion were everywhere. Love, the supreme illusion, was the name we gave our greatest need.

Into these large opinions fed small complaints. Rudeness seemed to be pervasive. The kid at the information booth, when asked where the museum was, had pointed to a wall in back of him without looking up from his book. The restrooms in my college building were dirty. My son's karate teacher had skipped town, several lessons owing. Around me, things seemed in decline.

No, I was not an old fogy, but I did suffer from the anger of the middle years. Everywhere I saw self-promotion, isolation, indifference. The whole world was getting a divorce, and so was I.

In this black mood I was the universe's least likely person to do what most of my newly single friends did: look for a partner. But of course I did. I traveled the singles' circuit, attended workshops on meditation and discussed in successive weeks the benefits of expressing emotions and the advantages of controlling them.

One Friday evening, I found myself at yet another singles' dance. A brief talk, "Charting Your Financial Course by the Stars," had taken place. The host of this event, a smiling fellow, had given us all, the young and the middle-aged, a quick disco lesson. I had danced with a sullen-looking woman who declared that she never went anywhere to meet a new person. The burly man whose voracious consumption of cookies I had noted at other events was telling me that he lived at the local Buddhist monastery. An old, sweet-faced man was doing a polka to a sultry woman's rock 'n roll. The week before he had told me "in confidence" that he didn't know how to dance.

I looked around. I was as out of step as he. The thought that I would never meet anyone here, and that I was a fool for having come, seized me like a pain.

As I made my way to the front door, a handsome young man pushing a wheelchair came through. The young woman in the chair looked weak, her color matching her long beige dress. With the greatest caution, as if he were lifting something expensive and precious, the man drew her upright. She leaned forward, her arms around him, her body inert but not without grace. He rocked her slowly back and forth, and she rocked on her own as well. His beat quickened, and the motion of her upper body did too. She never moved her feet, but her body seemed supple in his arms. When the music stopped, he lowered her in the chair, and she smiled at him, blushing. Calmly he maneuvered the chair to the refreshment table and poured her a glass of wine, and when she was done, he just as calmly wheeled her out of the hall.

No one gave any sign of looking. If people looked, they didn't stare.

I headed for the exit. For once, the coatroom's unholy chaos did not annoy me. Nor did the piece of bright green gum stuck to the wall by someone too impatient to dispose of it in a more conventional way. I walked to my car and thought that in my irritation with dirty public facilities, in my anger over people's self-promotion, in my despair over human callousness, I had blinded myself to the kindness and selflessness that were all around me.

And that couple—who could believe in the impossibility of love after seeing these two?

I am glad that I did not give the Last Lecture and pronounce that convenience underlies our morality or that anger triumphs over shared concerns, for, at best, these things would have been only half true.

Of course, I did not meet anyone at the dance that night. But some sense of possibility was healed, some belief in love restored—along with the realization that despair and depression sometimes need just one more day, one more experience, to be overcome.

1986

Letters to No One in Particular, from Anonymous

Carefully, I address the envelope: "Alfred Okomoto, Poste Restante, General Delivery, Abidjan, Cote d'Ivoire, Ivory Coast, Africa." Inside my typewritten message, I enfold $2, seal the envelope and affix an 80-cent stamp.

I send the same message to "Yzedin Goca" in Tirana, Albania, Europe's poorest country. Next comes "Rosa Hernandes," in Bahia, Brazil, and then "Juanita del Valle" in Mérida, Mexico. Also "Héloise Boigny" in Antananarivo, Madagascar, and "Juan Portillo" in Lima, Peru.

There is no limit to the cities in which poverty reigns. This gift will do nothing to avert it, merely make one person feel a little less poor for a few hours.

I bend over my map of Lima, the capital of Peru: Avenida Nicolás de Pierola. I think I'll send $2 to "Carlos José Ramirez" at No. 216. I wish I had a zip code, but it will get there without one. I hope that address is not in a prosperous neighborhood. Why not another one? Lima is a big place. "Maria Concepción Sanchez," Avenida Arequipa 339. In a few days, some towns in the Chiapas region of Mexico, some in Belize and Cuba, then a number of even poorer places in Africa. Perhaps Freetown in Sierra Leone, a war-torn and desperately poor country.

I will get myself more maps and address more letters, but I don't actually need addresses. Years ago I heard the slogan "random acts of kindness." I forget how the rest of it went, but it was sufficient onto itself. Why should there be only random evil in the world? Why not an occasional unexpected good deed? Nothing startling about the idea, but the word "random" in this context was new. It's usually associated with bad things. Not this time: something nice happening for no reason; good things falling out of the sky.

Once after a trip to Israel, I mailed all my leftover shekels to an Arab employee in a Jewish hotel in Jerusalem. I do not know if he received it. He had served me kindly; we had talked. He was an older man with a melancholy, despairing look in a manner reminiscent of my late father. He sighed when he spoke of the hotel business and how awful war was for tourism. It was clear that he took pride in the hotel for which he worked and that all he wanted was to earn a living, to support his family and to lead a quiet life. I hope he got my modest gift.

Then it occurred to me: if he did not receive it, someone did. Maybe someone less deserving, maybe someone more deserving. The important thing is it found its way.

I wouldn't have to know the recipients. I could send people small gifts, and they would have them, a random gift from nowhere. No one's life would be changed, but someone's day would be improved by a happy surprise.

Someone such as Alfred Okomoto. There is no Alfred Okomoto, but someone, maybe in the post office, maybe even the carrier on the way to the post office, maybe the clerk in charge of wherever dead letters go in Abidjan, would find it. Unlikely that they would destroy the letter unopened. The postal clerk would think, looking at the letter no one had picked up, "Here's something from America. No return address. Let's have a look." And then he'd find my gift, liberate the bills from the envelope. He would be my Alfred Okomoto.

It's my version of foreign aid. I've always wanted to have my own foreign policy. After sending six or seven letters, I'm too excited to stop. Making up names, finding a new target country, seems to be my version of the warrior peering at his battle maps. My invasion is definitely less costly.

The message I insert in each letter reads:

"The name on this envelope is not real. You who open this letter are the legitimate recipient of my gift and the owner of the small sum I enclose. I will remain anonymous. The only thing I ask in return is that you perform one act of kindness for someone. It does not matter who it is or what you do, as long as you have gladdened him or her for a few moments, as you may have been gladdened by receiving this."

Occasionally, I long for a response. I toy with the idea of enclosing my return address so that a recipient could actually write me back.

But I wanted to protect myself from disappointment. What if nobody wrote back? And why should they waste a stamp almost as costly as the sum they have received? Worse still: what if they wrote back, asking for more, much more, burdening me with their troubles? This I want to avoid at all cost: I am not a truly charitable person.

Still, it would be nice to know more.

I brood over all this in the streetcar on my way to work. Awkwardly, the passengers descend right into traffic. I am the last out, and a car zooms toward me. I quickly get out of the way, somewhat shaken. Instantly, a young man comes over and asks if I'm all right. His eyes are kind and attentive. It is a random act of kindness, as much thanks as I could have had from Alfred Okomoto, Yzedin Goca, Rosa Hernandes or Juan Portillo. Actually, it is their thanks.

2001

Related Aphorisms

Do three favors for someone and he will wonder why you're taking so long with the fourth.

'To understand all is to forgive all' is both profound and shallow—the former for its stress on imaginative understanding, the latter for its assumption that people necessarily forgive what they understand.

Even difficult people can't tolerate difficult people.

Almost a Foreign Country:
Time and Aging

LOSING OUR COMFORTS, SMALL AND LARGE

"That salmon, you know, that's farm-raised salmon," said a dear friend. "You know what they feed them? Garbage."

I gulped. Whether she's correct or not, I haven't had non–ocean-caught salmon since that conversation.

Which means that I haven't been to my favorite low-cost neighborhood restaurant in a long time.

The next blow was tofu. For twenty-five years I've been eating tofu dishes. Not only was tofu healthful, I had always been told, but I could order it in restaurants, mixed with vegetables, without salt or soy sauce.

No more. Tofu, I read somewhere, has been implicated in prostate cancer. It has something to do with estrogen. I have no other details, but reports of this study sounded authoritative. I've not had tofu for a while.

Then came the edict on what I've been eating for lunch the last three decades: tuna.

I consider tuna one of the four food groups. I can't do without it.

Evidently the consumption of tuna brings with it the risk of excessive quantities of mercury. Pregnant women are urged to avoid it.

I'm not a pregnant woman, but I now avoid my beloved low-sodium tuna.

I was musing about all this, walking past my favorite cafe, now closed, and feeling a bit bereft. I realize this is not an earthshaking problem, not like losing a fortune in the stock market and certainly not like enduring the trials that people in the Middle East face. (Though I should say, I've often, while eating these foods, jotted down my thoughts on various world crises, which the *West Portal Monthly* then sent out into the world).

What did my musing lead to? Well, I quickly realized that these losses, these gradual and sudden removals of my comforts, are comparable to the losses we all face during aging.

Our comforts are taken away one by one.

We lose the ease of our bodies. Rarely do we have in the older years the sense of well-being we had while younger.

Also, the future is taken away. Instead of thinking, "Oh, I'll take care of that sometime," you feel the "dark encroachment of that old catastrophe," as the poet Wallace Stevens described the thought of death.

And maybe even more to the point: gradually your friends are removed, one by one. And your environment grows less recognizable, as young people do strange things to it.

This is not a cheery column. It's not about how age brings wisdom or fulfillment. No, it's about loss, large and small. It's about having to do with less.

As the eighteenth-century poet Samuel Johnson put it:

> Condemned to Hope's delusive mine,
> As on we toil from day to day,
> By sudden blasts, or slow decline,
> Our social comforts drop away.

2002

A Melancholy Poem about Love and Aging

Every once in a while, I turn to William Butler Yeats's poem "After Long Silence," not exactly for the comfort it brings, nor for the knowledge it affirms, but because it is such a jewel of compression, so agonizingly precise and so breathtakingly clear. I do not deny that I am left more melancholy after rereading it, but it also somehow braces me with its pointedness.

Here is the poem:

> Speech after long silence; it is right,
> All other lovers being estranged or dead,
> Unfriendly lamplight hid under its shade,
> The curtain drawn upon unfriendly night,
> That we descant and yet again descant
> Upon the supreme theme of Art and Song:
> Bodily decrepitude is wisdom; young
> We loved each other and were ignorant.

Two aging lovers, now that all their other lovers are gone or have died, turn to each other, speak to each other "after long silence." Of course the lamplight is "unfriendly," and even more "unfriendly" is the night—one is unkind to their appearance, the other is menacing in what it portends for both of them.

What shall they speak about? Only one thing seems left, "the supreme theme of Art and Song." It's not only that they speak of what is lasting, the permanence of art, but also that they have found an impersonal subject, a worthwhile subject that has defied time. They can be distracted by it, lose themselves in it, live through it.

The last two lines I have always found devastating. Love is for young people, or, to put it differently, a condition for loving is youth. Age does not favor love but instead brings wisdom. Is there a loss and a gain? Certainly, but who wouldn't rather be young and in love?

The great Irish poet answers that implicit question in the sadness of those lines. No one can really say that "decrepitude" is a good thing, even if it brings wisdom. Had Yeats found love and wisdom to be fully equal, he would not have used that word.

And certainly "ignorance" seems a small price to pay for love.
1998

A Serene Old Age?

Serenity is not the name of the game among my aging friends. Few of them are dreadfully unhappy, but most find something wanting in the way they live now.

John still wants to have the great sexual relationship he never really had. The older he gets, the less likely he is to attain it. Knowing this makes him feel worse, of course.

Another, Roberto, cannot stand being old. He laments—as we all do to a lesser extent—his lost youth, his lost middle age, even his lost early old age. Oh, to be sixty again.

Janet has wanderlust. She wants to see all the places she has never been to: Morocco, China, Nepal. Money permitting, she would be ready to set off at a moment's notice. When she was in her twenties, she traveled around the world and had many adventures. Why not now?

Francine wants her name to be a household word. She has achieved some fame with a few books and a radio show, but it is not enough. For a brief period she seemed about to go national, but it did not happen. She is a bit too old now for that to happen.

It's not that these people have no pleasures, do not enjoy their children and grandchildren, or aren't grateful for what health they have. I'm not talking about chronic malcontents or voracious, ego-obsessed people; no, these friends are relatively normal. True, they're not models of sainthood, and not one of them feels the lack of having attained greater spirituality, though some lament not having done enough for others.

What about me? It would take several columns to delineate all the things I'm discontent about (readers beware: these columns may be on the way), but one thing bothers me greatly: while I have had a very good career as a college teacher, I occasionally lament all the talents I have not been able to use.

For instance, I fancy I have a gift for diplomacy, and while that is helpful in the classroom, I wish I could have used it on a larger stage. I took on many diplomatic missions while I was married, traveling tirelessly in a kind of shuttle diplomacy between my mother-in-law's house and my own to make peace between mother and daughter. But it wasn't quite the Balkans or the Middle East.

In my fantasies, Kofi Annan calls on me to be his deputy: there is a nasty but dangerous dispute brewing among various peacekeepers, and I'm dispatched to speak to all sides, using the various languages I happen to know, sound out the quarreling sides, consult at length, draw up possible solutions, call Kofi (we're on first-name terms), and hammer out an agreement acceptable to one and all. Very few people hear of my accomplishment, but even the State Department is happy with my work and wants to send me on to the next trouble spot.

The fantasy is pleasurable, but it is distressing to think that there is something you could have done well but did not get the chance to—and never will.

So what to do with my dissatisfactions? What to do with *our* dissatisfactions?

I want to say: accept what you have been able to accomplish, dwell on what you have attained, take satisfaction with what you can still achieve. It is the Path of Wisdom.

But another, more vocal part of me says: continue to seek what you have not yet found. Travel to Nepal in your sixties. Reach for perfect sex at an age when few have any sex. As for me, it's just possible that the letter from the United Nations will come—or that a new president, in desperate need of diplomatic talent, will seek me out for deputy secretary of state.

2000

AGING MINDFULLY?

Oscar Wilde once said, "The tragedy of old age is not that one is old, but that one is young." It's a heartbreaking aphorism. We older people are the same young people we ever were, with the same drives and needs, but we are trapped in these ancient bodies.

All the more heartbreaking for Wilde himself, who—though never reaching old age—felt keenly the loss of youthful beauty, imbued as he was with the aesthetic youth culture he himself had a role in shaping.

And we too live in a youth culture. We too discover that as we get older we don't ever turn heads, not even once or twice. We become invisible.

Perhaps women suffer most from this, especially attractive women who once got plenty of attention. True, any number of them will tell you that it doesn't matter, they're "glad to be done with that nonsense," and that now finally they don't have to watch their waistline. But there is an element of false bravura in that declaration, and a certain regret for things that are no more.

A formula we frequently hear—almost by a kind of compensation—is that "old people are beautiful." But that comment has about it a sort of willed distortion, a deliberate contrarianism, and the effect seems condescending. Most of us, young or old, know that old people are not beautiful, and while some famous older people, like Katharine Hepburn or Jimmy Carter, may have marvelously arresting faces, we know they are not what the world calls beautiful. So these are comments about their character far more than their appearance.

And we live in a world of appearances. Whether aesthetes or not, we are drawn to the unlined face, the shapely body, the muscled slenderness. So what is to be done? How do we handle the sense that we are increasingly dismissed as "old"?

We can begin by being mindful, as the Zen masters say, by noting, just noting, not with distress or sorrow—but with attention. We can try watching changes in ourselves with interest rather than regret. Observe them, do not judge them. Attempt to register them attentively, but do not ascribe a sorrowful meaning to them.

Easier said than done, of course, but you have all the time in the world to practice, day by day.

Sooner or later, this new habit will stand you in good stead. It will increase your appreciation of what *is*. It will strengthen your command over the present. You may still prefer to be young, but you will not despair over being what you are.

2000

Random Thoughts on Growing Old

"As we get older," says a good friend of mine, "we have to learn to live on less." Yes, of course, it's not money she was referring to: we may have the same amount or even more money—but everything else will certainly be less. When it comes to love, respect, prestige, inevitably you'll not get what may have come your way routinely a mere decade ago.

Most older people I know suffer from this but have other things to worry about. After all, there's also less health; they're usually concerned with retaining what health they have. So despite the smaller emotional scale on which older people live, they choose to focus on other things and aren't necessarily more unhappy. Or if they are, it is still not an overwhelming unhappiness they feel.

What has increased, though, is a malaise resulting from a certain dislocation. Everything around them is beginning to feel really odd. John Updike's recent novel, *Toward the End of Time*, about growing older, is deliberately set in 2020 so that Updike can increase the sense of dislocation his main characters—and all his readers—feel. Following the Sino-American nuclear war, the U.S. is utterly changed. The federal government is weak, and UPS has taken over many law-enforcing functions. California and New England hardly communicate. Nothing is as it was.

This, Updike seems to say, is the landscape older people live in: somewhat recognizable but largely so different from the country of their youth that it is barely the same place anymore.

True, but so bleak. What, then, do we do? Oddly, this dislocation, these losses, generally require from us pretty much what life has always required.

It is harder to do what we must do, but the task is no different. Since we are out of our element, since we have to live on less, since we exist without much of a future, we must live for the present, we must embrace what is still ours. More than ever, our task is Zen-like: to apprehend the present so vigorously that our losses become irrelevant.

"I don't have a support group," laments an old friend of mine.

I remind him that a support group is nothing more than people you have been nice to and who can now occasionally be relied on to be nice to you.

But if he has been too careless, too neglectful, to build such a group, if he has not been kind to anyone, let him begin now, and maybe give to those who need it—give skills, or affection, or concern.

And the minute he does not expect anything in return, he will get it all back. In this, being old is no different from being young.

1999

Zen and the Art of Growing Older

Older people will often interrupt even their mild complaining by saying things like, "Well, I can't complain. At least I'm still here," or "Let's face it. I have nothing to worry about; I'm alive."

In that respect, and maybe in that respect only, age brings a certain wisdom. I call it wisdom, because these comments of older people reflect, almost unwittingly, a keen sense of how one should live.

No, they haven't thought about the matter in such terms. It just seems sensible to value life and living when so many of one's contemporaries are gone. Those departed ones are forever separated from the pleasures we still have. It is only the living who are here to enjoy—or to sigh. How then can they—we—find fault with what is, however imperfectly, still available?

Not everyone feels this way, of course. There are some who are bitterly disappointed with their own advanced age, their unfulfilled lives before reaching that age, their despair at never being able to realize the dreams that are now more elusive than ever. They are blamers and regretters: angry beyond measure, they will not be consoled.

I am sometimes in their camp, but—thankfully—most of the time I'm more serene, more inclined to be grateful for just being alive. And I think most of my aging friends are too. They have almost intuitively come to the greatest lesson of them all: that the major value in life is life itself, and that living well is mostly a matter of appreciating the being that runs through us rather than achieving the goals or fulfilling the desires that we cling to so tenaciously.

People who know how to live know this early on. Others have to wait a long time to begin to realize that our experience of being alive transcends our wishes, hopes and wants—that, as the Zen masters tell us, there are few real needs beyond the experience of living.

In some way, it is nothing more and nothing less than a celebration of what IS. In the year he died, the Victorian poet Robert Browning wrote, with a certain contentment, about his old age:

> And now a flower is just a flower:
> Man, bird, beast are but beast, bird, man—
> Simply themselves, uncinct by dower
> Of dyes which, when life's day began,
> Round each in glory ran.

This celebration of life did not come easy to Browning, and it doesn't to almost anyone else. But it is the path to happiness in life, in living—as it is in death, and dying.

2001

Related Aphorisms

It's hard to separate old people's astonishment at the times they live in from their astonishment at being old.

Though we age, maturity continues to elude us.

The next generation is always perceived as playing at adult life.

All experience, like all medicine, has side-effects.

We may spend months, or years, on trivial decisions, and minutes, or none, on important ones.

Distractability is the major antidote to suicide.

Eighty is the new sixty, but even sixty is too old.

We can accept death, but not imagine it.

p 44 Tina Martin poem
p 76 - George Tenet -
p. 168 fewer things - less gadgets
p 181 - first boarding impression
p. 333 - Kiffe Kiffe Tomorrow - Faïza Guène
p. 239 Culture is a mode of perception
i.e - culture is a way of seeing (the other? -
the self"?

p 247   Semiotician -
         Jean Beaudrillard 1989 - America

p 248 - definition of the American desert

p 251 - Mexican - American culture -
        are coming early to the party

p 253   "centering yourself" as a
        California cliché - need for
        teachers facing classes & for me -
        stop and put into action" reflection
        in action" (Schoen)?

p 258 - me & Claude Pepper

p 329 - "Satchimelita"
343 - - Old age is not beautiful
      (to the old) but it too has occasional
      moments of beauty - A glance, a smile
      & word to another -

Printed in the United States
138042LV00006B/70/P